I0605300

THE MOST CONTROVERSIAL STATE PARK

THE MOST CONTROVERSIAL STATE PARK

Jekyll Island

C. Brenden Martin

The University of Georgia Press *Athens*

Publication of this work was made possible, in part, by support from the University of Georgia Press Friends Fund

page ii
Driftwood Beach
Jekyll Island, Georgia
by Ron McKenzie,
Adobe Stock

page vi
Aerial view of Jekyll Island, Georgia
by Rodphotography,
Adobe Stock

Athens, Georgia 30602
www.ugapress.org

Designed by Mindy Basinger Hill
Set in ITC Galliard Pro
Printed and bound by Sheridan

The paper in this book meets the guidelines for permanence and durability of the Committee on Production Guidelines for Book Longevity of the Council on Library Resources.

Printed in the United States of America
30 29 28 27 26 C 5 4 3 2 1

EU Authorized Representative
Easy Access System Europe—Mustamäe tee 50, 10621 Tallinn, Estonia, gpsr.requests@easproject.com

Names: Martin, C. Brenden author
Title: The most controversial state park : Jekyll Island / C. Brenden Martin.
Description: Athens : University of Georgia Press, [2026] | Includes bibliographical references and index.
Identifiers: LCCN 2025028361 | ISBN 9780820373560 hardback alkaline paper
Subjects: LCSH: Jekyll Island Authority—History | Jekyll Island State Park (Ga.)—History | Jekyll Island State Park (Ga.)—Social aspects | Jekyll Island State Park (Ga.)—Environmental aspects | Jekyll Island (Ga.)—History
Classification: LCC F292.G58 M37 2026 | DDC 975.8/742—dc23/eng/20250904
LC record available at https://lccn.loc.gov/2025028361

CONTENTS

PREFACE

The first time I visited Jekyll Island was in 1984, when I was a young teenager. My mother and stepfather, June McCash and Bart McCash, had discovered the allure of Jekyll Island's historic district and had just begun a long-term research project to gather information on the Jekyll Island Club and the people associated with it. I still remember seeing the ramshackle clubhouse, which had been closed for about fourteen years. Two years later my family purchased a house on Jekyll, and we drove there nearly every summer. During those summers I learned to love the island.

My primary interest at first was in Jekyll's leisure activities, especially spending time on the beach. Then, as I grew older, I discovered an even greater attraction in the island's wildlife—the alligators and sea turtles, the live oak trees and the beautiful sunsets over the marshes. As I grew increasingly interested in history, I began to learn more about the island's past. The earliest people we know to have lived, hunted, and fished on Jekyll Island were Timucua Native Americans. After 1732, when General James Oglethorpe and his English Board of Trustees founded the colony of Georgia, the island would become an outpost, and the home of Major William Horton, one of Oglethorpe's most important military leaders in the British colony. During that time, it was still part of what has been called the "debatable land," which lay between Charleston, controlled by England, and St. Augustine, where the Spanish dominated. The "debate" ended in 1742 with the defeat of the Spanish by English forces in the Battle of Bloody Marsh on St. Simons Island, bringing Jekyll definitively into English hands. In a final gesture of hostility against the English, the retreating Spanish army paused briefly on Jekyll Island to burn down the house of Major Horton. (The shell of his rebuilt tabby home still stands on the island.) Following a peace treaty between Britain and Spain in 1748, Jekyll, no longer requiring a military presence, became a Sea Island cotton plantation. It would eventually be acquired by a family of French émigrés, who owned it for almost a century before selling it in 1886 to the Jekyll Island Club, which established the island as an exclusive winter retreat for America's richest families. The elite club closed in 1942 for the duration of World War II and would never open again.

Like most seaside resorts, until World War II Jekyll Island had been reserved for the nation's wealthy. Around the same time the Jekyll Island Club was founded and began to flourish, for example, Henry Flagler was beginning his efforts in Florida to attract the wealthy during the winter months. Only with the relative affluence of postwar America and the widespread use of the automobile did travel and tourism became possible for the average person.[1] It was during this period that Jekyll Island was transformed from a resort for the affluent to a state park for the middle class. In 1947, during the brief period of leadership by Governor M. E. Thompson, the State of Georgia acquired Jekyll, which Thompson envisaged as a state park for ordinary Georgians rather than a private island for the most prosperous Northern elite.

Thus it became possible for my family to spend its summer vacations at Jekyll Island. During those summers, I noticed various aspects of the island changing, but it was not until I became a professional historian and college professor that I began to consider what those changes meant or could mean to the people of Georgia. In writing my first book, *Tourism in the Mountain South: A Double-Edged Sword*, I became aware of the difficult choices, decisions, and controversies involved in bringing development and tourism to an area that previously had been unspoiled; while these changes may have helped the economy of the region, they were not popular with local residents, who resented the transfiguration of the beautiful landscape and slow-paced culture they had always known and loved. The concerns raised by residents of the Mountain South are not unlike those that residents of and visitors to Jekyll Island have raised over the past three-quarters of a century, though some concerns differ by virtue of the different locations and their distinctive histories.

Jekyll Island State Park was born out of a bitter battle between two gubernatorial candidates, one of whom had a vision of an island owned by the state that could be enjoyed by the "plain people of Georgia," unlike nearby Sea Island, which was more exclusive and reserved for the wealthy. The other candidate opposed the acquisition of Jekyll, arguing that the island was "sinking" and would be an albatross and a waste of money for the state. From the outset, controversies would mark every decade of the state's ownership of the island.

For many years, I was unaware of all the controversies the changes to Jekyll entailed. Then in 2003, when I published "From Millionaires to the Masses: Tourism at Jekyll Island, Georgia," an article coauthored with June Hall McCash, I noticed certain parallels with my earlier study of tourism in the Mountain South.[2] In the summer of 2014, I conducted a field study with my graduate students from Middle Tennessee State University's public history program in which we recorded oral histories, undertook archival work, and mounted interpretive exhibits for the Jekyll Island Museum. During that field study, I learned of a then-current dispute over the definition of "land" on Jekyll Island. Although it may sound ridiculous today, this controversy, which lasted for at least three years, would be vitally important in determining the scope of future development on Jekyll Island, as the state entity that manages the island prepared for what it called "revitalization."

Initially, I considered writing an article about Jekyll's controversial state history. However, I eventually realized that I had compiled so much information from my research that an article couldn't contain it. And so I decided that I needed to write a book to fully explore the battles that went on behind the scenes as Jekyll was becoming what it is today. As I interviewed people on both sides of the issues, it became apparent that, whatever their point of view, most people generally sought what they thought was best for Jekyll Island. They just didn't agree on what that was or how to accomplish it.

When the Georgia General Assembly authorized the creation of the Jekyll Island State Park Authority (JIA) in 1950, it gave the board a fifty-year lease on the island and "all rights and powers necessary to hold as a lessee, to improve, maintain, beautify, repair, rebuild, increase, extend, subdivide, and sublease no more than one-third of Jekyll Island State Park."[3] The assembly amended the legislation in 1953, extending the authority's lease to 2049 and allowing the authority to develop "one-half of the highland portion of Jekyll Island."[4] Eventually, the allowance for land development would revert back to one-third of the island above mean high tide, until it was redefined once again in terms of acreage in 2014.

How the authority might go about accomplishing the many-faceted task with which it was charged remained to be seen. And defining precisely what the island state park would become would prove to be a struggle. Those involved often had differing visions. Some wanted it to be primarily a natural preserve, open to the public, that protected its magnificent live oak trees, sand dunes, and forests, as well as its abundant wildlife of birds, deer, turtles, and alligators. Others believed it should be a recreational area, with attractions such as an amusement park, a "sea circus," a "super slide," an indoor pool, and a water park—something like Daytona Beach. Over time, some began to envisage it as a new, upscale Hilton Head. Still others wanted it to be a calm seaside residential paradise for middle-class retirees, where the material culture and history of Jekyll's past as a winter retreat for the nation's wealthiest families would be preserved. Finding an appropriate and satisfying balance among these goals would continue to be a challenge throughout the state era.

The evolving culture of the nation, and of the South in particular, would also create inevitable changes and controversies on Jekyll Island. With Jekyll having become a state park during the Jim Crow era, the Jekyll Island State Park Authority made no initial plans to allow Black Georgians access to the island's beaches and residences. However, the Black community soon argued that they had the right—granted to them by the Supreme Court in the 1896 *Plessy v. Ferguson* decision—to a "separate but equal" opportunity to enjoy the island. At that point the JIA began to allow a segregated development for

African Americans called St. Andrews on the island's south end, an area well delineated from the parts of the island enjoyed by white citizens. Even before the passage of the Civil Rights Act in 1964, however, the NAACP began to demand equal access to all areas of the island. While there was resentment among some white residents and visitors, once the decision had been made and integration of the island was required by law, there was relatively little resistance, as island businesses began to accede to the NAACP's demands.

Some misfortunes were the result of well-intended but uninformed endeavors such as the bulldozing of sand dunes to provide a better ocean view to seaside motels and cottages, thus exacerbating erosion problems that had begun even before the state era. Today scientists know that sand dunes help to protect the island from the ravages of storms and hurricanes, which have increased in frequency and become more severe with climate change. Fortunately, those in charge of making critical decisions have learned from their mistakes, and over time they have forged an island and state park unlike any other.

In many respects, Jekyll Island as it stands today is unique. It is one of the smallest sea islands on the Georgia coast—only about seven miles in length and less than two miles wide, and containing approximately 5,500 acres. It lies between the magnificent salt marshes of Glynn County (made famous in a poem by Sidney Lanier) on its west side and the Atlantic Ocean to the east. It is unlike islands such as Hilton Head and Sea Island, which for the most part have become fully developed resorts with elite gated communities. Nor is it like Cumberland Island or Sapelo Island, which remain largely undeveloped and allow only limited visitation. And it did not follow the model (suggested by a state official in 1957) of Daytona Beach, with its high-rise apartment buildings and hotels, arcades, and beach races.

While it *is* called a state park, Jekyll Island is not administered like most other Georgia state parks. Instead, like Stone Mountain and Lake Lanier, it is overseen by an independent governing board, in this case the Jekyll Island Authority, described in its current (2021) master plan update as "a self-supporting state entity responsible for the overall management and stewardship of Jekyll Island." The authority supports itself through leases, various fees collected from homeowners and businesses, parking passes, and admission fees to island amenities such as golf courses, a water park, and the Georgia Sea Turtle Center.

Members of the Jekyll Island Authority board of directors are appointed by the governor to serve four-year terms. The board's chair, also appointed by the governor, serves a one-year term. An executive director works with the board and is responsible for overseeing the island's day-to-day operations. This group's task is not an easy one. The authority included this mission statement in its 2021 master plan update: "As stewards of Jekyll Island's past, present, and future, we are dedicated to maintaining the delicate balance between nature and humankind."

Preserving that balance is complicated by the fact that, unlike most state parks, Jekyll Island allows private residences and businesses built on land leased from the state. It seeks to attract visitors not only with its beaches and wildlife but with such amenities as the popular water park known as Summer Waves, the Georgia Sea Turtle Center, golf courses, tennis courts, bike trails, a campground, and kayaking. There are also activities and facilities designed especially for children—a miniature golf course, a playground, a 4-H camp, a soccer complex, and the Tidelands Nature Center. The island also maintains a unique historic district that once housed the famous Jekyll Island Club. While the island must rely on public/private partnerships, all on leased land, to serve many of its visitors' housing, dining, shopping, and recreational needs, it also seeks to preserve a fragile ecosystem abundant with diverse wildlife. In support of that effort, approximately two-thirds of the island remains undeveloped, except for nature trails and bike paths.

In preparing this book, I was fortunate to interview people who experienced some of the island's events and controversies over the years but who have since passed away. Among them were Johnny Paulk, a beloved figure on the island who served for many years as Jekyll's director of golf and tennis. He provided me with a wealth of information he had collected over the years. I was also fortunate to interview Andre Steiner, who worked for the architectural and engineering firm Robert and Company and did the original design for Jekyll Island State Park. He was almost a hundred years old when we met, but his mind and memory were still sharp. One of my most important interviews was with Charles L. "Charlie" Gowen, a lawyer and legislator who played a major role in the state's acquisition of the island and its transition from a private club to a state park. Another important interviewee was John McTier, a longtime chair of the JIA who served with executive director George Chambliss during a difficult time, when Chambliss was under fire for actions that resulted in his resignation. Finally, I was able to interview Larry Evans, the architect who undertook the restoration of the Jekyll Island Clubhouse and made it the gem it is today. Those interviews would all be impossible to conduct now.

I also benefited from oral interviews recorded and preserved in the Jekyll Island Museum Archives. Among them were interviews of Jim Bacote—who spoke of his teenage years on Jekyll and of his testifying in the civil action case the NAACP brought against Jekyll Island demanding integration—and Ray Hill, whose extended family had for many years worked for the Jekyll Island Club and who was later hired by the authority as a sort of "peacemaker" between the authority and the Black community.

More recently, I was fortunate to have interviews and discussions with the last two executive directors, Bill Donohue and Jones Hooks, both of whom met with many difficult issues as they oversaw major updates and changes on the island during their tenure there. Concerning the restoration of the Jekyll Island Clubhouse and the historic district in general, Vance Hughes, who partnered with Larry Evans in the clubhouse project, and Warren Murphey, who helped in the restoration of the historic district and served for a time as director of operations for the Jekyll Island Authority, were both generous with their time and knowledge. John Hunter, former director of historic resources at Jekyll and now director of planning, development, and codes for Brunswick, Georgia, proved knowledgeable about efforts to enhance the interpretation of the island's south end, including the first *Wanderer* exhibit to help tell the story of enslaved Africans on the island. Andrea Marroquin and Gretchen Greminger, curators of the Jekyll Island Museum, helped by allowing me access to the historical collection, including oral histories, images, and state-era documents.

A number of present and former island residents who were deeply involved in some of the island controversies shared their recollections with me, including the late Jean Poleszak, president of the Jekyll Island Citizens Association during a critical time; David and Mindy Egan, who cofounded the Initiative to Protect Jekyll Island; Bonnie and Steve Newell, who were especially concerned about the island wildlife, in particular the deer and sea turtles; and Joseph Henry Armstrong, who had once worked as a bellhop for the Jekyll Island Club and who went on to build a house in the St. Andrews subdivision on the south end of the island, the area set aside for Black Georgians during segregation. Many others shared their stories as well.

Fortunately for Jekyll, many people throughout the state era have cared deeply about the island. They did not all have the same ideas, nor did they always agree, but they were able to move toward compromises that helped the state-owned island to find the balance among many interests that it has finally achieved. How they got there was not always pretty or pleasant, and there is no doubt that seeking equilibrium among the many interests the Jekyll Island Authority must serve—residents, business owners, visitors, environmentalists, and state officials—will be an ongoing task. Their conflicting ideas and disputes have made for a colorful and rocky road for the island during the state era, from 1947 to the present. It is their stories, perspectives, and disagreements that I intend to explore in this book.

THE MOST CONTROVERSIAL STATE PARK

The Jekyll Island Club was one of the most exclusive clubs in the world. The clubhouse opened to guests in 1888, and the annex wing was completed in 1902. (Courtesy of Mosaic, Jekyll Island Museum)

WORLD WAR II AT JEKYLL ISLAND

1

An oft-quoted passage from a 1904 issue of *Munsey's Magazine* touted the Jekyll Island Club, founded in 1886, as "the richest, the most exclusive, and the most inaccessible" club in the world. Those words no longer provided a fitting description by the outbreak of World War II in 1939. In fact, the club had been in decline for the previous decade. Such circumstances as the Great Depression; the resignation of Ernest Grob, the club's longtime and beloved superintendent; the aging of club members; and a decline in membership brought the need for drastic changes to shore up the club's woeful financial condition. In response, the Jekyll Island Club formed a new and less expensive "associate membership" that brought in new members who were less familiar to the general public than many of its original members, whose very names evoked images of wealth—names such as Rockefeller, Morgan, Vanderbilt, Gould, Astor, and Pulitzer. As a consequence, the Jekyll Island Club limped on until 1942, when the difficulties of World War II eventually led to its demise.[1]

By the spring of 1940, World War II was underway in Europe. As the German blitzkrieg rolled over Poland in 1939, and then Denmark, Norway, Belgium, the Netherlands, Luxembourg, and France by May 1940, most Americans continued to favor U.S. neutrality in the conflict. Nevertheless, President Franklin D. Roosevelt prepared the nation for entry into the war by instituting the Lend-Lease program, the nation's first peacetime draft, and the beginnings of large-scale training maneuvers. The shocking attack on Pearl Harbor on December 7, 1941, led to the United States entering the war. The next day, Roosevelt convened a joint session of Congress to declare war against Japan. Three days later, Germany declared war against the United States. Starting on January 13, 1942, German U-boats attacked several merchant ships along the Eastern Seaboard of North America, off New England, Connecticut, and Long Island and near New York Harbor.

Despite the declarations of war against Germany and Japan and the U-boat attacks in the North Atlantic, the Jekyll Island Club opened in early January as usual, but its 1942 season was problematic from the start. The onset of the war put tremendous pressure on club president Bernon Prentice, who needed to address multiple problems to keep the club operating. Transportation was a major issue because fuel was suddenly scarce. Not surprisingly, most of

Bernon Prentice (third from left) relaxes at the Tea House at the Great Dunes golf course in 1940. With him are his wife, Josephine Prentice (far right); Felipe A. Espil, Argentina's ambassador to the United States from 1931 to 1943 (far left); and Hugh Dudley Auchincloss Jr., a wealthy stockbroker and lawyer (second from left). (Courtesy of the Coastal Georgia Historical Society)

the club members and their guests chose not to travel to Jekyll Island in the midst of war, in part because the island was remote and vulnerable. Another major problem was the lack of available workers, who were increasingly being diverted to the war effort. Without a sufficient number of cooks, servers, maids, and other essential employees, club operations were debilitated in many ways. With far fewer guests, it was clear that this season would be a very different experience for the Jekyll Island Club.

Charles and Charlotte Maurice's daughters, Marian and Margaret, the latter of whom who had inherited their father's membership, still journeyed to Jekyll for the fifty-fourth club season. Within a few years, they would be among the last remaining members of the Jekyll Island Club. The sisters quickly realized that the club season in 1942 was unusual compared with previous seasons. Nevertheless, they loved the isolation of the island and enjoyed spending time at their family's Hollybourne Cottage, visiting the beach, and socializing with other club members. While they likely were cognizant of the club's fiscal problems, they were not fully aware of the seriousness of the situation until March 3, when they met with Josephine Prentice, the wife of the club president, who gave them a "long account of the club's finances."[2]

Three days later, Bernon Prentice announced an early closing of the club's season. Prentice left the island a few days after his announcement, but he arranged with the Sea Island Company, which was overseeing the landscaping of the club's grounds, to extend the club season to Easter. Prentice initially hoped to reopen the following year, but in a September 1942 letter to Bill Jones, president of the Sea Island Company, he wrote, "On account of difficulty for fuel, transportation and labor, and supplies [the club] will not attempt to open Jekyll Island this next winter."[3] In spite of Prentice's intentions, the Jekyll Island Club would never open again.

Given the circumstances, Marian and Margaret Maurice must have realized that once the club closed for the season, they might not be able to return to Jekyll Island until the war was over. So as they began formulating their plans to depart by the end of March, it was with the idea that they would be away for an indefinite and perhaps prolonged period of time. Still, despite the island's vulnerability, they were not in any rush to leave Jekyll, as they intended to pack most of their belongings, including family heirlooms, pictures, china, books, papers, and some of their furniture. Even after the movers arrived on March 15, the sisters stayed another twelve days, storing teacups and airing blankets and other sundries. On March 27, they left Jekyll to visit the Hofwyl Plantation, and two days later, they attended a Palm Sunday church service at St. Mark's Episcopal Church in Brunswick, after which they crossed the St. Simons causeway to eat lunch at the Cloister. Later that day, Marian Maurice commented in her diary, "Beautiful plantings good lunch, but oh! The contrast to Jekyll."[4] The next day they boarded a train and left the Georgia coast to return to their home in Athens, Pennsylvania.

One week later, World War II finally came to the Georgia coast in a shocking manner. Near midnight on April 8, 1942, German Lieutenant Commander Reinhard Hardegen ordered his submarine, *U-123*, to approach St. Simons Island. He was pleasantly surprised to find no blackouts in Brunswick or on the sea islands, which made it much easier to spot ships, as they would be silhouetted against the coastal lights. Shortly after midnight, Hardegen's U-boat fired a torpedo at the SS *Oklahoma*, a 9,200-ton tanker. Years later Hardegen remembered, "The lights on shore were illuminated. She was a sitting duck." As the boat sank, the German submarine surfaced to fire its machine guns. Half of the *Oklahoma*'s thirty-two crew members died as the ship went down in shallow waters ten miles offshore St. Simons Island; most of them were asleep in their quarters when the ship was attacked.[5]

The explosions awakened people on St. Simons and Jekyll. Less than an hour later, *U-123* torpedoed another tanker, the *Esso Baton Rouge*, off the northeast coast of Jekyll Island. One witness account from Jekyll recalled that the submarine "thrust a torpedo into the side of a tanker in plain view of Jekyll Islanders on the beach."[6] Not long after, in the early morning hours of April 9, Hardegen's U-boat sank the SS *Esparta* off the coast of Cumberland Island. *U-123* went on to destroy more American ships farther south, including the *Gulfamerica* steam tanker near the pier at Jacksonville Beach on April 10, 1942.[7]

The SS *Gulfamerica* steam tanker sinks near the Jacksonville Beach Pier following a German U-boat attack in 1942. (Courtesy of the collection of the Beaches Museum, Jacksonville Beach, Fla.)

Rufus Bennett, caretaker of Jekyll Island during the war years, sits on the Jekyll Island dock with the club steamer in the background, around 1942. (Courtesy of Harold Schaitberger)

The next day, debris from the attacks washed up on Jekyll's beach. Rufus Bennett, soon to be the island caretaker, went to the beach with his daughters to investigate. Almost sixty years later, Bennett's oldest daughter, Lillian Schaitberger, still remembered the scene vividly: "We had all kinds of things floating in on those tankers . . . crates of chickens, quarters of beef, cans, everything you can imagine." Even a part of the hull "washed up on the beach," she noted. "It sounds cruel. Daddy would go down and just kill them [the chickens]. . . . We couldn't leave them there just to let them starve to death."[8]

These brazen attacks exposed the complacency of the Office of Civilian Defense on the Southeastern coast. It was clear that Brunswick and the Golden Isles were vulnerable to enemy strikes. From that point forward, mandatory blackouts were frequently imposed, and military leaders realized that they needed to bolster the area with more troops and better ways to counter U-boats. As early as mid-April, Coastal Patrol 6 of the Civil Air Patrol, commanded by Major Thomas H. Daniel, gathered civilian pilots and private planes on St. Simons to search for German submarines off the coast.[9] About a week later, army military officials ordered troops to guard the region and to search for German U-boats. Many of these army camps were deliberately located throughout the Southeast to enable year-round training and to reduce construction and building maintenance costs.

In late April 1942, the first group of soldiers arrived in Glynn County: Company G from the 104th Regiment of the 26th Infantry. Charged with protecting defense industries in Brunswick, they initially established camps near the Hercules Powder Company plant in Brunswick, which extracted rosin, turpentine, and pine oil from pine tree stumps to produce a range of chemicals for industrial and military products, including explosives.[10]

Starting in late April of that year and continuing to the end of the war, the navy and the coast guard used the sea islands, including Jekyll, for their coastal patrols. In the first few months of the war, the soldiers of the 104th were typically broken into teams of eight soldiers and two radio operators that were sent to each of the sea islands. On Jekyll Island, Rufus Bennett allowed soldiers to use some of the facilities, including the club boardinghouse for male servants, the dining hall, and an employee house on Pier Road. After the soldiers erected an observation tower near Shell Road to watch the dunes, the beach, and the ocean horizon, they ran a telephone line from the tower to the house on Pier Road. The soldiers posted at the tower patrolled the shores along the beach. Bill Jones, president of the Sea Island Company, notified Prentice in August 1942 that "the Army just has a beach patrol on Jekyll as they have on all islands up and down the coast." He also added, "Each island either has or will have portable radio communication with the central headquarters in Brunswick and they have equipment for properly patrolling the areas."[11] At Jekyll Island, the employee house connected by telephone to the watchtower on the beach was nicknamed "radio shack." By the end of 1942, another tower, one that was significantly taller than the tower off Shell Road, had been built on the south end of the island to identify ships and suspicious activity.[12]

In July 1942, the coast guard began patrolling the shores along the beaches. The 104th, the coast guard, and other military detachments frequently coordinated their patrols. In 1943, troops patrolled the island on horseback. They could not routinely bring vehicles on the island since there was no access except by boat. On occasion Rufus Bennett, who kept a car on the island, loaned his Lincoln automobile to the coast guard to use on their patrols. Approximately twelve coast guards-

The Hercules Powder Company plant in Brunswick, Georgia, contributed significantly to wartime munitions. (Courtesy of the Science History Institute)

LEFT Watchtowers used for surveillance for German U-boats were located on the north and south ends of Jekyll Island. This is an image of the south end tower. (Courtesy of Harold Schaitberger)

RIGHT Turtle tracks spotted on the beach at Jekyll Island in 1944 were mistaken for tank tracks. (Courtesy of Ed Friend Visual Materials Collection, Richard B. Russell Library for Political Research and Studies, University of Georgia Libraries, Athens, Ga.)

men were stationed on Jekyll at a time. As it turned out, however, there were no more direct incidents along the shore of Jekyll Island; there was a report of tracks on the beach indicating that a tank had landed there, but Bennett explained it was the trail of a loggerhead turtle, whose tracks resemble tank tracks.[13]

Besides the rotating teams of army, navy, and coast guard personnel on Jekyll, a few civilians still lived or worked on the island. Rufus Bennett was the most important employee of Jekyll Island during the war. He began working on Jekyll in 1939 as a mechanic, but over the next few years he took on additional responsibilities, such as working in the power plant and serving as the island's boat captain. By early August 1942, he was the caretaker of the island, and during the war years his family would visit Jekyll on weekends and holidays. A few African Americans also resided on the island. Normally, after the club season ended, the island was largely populated by Black men and women, club workers who lived there for most of the year. During World War II, however, only a handful of Black employees stayed on Jekyll, among them seventy-year-old Ophelia Polite and Charlie Hill, who had spent most of their lives on the island, and Ralph Henderson, who was the night watchman.[14]

In the fall of 1942, the army's 725th MP Battalion replaced the 104th Infantry in guarding the coastal islands. The 104th remained in Brunswick,

Several African American families, among them the Hills, the Parlands, and the Polites, were prominent workers at the Jekyll Island Club. Charlie Hill, shown here, was coachman for the family of Charles Stewart Maurice. (Courtesy of Mosaic, Jekyll Island Museum)

and its troops were used primarily for mainland patrol. Both detachments bivouacked near the Hercules Powder Factory, but the 104th was transferred from the area in late 1943. The 725th took over the observation tower near Shell Road, as they continued the patrols on foot and by jeep. Lillian Schaitberger commented, "There were two companies called the 725th MP Battalion. They were stationed in Brunswick, and they rotated them . . . every two weeks. They'd be out here [on Jekyll Island], they would go back to Brunswick, and they'd rotate them around the islands on the Georgia coast. And then later 'A' company went back, and a 'B' company came back."[15] Schaitberger claimed that near the end of the war, "they did end up . . . having some lady guards here"; these were likely WAVES (Women Accepted for Volunteer Emergency Service), members of the women's branch of the U.S. Naval Reserve.[16]

One evening, a soldier thought he saw a light above the ocean's horizon and was worried that it was a submarine recharging its batteries. An airship from Brunswick flew over the area and dropped some depth charges, but no enemy vessels were located that night. Indeed, there were never any documented enemy ships found in the area while the 725th was on the island.[17]

Perhaps one reason they did not detect any enemy ships was that the island patrols were increasingly needed to protect the wartime industries and military facilities that were developing in Brunswick. First and foremost was the incredible effort to build the famed Liberty Ships. The first keels were

Thousands of men and women worked tirelessly in Brunswick, Georgia, building the Liberty Ships. (Courtesy of the Coastal Georgia Historical Society) Between 1942 and 1945, the workers at the J. A. Jones Shipyard in Brunswick built ninety-nine Liberty Ships. (Courtesy of Brunswick–Glynn County Library)

Between 1942 and 1945, the workers at the J. A. Jones Shipyard in Brunswick built ninety-nine Liberty Ships. (Courtesy of Brunswick–Glynn County Library)

Liberty Ships were important to the war effort. (Courtesy of Brunswick–Glynn County Library)

laid at the J. A. Jones Shipyard in July 1942. People from all over Georgia flocked to Brunswick to take good-paying jobs and contribute to the war effort.

At its peak between 1943 and 1945, the shipyard employed sixteen thousand men and women. The workers constructed ninety-nine cargo ships, each one measuring 447 feet long and weighing 3,500 tons. These ships played a crucial role in winning the war in Europe because they transported tanks, planes, guns, ammunition, trucks, bombs, and jeeps to England and other Allies, thus bolstering Allied operations in the European theater of the war.

Another critical development was the creation of the Glynco Naval Air Station that helped protect the Liberty Ships. The U.S. Navy purchased 2,400 acres in Brunswick on which to build a facility for housing and maintaining airships, commonly called blimps. Robert and Company, an architectural and engineering firm in Atlanta, designed enormous structures to house the airships. The hangars at Glynco were the largest wooden structures in the world at that time, and construction workers assembled them in only six months. At the peak of the base's construction, 2,300 civilian workers were laboring ten hours a day Monday through Saturday. Incredibly, the entire project was built in fourteen months, and the Glynco Naval Air Station was commissioned in January 1943. This air base was one of five strategically placed air bases on the East Coast. Once the airships housed at these bases were fully operational and implemented, the U-boat threat essentially ceased.[18]

Meanwhile, Bernon Prentice had not been to Jekyll Island since he closed the club at the end of the 1942 season. Prentice was a Wall Street stockbroker in his early sixties whom both the French and Italian governments had deco-

Blimps were used for surveillance to protect the various wartime industries in Brunswick. (Courtesy of Brunswick–Glynn County Library)

rated for heroism in organizing ambulances on the Italian front during World War I. His correspondence shows that he spent most of the World War II years at either the Homestead spa in Hot Springs, Virginia, or his residence on Wall Street. Despite his absence from Jekyll Island, he was clearly thinking about Jekyll's future and was troubled by the club's diminishing funds. During this time, he was primarily dependent on Bill Jones of the Sea Island Company for information about conditions on Jekyll. Luckily, Jones had designated his executive secretary, James D. Compton, to oversee Jekyll Island and its employees during the war years and beyond. Just as Glynco was fully opened, Bernon Prentice sent a letter to Bill Jones expressing his belief that "the Marines might be interested in leasing Jekyll Island."[19] Jones, who had investigated the military leases in Florida, responded that such an arrangement was not likely to generate significant income and might be detrimental to the island. Prentice followed up by writing that he was "most anxious to have Jekyll continue as a club after the war, and since the Army and the Navy both know it's available, I think we should let nature take its course."[20]

Bill Jones (1902–1982) was president of the Sea Island Company, which oversaw Jekyll Island during World War II. (Courtesy of the Sea Island Archives)

Six months later, while still at the Homestead, Prentice reached out to Jones about "forming a syndicate to purchase Jekyll Island" with financial support from some twelve Jekyll Island Club members, Frank Miller Gould being the largest investor. Prentice ended the letter with these words: "Have funds on hand to carry on through Feb. 1944."[21] After this correspondence, Prentice seemed to become more and more desperate, but it appears that, for unknown reasons, Bill Jones did not respond to nine letters and a telegram from Prentice between August 5, 1943, and November 1943. Finally, in late November, Jones composed a letter to Prentice in which he apologized for "the long delay in answering your recent letters"; however, his response was not at all encouraging about the situation. He wanted to "set down a few facts" about the problems with Jekyll. First, he believed that Jekyll could now become viable only with the construction of a causeway, which would cost at least $500,000, plus the cost of erecting a drawbridge over Jekyll Creek. He also pointed out that getting power lines to Jekyll would cost another $75,000. Then many thousands of dollars would be needed to build roads on the island and enlarge the water system. Jones also informed Prentice that a recent storm had caused much damage to the island, especially to the famed Great Dunes golf course designed by Walter Travis, which Jones claimed had eroded almost to the beach. He added that "the buildings, furnishings, [and] layout there at Jekyll are old," and he ended the letter pessimistically: "As much as I hate to say it, we are of the opinion that a successful operation of the present club facilities would be very difficult after this war . . . unless some fairy godfather could make up operating deficits."[22]

Prentice was clearly running out of options. In his absence, Bill Jones worked to arrange for some Miami investors to tour the island in a jeep, but they left quickly to check out beachfront properties in Jacksonville. Roy Hawkins, one of the prospective investors, sent a letter to Bill Jones stating that "it [the island] is one that is most inviting, but to be successful, it presents quite an operating problem and I am not sure we are in a position to handle it."[23] Jim Stockton, who owned a Florida resort at Ponte Vedra and was an associate of Hawkins, wrote that "we are in a fog regarding our views concerning Jekyll Island. . . . [T]he development of the island would be difficult without a causeway."[24] A few days later, Prentice received a letter from his Brunswick attorney, F. M. Scarlett, notifying him that U.S. Navy Captain H. F. Lawrence, who had recently been to Jekyll Island, had "made an investigation relative to using the island for the wounded boys who are being brought back from the front." Scarlett said that Captain Lawrence was "going to make a recommendation that the Government use the island for this purpose," because he thought the club would not charge very much rent for "these wounded boys as the Club was not using the Island at the present time."[25] Based on a telephone conversation between JIC superintendent Michael DeZutter and Jim Compton in July 1946, it appears that Prentice made a temporary agreement with Captain Lawrence to allow wounded navy members to convalesce at Jekyll Island.[26] Additionally, in late 1944, the army leased Jekyll Island to practice maneuvers by simulating beach landings, with the goal of preparing for amphibious assaults in the South Pacific theater of World War II.[27]

On April 4, 1944, a group of Jekyll Island condominium owners—the remaining shareholders of the Sans Souci Association—met at 230 Park Avenue in New York City. This special meeting brought them together to sell the Sans Souci, a three-story building that stood adjacent to the clubhouse, to the Jekyll Island Club for one dollar. The meeting ended with a unanimous vote to dissolve the association, which further eroded the hope that the Jekyll Island Club would ever open again. This action demonstrated the eagerness of Jekyll Island Club members to bail out of the club.[28]

On April 30, 1944, Arthur Young and Company, JIC accountants, provided the club's balance sheet to the JIC board of governors. The report revealed the stark reality of the club's fiscal problems. The club had been closed since April 1942, and the 1943 and 1944 seasons were cancelled because of the war. The lack of membership dues and the expenses of upkeep for the clubhouse, golf course, stables, grounds, and gardens made this period a major loss. The accountants admitted that they did not have time for a physical inspection of the buildings, nor did they have the club's inventory from the last few years. As a result, they had to use prior numbers from 1941 and 1942, likely inflating the bottom line, which amounted to $54,000. Interestingly, most of the income for the Jekyll Island Club came from the American Creosoting Company, which periodically cut down pine trees at Jekyll between 1941 and 1944.[29]

In a desperate effort to save the Jekyll Island Club, Frank Gould and Bill Jones launched a campaign to buy club bonds owned by other shareholders. Frank Gould was the grandson of Jay Gould, a railroad magnate in the late 1800s. The Gould family owned three houses in the cottage colony at Jekyll, and Frank Gould, who had come there since he was a small child, loved the island. He was perhaps the only long-term member, besides the Maurice sisters, who wanted to see the Jekyll Island Club resurrected. By August 1,

Frank Miller Gould was the grandson of railroad magnate Jay Gould. His family owned three houses at Jekyll Island: the Gould cottage (now only ruins), the Villa Marianna, and Cherokee, which had been built for Frank Gould's maternal grandparents, Dr. George Frederick Shrady and his wife, Hester. (Courtesy of the McCash Collection)

Gould and Jones had accrued $185,000 and were in the process of buying out other bondholders. The syndicate plan seemed to be working, but then Frank Gould died suddenly of a heart attack at his breakfast table on January 13, 1945. He was the only remaining club member with access to sufficient funds for building a causeway to Jekyll Island.

At this point, Jim Compton, the new president of the Sea Island Company, and Bill Jones, now chair of the Sea Island board, seriously considered buying Jekyll Island to prevent it from falling into the wrong hands, which might have had an undesirable impact on Sea Island. Within three days of Gould's death, Jones hired New York attorney Marion N. Fisher to study the pros and cons of acquiring Jekyll Island. Fisher carefully investigated the possibility for several months, including hiring a New York appraisal company and making sure the deeds were in order. He also reached out to Frank Gould's estate to determine the status of Gould's bonds, and he designated the year 1913 to be the base of depreciation of the property owned by Jekyll Island. The study highlighted some of the beneficial aspects of the purchase, which included an immediate enlargement of the resort facilities for Sea Island, the international reputation of Jekyll Island, and other tangible and intangible factors.

Curiously, Prentice was mostly out of the loop during this critical period, but in the meantime, Bill Jones and Jim Compton were quietly continuing to work on the possible acquisition of Jekyll. The correspondence is a bit murky, but it seems that Prentice and Jones were trying hard to buy out and consolidate the JIC bonds. It was clear to Prentice that the Jekyll Island Club was faced with foreclosure. It appears that there were serious conversations about demolishing some of the iconic structures in the cottage colony. On May 1, 1945, F. M. Scarlett sent a letter to Prentice about the possibility of the Sea Island Club purchasing Jekyll. He discussed plans for the existing buildings on the island. Referring to a prior letter, Scarlett stunningly wrote, "Don't you think it would be wise for us not to say anything about demolishing the club house or Sans Souci until we make the proposition of settlement of taxes?" He also mentioned that "there might be a possibility of cancelling out these old leases by making a conveyance of the Jekyll Island Club properties to some company and then letting the charter of the Jekyll Island Club expire . . . on the 18th of January 1946 and then there would not be any [negative] publicity of the Jekyll Island Club going out of existence."[30]

Bill Jones was mostly concerned about the Gould estate, especially when the attorney for Gould's widow stated to Scarlett during a visit to Jekyll that "there might be complications." Scarlett recommended Charles L. "Charlie" Gowen, a Brunswick attorney and state representative from Glynn County, to represent the Gould estate if there was a conflict. Although Gowen never advocated for Mrs. Gould, he would become an important player in the story of Jekyll Island.

Despite all the challenges surrounding the messy situation for the Jekyll

Admiral Chester Nimitz signs the Japanese Instrument of Surrender, as General Douglas MacArthur (closest to camera at left) looks on. The surrender ceremony took place aboard the USS *Missouri* on September 2, 1945. (Library of Congress)

Island Club, somehow Prentice still wanted to go ahead and open the club in 1946, which was a big problem for Compton and Jones in their effort to acquire Jekyll Island. Scarlett commented to Jones, "How any person could think . . . that the Club could be operated for any length of time on the basis on which they are operating it is to me wishful thinking."[31]

Eleven days later, World War II formally ended when the Japanese emperor signed surrender documents aboard the USS *Missouri*. V-J Day sparked jubilant celebrations around the country. At Jekyll, the navy still occupied the island, and its fate was still undecided. In the months ahead, Jekyll Island would become embroiled in one of the most tumultuous periods in Georgia politics.

This photograph of the Jekyll Island Club in 1944 shows the unkept grounds and poor condition of the clubhouse. (Courtesy of the McCash Collection)

THE END OF SPLENDID ISOLATION

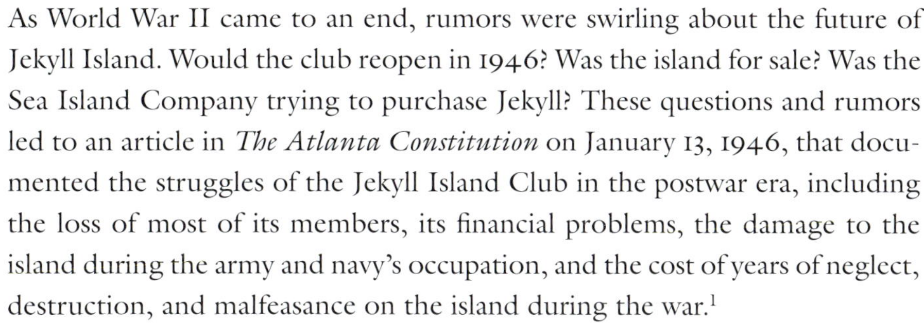

As World War II came to an end, rumors were swirling about the future of Jekyll Island. Would the club reopen in 1946? Was the island for sale? Was the Sea Island Company trying to purchase Jekyll? These questions and rumors led to an article in *The Atlanta Constitution* on January 13, 1946, that documented the struggles of the Jekyll Island Club in the postwar era, including the loss of most of its members, its financial problems, the damage to the island during the army and navy's occupation, and the cost of years of neglect, destruction, and malfeasance on the island during the war.[1]

Only a handful of people knew what was really happening. Since the death of Frank Gould in 1945, Bill Jones and Jim Compton had quietly considered the possibility of purchasing Jekyll Island to expand the operations of the Sea Island Company. Compton had commissioned a study about Jekyll in early 1945 so that he and Jones could evaluate the viability of acquiring the neighboring island. Compton, who oversaw Jekyll during the war, knew its condition. He personally developed a comprehensive Jekyll Island survey for Bill Jones and the Sea Island board. On March 29, 1946, he released his recommendation "that Jekyll Island be operated under the name of Jekyll Island Club, but in actuality [it will] be a public inn and a resort catering to a selected and restricted clientele," to be operated by the Sea Island Company. Compton warned that it would take years to make any profit, as the costs of operations and the backlog of repairs were problematic. He also pointed out that the tax consequences of integrating Jekyll Island into the Sea Island Company would complicate the issue of outstanding Jekyll bonds. On top of all that, the low estimate for the cost of a partial opening of Jekyll Island was nearly $604,000, and that number did not attempt to include the expenses of new employees, termite treatment in the clubhouse, and addressing the deteriorating condition of many of the structures. He examined the possibility of acquiring the island through a shell corporation, but the corporate taxes were likely to rise dramatically after the war. After two years of debate, Compton's survey finally made it clear that the Sea Island Company was not in a position to acquire Jekyll Island.[2]

However, on June 27 Prentice sent a telegram to Jones that read, "IN ACCORDANCE OUR CONVERSATION IN NEW YORK WOULD APPRECIATE SEA ISLAND COMPANY TAKING OVER RESPONSIBILITY DAY BY DAY

MANAGEMENT JEKYLL ISLAND IMMEDIATELY."[3] Over the next few days, Compton made several phone calls to some of the key people involved with Jekyll Island. Perhaps the most telling was a long phone call on July 2 with Michael DeZutter, the JIC superintendent, who was then living in New York. Compton was trying to get a grip on the operations on Jekyll, and his conversation with DeZutter exposed many problems. First, Compton questioned DeZutter about his outgoing island caretaker Rufus Bennett, commenting, "I found out that all during the summer Bennett has been entertaining down there, presumably paying guests with great numbers from Atlanta. . . . I think Bennett has been renting the cottages out to them." DeZutter claimed that Bennett also "charged local people to golf" and that he was "making some side money."[4] This conversation explains why Compton had created a press release announcing Bennett's resignation, effective July 6, 1946. The press release also announced that "Prentice has arranged with the Sea Island Company to augment the supervisory service, which has been rendered by its landscaping department during the last ten years in maintaining the golf course and club grounds, to include . . . general property supervision." Another issue that Compton brought up was the mounting debt from ten years of the Sea Island Company maintaining the costs of landscaping. It was clear that Prentice was in arrears and that DeZutter, who had not been to Jekyll since 1942, was in the dark about almost everything, including insurance policies, telephone bills, and numerous contracts.[5] Jekyll Island's future was more uncertain than ever before.

Ellis Arnall, governor of Georgia from 1943 to 1947, was in favor of the Jekyll Island acquisition. (Courtesy of Brunswick–Glynn County Library)

At this most critical time, the State of Georgia proactively stepped into the picture. In August 1946, the Georgia revenue commissioner, Melvin E. "M. E." Thompson, who at that time was also campaigning for lieutenant governor, publicly announced that he wanted to purchase a coastal island for the state to create a public beach park. Governor Ellis Arnall was initially in favor of the idea of a state beach park, so he appointed Thompson to lead a special commission to investigate suitable coastal islands for the proposed park. Thompson made numerous phone inquiries about Blackbeard Island, St. Simons, Sapelo, and Ossabaw.

On August 16, 1946, Thompson called Charles L. "Charlie" Gowen, a lawyer, judge, and member of the Georgia House of Representatives for Glynn County, for advice. Thompson was seeking reliable contacts to help him determine the possibility of acquiring Ossabaw Island or Blackbeard

Island. Gowen suggested he contact Bill Torrey, whose family owned Ossabaw, and, curiously, L. H. Smith of Savannah about Blackbeard, though the latter island was never actually an option since an executive order by President Woodrow Wilson in 1914 had made it a wildlife preserve, and a decade later it was established as a permanent national wildlife refuge.[6] Ossabaw, however, was another matter. A few days later, Thompson called Gowen again to let him know that Torrey had reported that Ossabaw Island was available for a price of $750,000. Gowen responded that "if the State was going to spend anything like that amount of money . . . Jekyll Island might be available." Gowen immediately called Compton to provide a synopsis of these phone calls with Thompson, because Gowen knew that the Sea Island Company had taken over the maintenance and general supervisory operations of Jekyll Island. Gowen asked Compton what "might be a fair price for Jekyll," and Compton replied, "in the neighborhood of a million dollars. . . . I'm not sure it can be bought at all, but I am quite sure it couldn't be bought for $750,000."[7] Gowen then contacted Thompson to let him know that Jekyll would cost at least a million dollars. For a while it seemed that Jekyll was unattainable, especially since Prentice made it clear publicly that he was looking forward to reopening the Jekyll Island Club in 1947. But Prentice knew the Jekyll Island Club was faced with foreclosure of the mortgage, and he acknowledged privately to Jones that "there is no way that I know of for the club to go on as it has been."[8]

Charles Gowen, a prominent lawyer and Georgia state congressman, played an important role in the state's acquisition of Jekyll Island. (Courtesy of Charles L. Gowen Papers, Richard B. Russell Library for Political Research and Studies, University of Georgia Libraries, Athens, Ga.)

Thompson may have received inside information about the financial problems of the Jekyll Island Club over the next few weeks. On September 5, Thompson called Compton directly to discuss the possible acquisition of Jekyll. Thompson explained that he had talked to Governor Arnall and to Eugene Talmadge, who was almost certain to win the gubernatorial election in November, and he declared that both men were on board with acquiring Jekyll: "I think I've sold them on the idea that if we could obtain Jekyll, we'll do it." Compton responded, "Well, that puts it right up to us and the question of putting the matter up to Mr. Prentice." He continued: "I've never said a word to him about this yet, I didn't want to get him even thinking along the lines until I knew there was something definitive. . . . I am not sure, Mr. Thompson, how Mr. Prentice will react to this." Thompson was optimistic, however, that the state could start a condemnation process in late November.[9]

Eugene Cook (at right) served as attorney general of Georgia from 1945 to 1965. (Copyright Atlanta Journal-Constitution. Courtesy of Special Collections and Archives, Georgia State University Library)

Four days later, Bill Jones received a telegram from Governor Arnall stating that "AFTER FURTHER LENGTHY DISCUSSIONS REFERENCE BEACH PARK INCLINED TO BELIEVE PROPOSITION HAS MORE MERIT AND POSSIBILITIES THAN FIRST APPEARED."[10] Charlie Gowen had recently spent a day at Jekyll Island with Eugene Cook, the attorney general of Georgia, and a few days afterward, Cook wrote a letter to Jones expressing that he was "personally ready to recommend that this be done immediately."[11] Sometime in mid-September, Gowen arranged for a boat trip to Jekyll Island, bringing box lunches from the Cloister for the members of the beach park commission, including M. E. Thompson and Glynn Phillips, a representative of Columbia County. After that tour, Thompson became even more excited about the possibilities of Jekyll Island.[12]

By this time, it was clear that Jekyll was the main target for the proposed beach park. In the weeks ahead, newspaper editorials from all over Georgia were mostly supportive of the state acquiring Jekyll Island, but there were some lingering concerns about the cost of purchasing an island that was not accessible by car from the mainland. In the midst of these newspaper articles, Prentice, who was somewhat blindsided by all the press, asked John Gilbert, his Brunswick attorney, to send out a press release with the following statement: "The officials and members of the Club are disappointed that the Committee which made the recommendation to Governor Arnall did not make an effort to get in touch with those in authority and ascertain the Club's plan and the availability of the Island before giving the proposed condemnation such publicity." The release also claimed that "the Club is making plans to reopen shortly." However, near the end of the press release, it acknowledged that "the State has the absolute right to condemn the Island" and "if condemnation is decided upon, the Club will cooperate insofar as its interests."[13]

A second wave of newspaper articles about Jekyll Island reflected another divisive issue. Many Georgia state representatives, especially those who were Talmadge supporters, wanted to slow down the process of acquiring the island so that the anticipated new Talmadge administration could oversee the costs and administration of the proposed new park. Eugene Talmadge, who had preceded Arnall as governor and was now running to replace him, was on record as being in favor of the park, but there were questions about how the state should acquire Jekyll Island, and he had worries about the process of condemning the island. As a consequence, Governor Arnall called a halt to the acquisition.

Throughout October and into November 1946, Thompson put aside the beach park commission to fulfill his obligations as state revenue commissioner and to turn his attention to campaigning for the position of lieutenant governor. Thompson won the race, making him the first person to be elected

Melvin E. Thompson was the first person elected to the office of lieutenant governor of Georgia. He served as governor of Georgia in 1947–1948. He is remembered not only for acquiring Jekyll Island for the state of Georgia but also for his role in the "three governors controversy" after the death of governor-elect Eugene Talmadge in December 1946. (Courtesy of Kenan Research Center at the Atlanta History Center)

After the death of his father, Eugene, Herman Talmadge claimed to be the rightful governor as a result of a write-in campaign and a vote by the General Assembly. Here he is shown campaigning in 1947. (Courtesy of Ed Friend Visual Materials Collection, Richard B. Russell Library for Political Research and Studies, University of Georgia Libraries, Athens, Ga.)

Georgia's lieutenant governor, which was a new position codified in the 1945 Georgia Constitution. Eugene Talmadge had won the Democratic primary for governor back in July; since there was no Republican candidate for governor, he was assured a victory in the gubernatorial election in November. However, Talmadge was dying of hepatitis and cirrhosis of the liver, and his supporters were worried that he might pass away before his inauguration, so they studied the state constitution and concluded that if the governor-elect died before the inauguration, the General Assembly could choose a new governor from among the candidates who placed second and third in the election. The party arranged for a secret write-in vote campaign for Talmadge's son, Herman. Eugene Talmadge passed away on December 21, 1946, just a few weeks before he was to be inaugurated in January 1947. The aftermath of his death created one of the most bizarre political spectacles in American history and put Jekyll Island's fate into the hands of partisan politicians.[14]

When the assembly met on January 15, 1947, the pro-Talmadge faction immediately pushed for the legislature to elect Herman Talmadge on the basis of the write-in ballots. Under the new state constitution, ratified in 1945, the lieutenant governor would become chief executive if the governor died in office, but the constitution was unclear about what would happen if the governor-elect died before the inauguration. The constitution stipulated that election results would not be official until certified by the General Assembly. Thompson wanted the legislature to certify the vote results, which would have given him a strong claim to the governorship, but Talmadge supporters prevented the certification in a narrow vote, and they moved on to selecting the new governor. The assembly elected Herman Talmadge, and Thompson immediately started legal proceedings to appeal the election outcome to the Georgia Supreme Court.

Ellis Arnall, the outgoing governor, proclaimed that he would not resign his office until it was clear who would become his successor. This announcement infuriated Talmadge supporters and triggered physical confrontations between members of the state legislature. Herman Talmadge demanded that Arnall honor the assembly's election, but Arnall insisted that the state legislature had no right to elect a governor, and he refused to step aside.

Amid all this chaos, Herman Talmadge ordered state troopers to physically remove Arnall from his capitol office, and both Talmadge and Arnall

Legislators sleep during the chaos and uncertainty of the three governors controversy. Photo taken March 20, 1947, at 11:30 a.m. (Courtesy of Ed Friend Visual Materials Collection, Richard B. Russell Library for Political Research and Studies, University of Georgia Libraries, Athens, Ga.)

now claimed to be governor of Georgia. The next day, Talmadge took over the governor's office and changed the locks on the doors. Meanwhile, Arnall became the governor-in-exile, setting up office in an information kiosk in the capitol rotunda. In the weeks ahead, Arnall renounced his claim to the governorship and threw his support behind M. E. Thompson's claims to the office. Over the next two months, chaos reigned in Georgia politics. During the uproar, Georgia Secretary of State Ben Fortson, who controlled the state's seal, which was required for any government action, hid it in the cushion of his wheelchair until the matter was decided.[15]

During the first troublesome months of the new year, Thompson's attention was focused on the contested political controversy in the election, which attracted negative national and international attention. Many Georgians were openly asking "who runs Georgia." In the contemporary account that decades later would be published as *Who Runs Georgia?*, Calvin Kytle and James Mackay found that "a few executives in a few corporations, together with a few skilled politicians, run Georgia."[16] From the perspective of Charlie Gowen, during the political crisis "Ed Thrasher [the state auditor] was running the state, and he did a splendid job."[17]

By early March 1947, Thompson was hearing rumors that he would likely win his case in the Georgia Supreme Court, which emboldened him to con-

Ellis Arnall performs his duties in the capitol rotunda while surrounded by reporters and onlookers after literally being carried out of the governor's office by state troopers at the order of Herman Talmadge. (Courtesy of Kenan Research Center at the Atlanta History Center)

tinue his push to acquire Jekyll Island for a public beach park. Charlie Gowen played an important role by arranging another VIP tour of Jekyll Island. Thompson, Glynn Phillips, and their respective spouses spent most of the morning touring the island with Gowen and discussing the possibility of a beach park at Jekyll. As they were returning to Brunswick, Thompson felt a renewed excitement and confidence about the acquisition. When Thompson and Gowen met again a few days later in downtown Atlanta, they had lunch at a restaurant on Luckie Street. At some point during that lunch, Thompson turned to Gowen and said, "Charlie, if I win this governorship, if I don't do another damn thing, I'm going to get Jekyll Island!"[18]

Finally, on March 19, 1947, the Georgia Supreme Court ruled in a 5–2

ABOVE Protesters at the state capitol during the three governors controversy. Students had worked hard for Ellis Arnall in the 1942 gubernatorial election, when Arnall defeated Eugene Talmadge, whose views the University of Georgia's *Red and Black* student newspaper had described as being "hand in hand" with Nazism and fascism. Now they opposed his son, Herman. (Courtesy of the Kenan Research Center at the Atlanta History Center)

LEFT B. E. "Ed" Thrasher Jr., Georgia's state auditor from 1941 to 1964, was a major factor in the conduct of state business during the three governors controversy. (Courtesy of Ed Friend Visual Materials Collection, Richard B. Russell Library for Political Research and Studies, University of Georgia Libraries, Athens, Ga.)

decision that M. E. Thompson was the rightful governor because he was the lieutenant governor when Eugene Talmadge died. The justices ruled that Thompson would be the acting governor until a special election could be held to decide the remainder of the original term. Within two hours, Herman Talmadge left the governor's office and began to campaign for the special election set for September 1948.[19]

After the verdict, Thompson quickly made plans for the acquisition of Jekyll Island. He notified Prentice on April 2 that the State of Georgia was "prepared to go forward with condemnation or otherwise." On April 7, Thompson arranged an informal closed meeting to discuss the terms of acquiring Jekyll. Bernon Prentice was not able to attend because his wife was sick, so Bill Jones essentially became the spokesperson for Jekyll Island. In these meetings, Gowen "did all of the negotiations to avoid accusations of money changing hands."[20] Gowen suggested that the state might pay as much as $800,000, but Jones insisted that Prentice would not consider anything less than $1,000,000. The meeting ended in a stalemate, but they agreed to convene again on April 28 in New York to continue the dialogue. By their third meeting, held in Atlanta on May 19, Thompson had reduced the offering price to $600,000 as fair compensation. Prentice thought the offer "quite inadequate," and he asserted once again that "the island was not for sale."[21]

On June 6, at the instruction of Acting Governor Thompson, A. J. Hartley, an assistant attorney general for the State of Georgia, filed the original condemnation proceeding in Glynn County Superior Court.[22] Herman Talmadge, who was campaigning for the special election in 1948, criticized Thompson about his dealings concerning Jekyll Island. First, Talmadge personally attacked the governor by nicknaming him "Me-too" Thompson, which caught on with Talmadge supporters during the long run-up to the special election. Next, Talmadge claimed that Jekyll Island was sinking. Talmadge's invective attacks also included the claim that his political enemies wanted an island "where they can go hide from the people and plan and scheme to spend the state's money for the favored few."[23] Talmadge supporters wrote editorials that denounced the Jekyll acquisition. The *Savannah Morning News* called it "unjust, confiscatory, undemocratic, and unAmerican," and another op-ed claimed that "the proposed acquisition of Jekyll Island stands as a monstrous intention to place the burdens of Hitlerism and Stalinism."[24] However, despite some negative editorials, the acquisition of Jekyll Island proved to be a popular move and received mostly positive press within newspapers around the state.

In this hyperpoliticized context, the condemnation proceedings began on June 26, 1947, in Glynn County Superior Court, with Judge Gordon Knox presiding. The State submitted that "it is the unanimous opinion of M. E. Thompson, Acting Governor, B. E. Thrasher, Jr., State Auditor, and Eugene Cook, Attorney General, that it is necessary and desirable to take property . . . to be used by the Department of State Parks . . . for enlarging and expanding the State Park System of Georgia by providing a State Seashore park to give seashore recreational facilities to the citizens of Georgia." The petition continued by pointing out that "the State has no beach park or seashore recreational facility on the seashore for the use of its citizens."

Jekyll Island Club officials thought that the price of $600,000 for acquiring the island was entirely insufficient, but they did not allow their attorney to take any action that might stop the state takeover. In fact, they made it clear that they wanted their lawyer to use "every fair and legitimate persuasion" to keep condemnation from being voluntarily dismissed by the state. Prentice and Jones had a lot on the line, because they were the primary people to be financially burdened with the cost of maintaining the island. They simply wanted to settle the matter. While they had hoped to get more money for the island, they felt that $600,000 was better than nothing.

To complicate matters, Lawrence Condon, the lawyer for the Gould estate, and the Maurice sisters wanted to stop the condemnation of Jekyll Island. Condon, who had recently acquired Frank Gould's cottage, the Villa Marianna, was "very unhappy about the State taking the property[,] and I have requested my counsel in Brunswick to see if it is not possible to retain my property."[25] Marian and Margaret Maurice, who had intimate ties to the island after sixty years of family ownership, were quite bitter about the state's actions, but they realized that if the state was determined to take control of Jekyll, they could do nothing to prevent it.[26] By late June, it was clear that the State of Georgia was going to go forward with the condemnation of Jekyll.

Talmadge supporters tried various tactics to delay the condemnation proceedings in an effort to make the island's acquisition by the State of Georgia an issue in the special gubernatorial election in 1948, but they were unsuccessful. Condon's efforts to sue separately also came to naught, and he was compelled to join the general condemnation proceedings. Thus a date was set for the condemnation hearing.

The last barrier revolved around how much the state was willing to pay. Two independent appraisers separately valued the property at $850,000, but the state appraiser set its worth at only $675,000. Judge Knox finally handed down his verdict on October 4, 1947, giving the State of Georgia the right to condemn Jekyll Island for a compensation of $675,000. Judge Knox also dispensed the value of the bonds and stocks from the Jekyll Island Club. The remaining JIC stockholders split $153,353, and the rest was divided among Lawrence Condon ($60,000), Margaret Maurice ($20,000), Bernon Prentice ($14,590, for tax liens he held against the Jekyll property), the Bankers Trust Company ($11,306), the New York Trust Company ($396,750), the Jekyll Annex Association ($18,000), and two Brunswick individuals who claimed ownership of Latham Hammock, a marsh island that club members had used for hunting ($500 each).[27] Within four days, the state took possession of the island. M. E. Thompson declared that Jekyll was now "a playground that be-

The aging Maurice sisters, Margaret (left) and Marian (second from left), stand on the front steps of Hollybourne Cottage with a few visitors. (Courtesy of the Maurice Family Papers, Southern Historical Collection, Wilson Special Collections Library, University of North Carolina at Chapel Hill)

longs to every Georgian." The cost of acquiring Jekyll was a good bargain for the state, despite Talmadge's complaints. As for the Jekyll Island stockholders, Jones thought it had been "a good solution to a difficult problem."[28]

Club members were allowed to remove their belongings from the island before January 1, 1948. Among the families that went back to Jekyll to claim their belongings were the aging Maurice sisters, who returned to the island for the last time. Marian Maurice wrote in her diary that the distressful chore of "dismantling our dearly loved house" was "heart-rending" for her and her sister. She mourned their loss and asserted that "when Jekyll Island was lost to us, we never wanted to see the coast of Georgia again."[29]

Most of the club furnishings were sold to Lawrence Condon, the Sea Island Company, and an antique dealer from Atlanta. On November 5, the last Jekyll Island Club stockholders meeting in New York resolved legal details, outstanding taxes, and the final settlement of accounts, which included compensation to the Sea Island Company for its multiple services over the previous ten years.[30] Michael DeZutter, the JIC's superintendent, who claimed that he had worked eight years without compensation, submitted a request for $36,000 but later settled for $15,000. On January 31, 1948, the Jekyll Island Club Corporation was legally dissolved. Among the stockholders was Bill Jones, who, after he received his cash distribution of $10,590, donated the funds to the Thomas and Jones Educational Foundation.

Bernon Prentice, the last president of the Jekyll Island Club, passed away at the age of sixty-six on June 12, 1948, just a few months after formally disbanding the club. It was clearly the end of an era of "splendid isolation" at Jekyll Island that the nation's wealthiest families enjoyed for more than sixty years.[31] But these wealthy families were not the only ones displaced by the state's condemnation of the island. Many people forget that after each club season ended, the island was inhabited primarily by year-round African American workers employed by the Jekyll Island Club. Some of them had lived on the island for many decades, including Charlie Hill and Ophelia Polite as well as members of the Parland, Clark, and Denegal families, who considered Jekyll their home. With the closing of the club, a way of life had come to an end on Jekyll, but the opening of Jekyll Island State Park on March 5, 1948, would usher in a new era.

The *Robert E. Lee*, a paddle wheel sternwheeler, was used to transport visitors from the mainland to Jekyll Island. (Courtesy of Mosaic, Jekyll Island Museum)

A STATE PARK FOR THE PLAIN PEOPLE OF GEORGIA 3

After Judge Knox ruled that the State of Georgia had the right to condemn Jekyll, the state took possession of the island on October 7, 1947. Governor Thompson knew he did not have much time to demonstrate the worth of Jekyll Island before the special election on November 2, 1948. Within two weeks, he had transferred a group of Black convicts to Jekyll to begin the difficult work of transforming the island from a privately owned property into the new Jekyll Island State Park, which in 1948 and 1949 would be operated as part of the Georgia state parks system. At that time, the director of the Department of State Parks was Charlie Morgan, who had hired John Messick as superintendent of Jekyll Island on December 1, 1947. On October 11, 1948, Governor Thompson gave a speech in which he optimistically predicted that a multimillion-dollar bridge and a highway project would be completed within a year and declared that these projects would "save" Brunswick.[1] In reality, the completion of these projects would take far more time and money than he originally thought.

The decision to utilize convict labor would prove to be controversial, especially among the African American community in Brunswick. Black convict labor had been a common feature of the Georgia penal system in the postbellum era, when enslaved labor was no longer legal. At first, convicts had been leased to private citizens as a source of income for the state. Later, the state abolished convict leasing to private citizens and developed the chain-gang system to serve on public projects, such as roadways. During his term as governor, Ellis Arnall had sought to reform the prison system and eliminate its cruel treatment of prisoners and use of the chain-gang system, while still allowing Georgia prisoners to work on public projects.[2] His efforts at eliminating inhumane treatment were only partially successful. For example, on July 11, 1947, there was an incident at the Glynn County prison camp in which guards shot and killed eleven convicts who were refusing to work in a snake-infested ditch.

Two months later, when Thompson professed that he wanted convicts "to do lots of work that may need doing" on Jekyll Island, the African American community in Brunswick protested the governor's decision.[3] The leader of the protest was Dr. Willard A. Patterson, who said, "We shudder at the thought of July 11th." He added that "Brunswick negroes are as much interested in the development of the resort as whites" and urged the state to hire local laborers, pointing out that "the use of convict labor deprives other mouths that should be getting fed." Patterson also worried that the transportation of convicts to and from the island might precipitate another incident like the one on July 11.[4] As a consequence, he suggested that the convict camp should be on the island itself. Governor Thompson had earlier claimed that, with the use of convict labor, the cost of transforming the park would reduce expenses by 60 percent. Responding to the recent protest, however, he announced that he would instead use white convict labor. Ten days later, he changed course again by pivoting to the use of free workers, who would "be faster and more efficient."[5] On November 11, Charlie Morgan, the state parks director, followed up by commenting that "every effort will be made to utilize the labor supply in Brunswick and the surrounding area in converting Jekyll Island into the finest seashore park in the United States."[6] Nevertheless, in the months and years ahead, the issue of convict labor would continue to be problematic and controversial.

Another major issue was the lack of state park personnel. Charlie Morgan spent significant time on the island, and he realized that Jekyll Island State Park could be the jewel of the state's parks department. He appointed Harry Glenn Jr. as the new superintendent of the park, replacing John Messick. Morgan also knew that the clubhouse and cottages needed special attention, so he decided to set up a private contract with Thomas Briggs Jr. for lodging services, with Briggs receiving a $6,000 annual salary plus 10 percent of the profits. Briggs, who was originally from Augusta, Georgia, was the owner of a seasonal hotel in the town of Manteo on Roanoke Island in North Carolina. During that first season at Jekyll, Briggs renamed the clubhouse and annex as the Jekyll Island Hotel, and he set the rate of renting a room at three dollars per person daily.[7]

As he rushed to open the island, Thompson was fortunate to have access to funds. Charlie Gowen explained that with the new Georgia sales tax, B. E. "Ed" Thrasher, the state auditor, "was able to get $800,000 for funds to purchase the island and still have another $150,000 that Thompson could use without legislative appropriations . . . so Thompson got it and turned it over to the park service."[8] Unfortunately, although the opening of Jekyll Island was originally scheduled for January 15, 1948, the park would need much more work before it was ready for visitors. After years of neglected maintenance, landscaping, and upkeep of the old clubhouse and other structures in what was a semitropical climate, it would take several additional weeks to make the property presentable to the public. Charlie Morgan announced a new opening date of March 1, but when that day arrived, they still were not ready to unveil the park. Finally, Jekyll Island State Park opened on March 5, 1948. Morgan announced that the clubhouse and the club annex could house 400

LEFT Parks director Charlie Morgan greets tourists who have arrived on Jekyll by ferry. (Courtesy of Mosaic, Jekyll Island Museum)

BELOW A bellman welcomes visitors into the "modernized" Jekyll Island Hotel. Among the bellmen of this era were Earl Hill, who served as bell captain, and John C. Newkirk; both men worked for the hotel in 1948. Hill went on to become a professional golfer, and Newkirk became pastor of a Baptist church in Garfield, Georgia. (Courtesy of Mosaic, Jekyll Island Museum)

Elizabeth, Joe, and Robert Ansley enjoy a bike ride on Jekyll Island on April 1, 1948. The Ansleys were among the first visitors to Jekyll in the new state era, arriving by ferry from Brunswick. (Courtesy of Frank and Elizabeth Allan)

Officials held beauty contests on Jekyll Island in the late forties and in several subsequent years as part of an effort to bring more visitors to the state park. (Courtesy of Mosaic, Jekyll Island Museum)

guests in 150 rooms, and the Sans Souci could host another 150 guests. A press release said, "There are approximately a dozen private homes, all of which could be used to house guests, with the exception of the Rockefeller House, which will be made into a museum."[9]

The island was inaccessible by automobile, but the Brunswick Chamber of Commerce and the City of Brunswick were fortunately able to lease the *Robert E. Lee*, an old Mississippi paddlewheeler, to provide free transportation to and from Jekyll Island.[10] By the end of April, more than six thousand people had visited the island, many of them greeted personally by Charlie Morgan. Governor Thompson had made it clear he was "determined to convert Jekyll Island, a gold-plated winter resort off Georgia's southeastern coast, into a state park for 'the plain people of Georgia.'"[11] Despite the enthusiastic response to the opening of Jekyll Island State Park, it was obvious that the park needed more funds, workers, resources, amenities, and attractions, and more time to succeed.

This editorial cartoon by Clifford H. Baldowski, who signed his work "Baldy," pokes fun at preening state politicians in a mockery of the Jekyll Island beauty pageants. ("Boardwalk at Jekyll Island," *Atlanta Constitution* [ca. 1961]. Courtesy of Clifford H. Baldowski Editorial Cartoon Collection, Richard B. Russell Library for Political Research and Studies, University of Georgia Libraries, Athens, Ga.)

In the summer of 1948, when they were about fourteen years old, Cannon Davidson and his friend Clyde Story came on a barge to Jekyll Island. Story's father was a prison guard on the island. Davidson remembered that there were about thirty prisoners housed inside the Morgan Tennis Court, an indoor facility, where cots were set up for sleeping. The prisoners were trimming palmettoes and cutting grass in the district. Someone was living in the Rockefeller Cottage, and the Brown Cottage was still standing. The only paved road on the island, Captain Wylly Road, went from Riverview Road all the way down to the beach. Davidson recalled that there were several barges loaded with cedar trees and pine.[12]

Throughout the 1948 summer season, Herman Talmadge continued attacking Thompson for acquiring Jekyll Island. In the months before the special election, Talmadge and his supporters pounced on the Jekyll takeover in an attempt to make it the central issue of the election. Thompson accomplished many positive goals as governor, such as improving highways, increasing teachers' pay, extending high school to the twelfth grade, and providing money for free textbooks for Georgia's public schools. Ignoring these achievements, Talmadge and his supporters fixated on what they called "Thompson's Folly." Charlie Gowen said, "Some of Thompson's friends were concerned about his

M. E. Thompson speaks at a campaign rally in 1948. (Courtesy of M. E. Thompson Papers, Richard B. Russell Library for Political Research and Studies, University of Georgia Libraries, Athens, Ga.)

chances of winning the special election, especially because he was so focused on Jekyll Island, which was a key issue in the election. Thompson deserves the credit, though he sacrificed any chance of becoming governor. . . . All of his friends begged him not to do it, . . . but he was determined."[13]

Talmadge won the special election on September 8, 1948. Twenty-two years later, *The Florida Times-Union and Journal* published an article entitled "Thompson's Folly Revisited" that spotlighted Thompson's perception of the 1948 special election. Thompson is quoted as saying, "I spent one night at McRae, and Eugene Talmadge was sick then. Herman was there, and I told them that I thought Georgia should buy Jekyll. Herman agreed that it was a good idea and suggested that it be financed through an authority." If Thompson's recollection was correct, Herman Talmadge was not at all truthful

M. E. Thompson congratulates Herman Talmadge on winning the special election in 1948. (Courtesy of Special Collections and Archives, Georgia State University Libraries)

during the campaign concerning the Jekyll Island acquisition. Nevertheless, Thompson admitted that "it was good politics to attack me on the Jekyll purchase, and the record proves he was right because Herman won the election."[14]

In the wake of the special election, the status of Jekyll Island was in limbo in terms of what would become of it under the Talmadge administration. Three days after the election, the governor-elect asserted that he "would be glad to sell the coastal playground openly, if the state could get its money back."[15] According to Charlie Gowen, there were rumors of Talmadge reaching out to Miami speculators who wanted to buy Jekyll Island, but he apparently changed his mind. In late 1948, Gowen "got a request from Herman to talk to him about [Jekyll]." When they met, Talmadge professed, "I'd like to see the state keep it. I suppose it could pay for itself. We can't appropriate money, so it has to support itself." From that point forward, Talmadge demanded that Jekyll Island be self-supporting, even though the Georgia state parks system was chronically underfunded, and Jekyll Island State Park was nowhere close to supporting its own operations.[16]

What followed over the next few months was a muddle of suggestions and proposals. During this period, Newton Moye, who had replaced Charlie Morgan as state parks director in November 1948, proposed the sale of lots on the island to private individuals "in order to obtain funds for developing the state park without an additional burden on the taxpayers." Herman Talmadge initially endorsed this idea, but M. E. Thompson vigorously denounced it. Using some of Talmadge's harsh rhetoric from the special election campaign,

Thompson charged that "it's a move to dispose of the island to big-shot politicians or friends of big-shot politicians." Even the members of the state House Game and Fish Committee, which had recently visited Jekyll Island, told reporters they "were opposed to the sale of any part of the island."[17]

In early February, after a few weeks of delay and indecision, the Talmadge administration was suddenly racing to get a Jekyll Island bill approved in the General Assembly within one week, but there were multiple obstacles. On February 9, 1949, Rep. W. C. McMillan and others introduced a bill "to transfer complete power over Jekyll Island to a five-man board" and empower "the board to sub-divide one third of the island of the state park and lease it to private individuals." The bill specified that the "Jekyll Island State Park Authority issue revenue certificates to improve, repair, and expand facilities on the island."[18] Two days later, Rep. Bernard Nightingale of Glynn County protested that a measure of the bill had been approved without a full meeting of the committee, since he had not attended. Consequently, the House of Representatives sent the bill back to the committee.[19] The next day, Rep. Iris Blitch, chair of the House Properties Committee, held another session, but Nightingale once again missed the meeting in an effort to delay the bill. Despite his absence, Blitch declared that "the Jekyll Island bill passed and . . . the bill was cleared for action on the following Monday." Her committee's vision for the Jekyll Island board was for a politically nonpartisan board that could make Jekyll Island self-sustaining. The committee also mentioned possible board members, including two physicians, an Atlanta preacher, and a writer, but no politicians.[20]

In mid-February 1949, Governor Talmadge decided to take the authority in a different direction and to instead "create a five-man investigative commission, appointed by the Governor to decide what to do with Jekyll Island State Park." Frank S. Twitty, a notable segregationist who was Speaker of the Georgia House, introduced a new bill that would permit the sale of lots on Jekyll to private individuals, with the goal of preventing complete power over the island belonging to the proposed Jekyll Island Authority.[21] The next day, when it looked as if that bill would not pass, Charles Gowen and Frank Twitty formed a coalition "to introduce a resolution to set up a committee to investigate [a] means of making the state park self-supporting." The committee would submit recommendations to the General Assembly in 1950.[22]

In a last-minute strategy, Talmadge shifted toward transferring complete power over the state park to an authority, which could lease lots and issue bonds for improvements. He insisted that the assembly should take immediate action "to halt the losses in operation of the park." He claimed that the park was losing $500 each week and that it "could not be continued without disrupting the entire Parks Department." Annoyed by the situation, Talmadge threatened once again to sell Jekyll Island, but in the end he embraced Newton Moye's plan "to sell lots to raise money to make improvements of the island

The committee appointed to oversee the creation of a board to govern Jekyll Island was chaired by Iris Blitch (center), the only female legislator in the Georgia General Assembly and later the first woman from Georgia to serve a full term in the U.S. Congress. In this photo, the committee members stand beside the swimming pool at the Jekyll Island Hotel. (Courtesy of Ed Friend Visual Materials Collection, Richard B. Russell Library for Political Research and Studies, University of Georgia Libraries, Athens, Ga.)

resort," claiming "it would lift a big load off taxpayers." M. E. Thompson immediately attacked the move as a "plot to sabotage, discredit, and finally sell the island." Charlie Gowen said that "before any property is sold, a master plan restricting its use should be drawn. Otherwise, it will open the door to encroachment by juke joints, bar rooms, dance halls, and the like." Gowen preferred leasing the property rather than selling it to retain state control.[23]

Clearly, Talmadge was frustrated with the politics surrounding Jekyll, so he hatched a plan to appoint yet another five-man committee to negotiate an outright lease of the entire island. Pursuant to this plan, Talmadge ordered Newton Moye to shake up the Jekyll State Park's leadership. Jekyll Park director James Page suddenly resigned. He was replaced by Harold Zell, the assistant park director, who would be the temporary manager of the island park pending its lease. Talmadge asked Moye and B. E. Thrasher, the state auditor, to recommend a group of "impartial outstanding citizens" (later identified as State Senator Braxton Blalock Sr.; Mike Benton, who owned an Atlanta radio station; State Senator Carl Rhodes; State Senator Gould Barrett; and Moye and Thrasher) whom he could appoint to negotiate a lease of the entire island. As state auditor, Thrasher called for competitive bids on the lease, and for the contract to remain effective for the remainder of Talmadge's term as governor. M. E. Thompson reached out directly to Talmadge to let him know that he would be willing to lease Jekyll Island from the state. In a tongue-in-cheek response, Talmadge publicly exclaimed he "had just as soon turn it over to Mr. Thompson as anyone else," but he went on to say that that he wanted to lease it to a private citizen. In a swipe at Thompson, Talmadge claimed, "We've already spent $5,000,000 to $7,000,000 on Jekyll Island. It would be crazy to spend millions more on it." These ridiculously inflated numbers differed from those of the state auditor. Thrasher rebutted that "the purchase price, all repair and maintenance expenses, and all roads directly attributable to Jekyll have cost $2,881,564."[24]

By mid-March, it had become clear that the state wanted to lease the entire island for only twenty months, making it a temporary, short-term lease. The lack of a long-term lease was likely to slow the development of the island's infrastructure and facilities. In mid-April 1949, however, the committee awarded the lease to Barney Whitaker, a veteran hotel manager from Augusta with strong political connections to Talmadge. He signed a contract that made him manager of the hotel and other facilities for the next twenty months, but he also had the power to sublease other services and tasks.[25] In the first five weeks, Whitaker was already losing money, because he was averaging only 120 guests a day. His lease specified that he would pay 20 percent of gross revenues to the state. However, since he was operating at a loss, he did not pay the state any revenue funds during that time.[26]

Whitaker employed several high school boys from Augusta's Richmond Academy and male students from the Junior College of Augusta to remove brush, clean the hotel, assist guests, serve as waiters, haul luggage from the ferry to the hotel, and complete other tasks. One of the Richmond

Academy students was Paul Murphey, whose parents were good friends of the Whitaker family. Murphey shared vivid recollections of the summer of 1949, when he and his friends lived in sparse quarters in the Villa Ospo. His first impression of Jekyll Island was that "it was obvious it had been a grand place . . . but it had really fallen into a state of disrepair. This was once a very fine resort, but in that summer of '49, there was mere curiosity for visitors more than coming there for its elegance." He also recalled that the island was "quite limited, having to rely on ferry service. . . . I don't remember large crowds at any time. Only eight to twenty people were [arriving daily] on the ferry. Most came over, they looked around, wandered around, maybe had lunch, and then they caught the ferry and went back." In his words, "it wasn't a tourist attraction yet. . . . It was a wild island and people were pretty well

Men on horseback on Riverview Road on Jekyll Island; the horses they are riding were left on the island after the war. (Courtesy of Mosaic, Jekyll Island Museum)

confined to the historic area." In Murphey's opinion, the main attraction on the island was Whitaker's daughter, Mary, who was beautiful and popular. In fact, Barney Whitaker employed most of his family members, including his younger brother Albert, who managed the hotel kitchen, and his wife, Valeria Orr, who served as the dining room hostess. Whitaker and his son Robert managed the young men from Augusta, giving them different orders each day.[27]

Despite the first few difficult months, Whitaker eventually turned things around in the summer and fall. Better advertising in key cities such as Atlanta, Savannah, Macon, and Augusta attracted some large conventions, including the annual conferences of the Georgia Education Association and the Southeastern Park Association. Whitaker also subcontracted leases for two horse carriages and two buses so that visitors could tour other parts of the island. Dudley Gay, the island's first state trooper, helped out by regularly regaling visitors with stories about the millionaires who used to stay on the island.[28] There were setbacks, mainly a destructive storm on August 30, 1949, that led to a conflict between Attorney General Eugene Cook and Whitaker about who would pay for the cleanup and repairs. After the state finally agreed to cover those costs, Whitaker was able to make his contractual payments to the State Parks Department for the rest of the year. Unfortunately for Whitaker, he mostly lost money trying to keep Jekyll Island open during 1950. By the time his lease ended in January 1951, he had lost over $25,000. In the end he and his family made up for their losses by moving back to Augusta and opening the Clarendon Hotel and a popular cafeteria that allegedly brought in more than $200,000 in 1952.[29]

At this point, Jekyll Island State Park seemed to be a failure, in part because Governor Talmadge was adamantly against appropriating funds for park development. From March 5 to November 15, 1948, under former Governor M. E. Thompson, the state had made a profit of $8,356 from its own operation of the resort. Under Talmadge, between November 15, 1948, and February 15, 1949, the park made only $769.[30]

In the meantime, plans were in motion to request that the legislature create a new Jekyll Island Authority (JIA), despite objections from State Senator W. B. Cochran, who still wanted to sell Jekyll Island. When the General Assembly convened in January, it passed a bill to create a five-man Jekyll Island Authority that could sublease lots for residential and commercial use for fifty years and issue certificates to finance and build the Jekyll Creek Bridge. Talmadge signed the bill on February 15, 1950.[31] The Jekyll Island State Park Authority Act of 1950 specified that the JIA "is empowered to divide, improve and lease or sell to the extent and in the manner herein provided and improve not more than one-half of the land which lies above water at mean high tide." This part of the legislation has long been debated and will continue to be debated for decades to come. Despite the wish of Rep. Blitch's committee to establish a nonpartisan authority, as well as Talmadge's pledge to create "a non-political

Jim Compton, the last person appointed to the first JIA board, had overseen Jekyll on behalf of the Sea Island Company during the war years. His experience and integrity were invaluable in helping to guide the early state era of Jekyll Island. (Courtesy of the Sea Island Archives)

authority . . . to remove Jekyll Island from politics," section I of the act defined the JIA members as mostly Talmadge-aligned politicians, including "the Secretary of State, the Attorney General, the Chairman of the Public Service Commission, the State Auditor, the Director of the Department of State Parks, and a secretary or treasurer who may not necessarily be a member of the JIA."[32]

After the act was approved, Herman Talmadge named Senator D. B. (Braxton) Blalock Sr., one of his strong allies, as chair of the authority's board of directors. To serve with Blalock, he appointed Mike Benton (vice chair), State Rep. Ben Tarbutton, and Senator Gould Barrett. Talmadge asked Charlie Gowen for another meeting to offer him a pick for the last JIA board member. When they met, Talmadge suggested Bill Jones from the Sea Island Company, but Gowen told him, "Jones can't do it. But I think [Jim] Compton would be good." Talmadge asked: "Who's that?" Compton was indeed the perfect choice, because he had been intimately tied to Jekyll for more than ten years as secretary and later president of the Sea Island Company; he was also a meticulous businessman who had broad insight into resort development and causeway construction, and he brought impeccable integrity to an inexperienced and politicized board. As Gowen later acknowledged, "It turned out that Compton was a lifesaver, because there were good men [on the JIA board], but they were scattered around the state; they didn't know what was going on, but Compton had been overseeing the island for the last five or six years."[33]

Over the next five years, Compton was by far the most active member of the board and the conscience of the Jekyll Island Authority. Without his guidance, experience, and expertise, Jekyll Island would very likely have developed in a different, more commercialized way. His knowledge of resorts drove the JIA toward master planning and resource management that continued for several decades.

Georgia State Highway Commissioner Downing Musgrove is featured here (at center) with his wife, Lyneath (in the white hat). (Courtesy of Ruby Webb Collection of E. D. Rivers Materials, Richard B. Russell Library for Political Research and Studies, University of Georgia Libraries, Athens, Ga.)

4

A NATURAL BEAUTY PLAN

The new Jekyll Island Authority board members held their first meeting on Sea Island on March 4, 1950. Members thanked Jim Compton for his "fine hospitality" as they convened the meeting. The earliest issues were planning for development and attaining funding for the causeway and a bridge over Jekyll Creek. Ray Whittle, a Glynn County commissioner, presented a resolution supporting "the prompt completion of an access highway by the bridging of Jekyll Creek." He pledged "cooperation of local officials . . . in your sincere efforts to serve Georgia's growing resort economy, by the exploitation of the limitless facilities of fabulous Jekyll Island." On behalf of the county commission, he offered "to build the bridge . . . this path of progress," an offer that would ultimately prove too expensive for the county to bear alone.[1] At the end of the second and final day of the board meeting, Jim Compton laid out a simple and straightforward plan: "First, we need easy access to Jekyll Island. Secondly, we need a master plan for development. And lastly, we need to gather all the facts about the park before we make any decisions."[2]

Since Governor Talmadge had recently said he "would not spend a dime on Jekyll Island," finding the money to complete the causeway, a bridge over Jekyll Creek, and other infrastructure projects would be a difficult task.[3] In effect, Jekyll would be closed for the next four years. Jim Compton spent a considerable amount of time inspecting the existing buildings and the contents of the structures, including the "Negro camp and kitchen," for insurance valuations, which came in at $979,300. After the first few JIA meetings, the authority met primarily in Atlanta over the next four years. The board's second meeting addressed the issue of lacking sufficient funds. Consequently, the board drafted a letter to Governor Talmadge requesting $30,000 for "professional and technical services, travel and incidentals to be repaid when the Authority's revenues permitted." Reluctantly, Governor Talmadge provided the requested funds from the governor's office, which enabled the authority to hire a few employees. Then board members began the process of reviewing engineering and preliminary master plan proposals. In their June meeting, Senator Blalock suggested "arranging for a convict camp and work upon the island." This proposal for the convict camp was agreed upon, but in the long run it came at a price.[4]

"Georgia's padlocked island" was lampooned by Clifford H. "Baldy" Baldowski in a cartoon illustrating an editorial that began, "The story of Jekyll Island continues to be one of bumbling and fumbling." ("Isle of Golden Schemes," *Atlanta Constitution*, April 26, 1965. Courtesy of Clifford H. "Baldy" Baldowski Editorial Cartoons, Richard B. Russell Library for Political Research and Studies, University of Georgia Libraries, Athens, Ga.)

Meanwhile, over the preceding several months, an unprecedented dredging project had been underway to create the causeway, the Highway 17 spur, and other roads. By February 1950, the Hendry Corporation of Florida had nearly completed the massive undertaking to remove muck, marsh grass, and sand so that the new spur of Highway 17, which was only partially paved at that time, could be built. After more than two years and $2 million of state and federal matching funds, it seemed that Hendry's crews were close to reaching their goal. When they finished the last eight hundred feet of the causeway in late February, the road abruptly ended where the Jekyll Creek Bridge was slated to be constructed.[5] Many people believed that the drawbridge would be completed within a year, but the onset of the Korean War in June 1950 led to President Truman issuing Executive Order 10161 on September 9, 1950, which essentially rationed steel for civilian purposes. Two years later, in the spring of 1952, a major steel strike that lasted fifty-three days created significant delays, especially after Truman issued Executive Order 10340 directing his secretary of commerce to seize control of the steel mills.[6] As a result, steel was not readily available for construction of the Jekyll Creek Bridge, because the bridge was not being built for defense purposes. While JIA members and the Glynn County commissioners advocated for the highway and the bridging of Jekyll Creek, both political foot-dragging and the federal government's wartime need for steel would delay construction of the bridge for another four years. In view of the delays, the JIA board decided at its October 1950 meeting "that the Island Facilities shall close on January 15, 1951."[7] The island remained partially open on a limited basis for day visitors who came over by ferry, but Jekyll would not fully reopen until December 1954, prompting some journalists and politicians to complain about inefficient administration on "Georgia's padlocked island."[8]

Despite the criticism, the authority had made significant progress on multiple issues over the previous few years. First, it had contracted Georgia Power to install power poles and lines and aboveground conductors along the causeway, which cost nearly $76,000. The authority also allowed the Georgia Forestry Commission to conduct reforestation and fire suppression training on the island in a limited manner. After the 1951 legislature appropriated $100,000, Governor Talmadge announced that the authority would receive those funds for upkeep and improvements to the park, which was the first time the authority had access to a substantial sum to apply to a variety of projects.[9] The JIA hired John Miller as the resident engineer at Jekyll, and he developed a topographical map of the island. The authority also purchased a large brush cutter to cut through the dense forests so that the process of creating lots could begin.

In late 1949 the authority had hired Hoke Smith, a former deputy sheriff, to clean up the park after a destructive storm. He demonstrated his multiple skills and was promoted to superintendent of maintenance. In April 1951, the authority appointed Smith to be the park's superintendent. He played an important role during the period in which the island was in "a closed-down status." Smith was also responsible for overseeing the convict labor camp that the State Board of Prisons had offered "to put . . . on Jekyll Island for general improvement purposes."[10] In late July, he reported that there were twenty-three convicts on the island, and he requested that their number be increased to fifty. By November, it was simply recorded that there were "a large number of prisoners working on the Island." They were apparently making progress "in repairing, repainting, and improving the houses and grounds and building up the road system."[11]

Among the road projects was the important causeway, which would connect Jekyll Island to the mainland. After two and a half years of work, it was finally completed, and a dedication ceremony was held on November 4, 1950.

Despite early problems, the park's superintendent, Hoke Smith, continued to use convict labor on the island. (Courtesy of Mosaic, Jekyll Island Museum)

At the time it was dedicated to the public and given no name other than the Jekyll Island Causeway.[12] In 1996 the Georgia General Assembly would rededicate the road and name it the Downing E. Musgrove Causeway. Governor Talmadge finally approved an annual budget for Jekyll Island State Park for 1952, which enabled the JIA to complete a survey of the island to support future developments and improvements. He would go on to provide yearly budgets for 1953 and 1954. After the initial dedication of the causeway, it would take another four years to complete the Jekyll Creek drawbridge. Despite the strong push for the bridge, not even Jim Gillis, the longtime director of the state highway board, could break through steel rationing during the Korean War. Talmadge threatened not to finish the bridge over the Turtle River that would link Brunswick with the new 17 route; Thompson claimed that the governor had "said it would remain a silent sentinel to the island that only could be reached by submarine, but he relented."[13] Despite the delay in building both bridges, the harsh criticism of the authority was unwarranted. Indeed, the partisan Georgia legislature passed a resolution in March 1953 commending the JIA "on its devotion and duty and the progress it had made."[14]

Perhaps the most important accomplishment during this period was the creation of the island's master plan. Even though the island was closed, some authority members were eager to cut corners and speed the process to lay out at least two hundred lots and build on top of the old existing roads, but Jim Compton advised them once again that creating an "overall development plan" first would help guide the future of Jekyll. He suggested that "200 lots [are] needed and needed right away," but he wanted the other board members to understand that it should be done according to a master plan and not in a haphazard way. Authority members agreed. They had already reviewed a proposed plan from the Vinson Company, but Compton, who always sought expert advice, encouraged the authority to instead hire Robert and Company Associates "to prepare an overall master plan for the development of Jekyll Island."[15] Robert and Company, which had developed the Glynco Naval Air Station in Brunswick during World War II, was a nationally known engineering firm with a wide range of expertise in architecture, civil engineering, military projects, and resort development. On April 26, 1952, the JIA approved the Robert and Company contract, which specified that the master plan must be in agreement with the topographical survey map developed by the authority's engineer to develop the "layout for roads, streets, natural drainage, lots, parks, allocation of land areas as residential, commercial, and amusement development on the Island." Andre Steiner, the company's expert in resort development, joined the meeting and brought in some preliminary sketches for the master development plan.[16]

Most people had no idea of Steiner's remarkable background as a Holocaust hero. He was born in 1908 in the Austro-Hungarian Empire and given the birthname Endre. His father passed away when he was four years old, and his mother remarried and moved to Bratislava, a provincial capital on the Danube River. Fortunately for Steiner, he grew up in an area that did not experience early anti-Semitic violence. Like many other Jews, his family had assimilated into the secular culture. After high school, he enrolled in the Czechoslovakian Institute of Technology's School of Architecture and was trained as a Bauhaus architect. By the late 1930s, he had become a noted modernist architect, but he was troubled by the rise of Nazi Germany, and he applied to immigrate to the United States. However, in 1939 Nazi Germany seized control of Czechoslovakia, and Steiner and his family, along with about ninety thousand other Slovakian Jews, were trapped and under siege by Nazis.[17]

Andre Steiner, a Jewish immigrant who survived the Holocaust, came to Atlanta in 1950 to work for Robert and Company. One of his first assignments was to create the original master development plan for Jekyll Island State Park. (Courtesy of Amy Nadler)

Almost overnight, the Gestapo began harassing the Jews of Slovakia. Steiner's notoriety as an architect may have saved his life, because he was forced to work with the collaborationist Slovakian government to design state resorts in the Tatra Mountains. In all, he developed four resorts where injured German troops came to recuperate. In March 1942, Nazi authorities began deporting thousands of Slovakian Jews to Polish concentration camps. Within seven months, they had rounded up some sixty thousand Slovakian Jews and sent them to Auschwitz and other camps. Soon there were reports and rumors of torture and murders at the camps. Steiner joined Rabbi Michael Weissmandel and other leaders in Bratislava to form an underground organization called the "Working Group" to save Jewish lives in any way possible. Not only did they smuggle out information about the ongoing genocide, but they also bribed German and Slovak officials to prevent the deportation of Jews. Since Steiner's professional connections gave him access to Nazi officials, he became the group's main negotiator. His closest contact in the Nazi government was a man named Dieter Wisliceny, an SS officer assigned by Adolf Eichmann to serve as Jewish affairs representative to the Slovakian government.[18]

Steiner convinced Wisliceny and the Slovakian government that deporting Jews was a waste of valuable resources and skills, and he persuaded them to allow him to design and build labor camps in Czechoslovakia to create a variety of workshops that could provide needed items for the Germans. The Slovak government permitted Steiner to design three labor camps, which abruptly stopped the deportations of Jews from Czechoslovakia, saving about seven thousand Slovakian Jews from almost certain death in concentration camps. Encouraged by this success, the Working Group attempted a much more ambitious proposal called the Europa Plan. Beginning in the summer of 1942 and continuing for a year, Steiner negotiated a deal with Wisliceny that promised $3 million in exchange for ending the German policy of deportation and extermination. At first, Wisliceny agreed to the arrangement, but when the promised payments from Jews in the United States and Europe had not been delivered by late 1943, Wisliceny suspended his dealings with Steiner and resumed deportations. Nevertheless, he allowed Steiner's Jewish work camps to continue their efforts. Still, by 1943–1944, Nazi death camps were killing thousands of Jews every day, and relatively few Slovakian Jews remained in Czechoslovakia, with roughly half of them living in the work camps developed by Steiner.

As World War II raged on, deteriorating conditions triggered the Slovak National Uprising in August 1944, but the Germans crushed the rebellion within a few months. This turn of events forced Steiner and his family to flee Bratislava and seek refuge in the Tatra Mountains. When Steiner's parents were unable to go any further, they decided to hide in a small village, where they were later discovered and killed by Nazi soldiers. Steiner, his wife, and their son spent most of the winter of 1944–45 in a tiny hunter's hut in the mountains, struggling to stay alive while listening to the sounds of distant guns. Some local Christian peasants found them there almost frozen to death and brought them bread and bacon, which helped them survive as they continued to hide for the rest of the war.[19]

When the war ended, Steiner applied once again for visas for his family to enter the United States. Although his father-in-law lived in Atlanta, obtaining a visa was a long process, so Steiner resumed his architectural career in Czechoslovakia. In 1947, Steiner and his family moved to Cuba, where they would wait another two years for admission to the United States. He finally obtained the required visas for himself and his family, but before they had left Cuba, Chip Robert, the president of the prominent firm Robert and Company, discovered Steiner and offered him a position. Shortly after Steiner arrived in Atlanta on October 26, 1950, he accepted the job. When the Jekyll Island Authority called for bids for Jekyll's master plan, Robert and Company was well positioned to respond. The firm entrusted the proposal to its newly hired Slovakian architect Andre Steiner, who quickly anglicized his first name as Andrew. He was well prepared to undertake the planning of a resort community, having spent many years working in difficult conditions while planning and constructing resorts in the Tatras.[20]

Authority members debated the direction of the island's development. Some wanted Jekyll Island to be like "a little Daytona." Others favored the model of Long Island's Jones Beach. But Steiner thought Jekyll should remain in a more natural state. He remembered his first impression of Jekyll and the natural beauty of the island. Jim Compton persuaded the JIA to accept Steiner's "natural beauty plan" rather than a more commercialized plan.[21]

After the JIA signed the contract, Steiner brought his family to Jekyll, and they stayed in the Villa Marianna. "The planning of Jekyll Island was one of my first experiences in the United States," he recalled. He was very conscious of "planning something for the middle class, not for the rich." Steiner spent six months studying the island in consultation with Compton and planning its future layout, including a network of roads, residential subdivisions, a shopping center, a small airport, golf courses, beachfront development of motels, condominiums, and amusement parks. Perhaps most notably, the master plan developed only one-third of the island, leaving the rest of the island in its natural state—one of Jekyll's treasured qualities even today.[22]

Not surprisingly given the times, the original master plan did not include developments for African Americans. This was perhaps an oversight, but clearly the JIA prioritized the initial 250 lots for white people, and it seemed to put off any development for African Americans. The authority was forced to confront the challenge of developing a state park for all Georgians within the framework of the state's Jim Crow laws, which required the segregation of whites and Blacks in public settings. In September 1947, before the park had opened, local Black leaders made it clear that they wanted facilities at the south end of the island. According to newspaper accounts in the 1950s, Jekyll Island possessed the only public beaches in Georgia accessible to African Americans. After initially announcing that it would lease 250 residential lots for whites on the island, the JIA then announced there would be an additional 500 lots for white lessees. The authority received letters "from the negro leaders of Savannah inquiring about the status of a negro development of Jekyll Island," and it responded that, "[i]n the formulation of the plans of development of Jekyll Island, the Authority has given careful consideration to the needs of the negro citizens of Georgia."[23] In consultation with the authority, Steiner designated the Black developments for the south end of the island, its most remote area. It would take another six months before the authority discussed the issue of building an access road to the south end, which delayed the plans for an African American subdivision. Indeed, the first Black-owned house was not built until 1962.

A persistent problem on the island was the presence of convict laborers, who all too frequently tried to escape. The authority once again requested at least fifty African American convicts, but the prison board denied the request because Black prisoners were needed for other state projects, so the JIA decided to continue using white convicts. From the beginning of the convict camps on Jekyll, there were numerous runaways. Two long-term convicts escaped in a motorboat on December 5, 1951, but were apprehended the next day.[24] In January 1952, three prisoners walked away from the prison camp and crossed Jekyll Creek in a stolen boat, but they were captured within a few days.[25] Two more convicts escaped in late July 1952, and *The Brunswick News* reported that there had already been eighteen attempts to escape the

The use of convict labor was a problem in the early state era of Jekyll Island but would continue into the late 1960s nonetheless. (Courtesy of Mosaic, Jekyll Island Museum)

The dairy barn where prisoners were once housed on Jekyll Island. (Courtesy of Mosaic, Jekyll Island Museum)

island.[26] In July 1953, the authority determined that there were about eighty prisoners on the island, but within another year the prisoner count would increase to ninety-five.[27] In early March 1953, two highly dangerous convicts with life sentences escaped by setting several forest fires so they could elude the bloodhounds. The convicts attempted to enter Hoke Smith's house to steal his guns and ammunition, but Smith's wife quickly called the camp headquarters, and a guard rushed to the residence to prevent a hostage scenario. The incident played out over a ten-mile radius of the state-owned island, and an estimated one hundred acres on Jekyll were burned.[28] A month later, another group of convicts escaped, but they were captured in Coweta County a few days later. The JIA board members raised

Herman Talmadge and Marvin Griffin were the first riders to cross on the causeway following the completion of the Jekyll Creek Bridge, which was renamed for M. E. Thompson in 1989. The drawbridge would be replaced in 1996 by the concrete bridge standing there today. (Courtesy of Mosaic, Jekyll Island Museum)

ABOVE Herman Talmadge and other prominent politicians attend the official opening of the Jekyll Creek Bridge in December 1954. (Courtesy of Mosaic, Jekyll Island Museum)

RIGHT Reopening ceremonies at Jekyll Island State Park in December 1954, with Herman Talmadge, Marvin Griffin, and members of the first Jekyll Island Authority. (Courtesy of Mosaic, Jekyll Island Museum)

Talmadge and Griffin cut the ribbon at the park's reopening ceremonies. (Courtesy of Mosaic, Jekyll Island Museum)

questions about the safety of the general public on Jekyll given the number of convicts "working on the Island under very light guard."[29] Meanwhile, the escapes continued to occur. Another prisoner tried to escape on March 29, 1954, but was stopped by guards who fired buckshot into his right leg, knee, and ankle.[30] Every time a convict escaped the island, it compounded the public relations problems for Jekyll Island State Park. Nevertheless, the convict facility remained on the island for years to come.

While it continued to tweak the details of the master plan, the JIA was mostly absorbed in preparing lots, finishing the Jekyll Creek Bridge, and preparing the island for visitors. Although some early bids for construction of the drawbridge were in the $200,000 range, the final cost exceeded $800,000. Press coverage indicated that the bridge's construction would be finished by late summer in 1954, but multiple delays pushed the bridge's opening to later in the year.

Finally, after years of delay and incremental progress, the Jekyll Creek Bridge was at last completed. Some five thousand people attended its grand opening on December 11, 1954, where ironically both outgoing Governor Herman Talmadge and governor-elect Marvin Griffin made positive comments, even though each was previously on record as being against the state-owned Jekyll Island State Park.[31]

In the years to come, Jekyll Island would continue to be a politicized issue that led to scandal and corruption.

Jimmy Dykes, a strong supporter of Herman Talmadge, was a controversial figure on Jekyll Island, as well as in the state legislature. He is shown here sitting in the chair of Governor Ellis Arnall during the three governors controversy. (Courtesy of Special Collections and Archives, Georgia State University Libraries)

THE WHITE ELEPHANT

5

In the first ten days after the island finally opened to automobiles in December 1954, the JIA received two hundred applications for residential lots. With another three hundred leases already in development, the authority planned to prepare for an additional fifteen hundred lots, making for potentially two thousand lots in all, though the number of lots never actually rose that high. The authority drafted rules that allowed one person to lease no more than three adjoining lots and required prospective lessees to make a deposit of $255 to deter speculative leasing. The cost of the leases varied from $100 to $400.

Within the first week of 1955, all oceanfront lots had been assigned. Jim Compton confirmed the strong demand for beach lots and claimed that the authority would "go to work at once on plans for making more ocean sites available in future subdivisions. Streets in the new subdivisions are being graded and water mains installed so there will be no delays to builders." By late February, leases were granted for the first motels and hotels, including two beachfront motels. D. B. Blalock announced that an unidentified Washington, D.C., hotelman was ready to spend $225,000 on the Jekyll Island Clubhouse and on improving Crane Cottage for use as a hotel. Blalock also promised that "in the near future, there will be general businesses, a gas station, and a building supply firm on the island."[1]

On May 25, 1955, *The Brunswick News* published the names of 104 individuals and firms that had leased lots on the island. The paper reported that nearly a third of the initial lessees were politicians or their family members, former lawmakers, active and retired judges, state government employees, and other people with political connections. Among those lessees was State Senator Everett Millican of Atlanta, State Rep. Ben Jessup of Cochran, State Rep. A. G. Swint of Orchard Hill, former State Senator Sims Alexander, State Rep. Roy Foster of Wadley, and many more who were well known in political circles. Some of the lots were granted to corporations; for example, the Roy Livingston Company leased three lots, and State Senator Jimmy Dykes of Cochran leased two lots for his business, the Bonded Building and Supply Company. At approximately the same time, in addition to his various concessions, Dykes also leased the Claflin Cottage, which had fifteen rooms and five baths.[2]

State Highway Director Jim Gillis (at left, with hand raised), here being sworn in by Governor Carl Sanders, helped Jimmy Dykes gain control of many of the island's leases. (Courtesy of James L. Gillis Sr. Papers, Richard B. Russell Library for Political Research and Studies, University of Georgia Libraries, Athens, Ga.)

Dykes began his political career as a state representative from Bleckley County, Georgia, serving from 1945 to 1948. He was a well-known Talmadge partisan during the "three governors controversy" in 1947. Amid the chaos of January 1947, Dykes sat in the chair of Governor Ellis Arnall, who had been forced to move his desk to the state capitol rotunda after Talmadge commandeered his office. When Dykes refused to get up, Arnall was forced to move to a downtown office building. As people around him booed, Dykes threw off his coat and challenged them to fight him one at a time. Dykes later served as mayor of Cochran from 1953 to 1956, and he served three terms in the Georgia Senate, in 1949–1950, 1955–1956, and 1961–1962. Clearly a strong supporter of Herman Talmadge throughout Talmadge's six-plus years as governor, he was also a staunch ally of the man elected governor in 1954, Marvin Griffin. Over the next few years, Jimmy Dykes would become a powerful and controversial person on Jekyll Island.[3]

As the JIA began to initiate the first major developments on Jekyll Island, Georgia politics again entered the picture, ushering in what many journalists and some politicians deemed to be a troubled period of corruption and political favoritism. In January 1954, the State Highway Department awarded a $207,893 paving contract for the Jekyll Island Causeway to Acme Construction Company, owned by former and future State Senator Jimmy Dykes. Just a few weeks before the reopening of Jekyll in December 1954, the authority called for bids to pave thirteen miles of roads, but when the board members convened via phone for a special called meeting on November 3, 1954, there was only one bid, from the Acme Construction Company. Ben Tarbutton moved "[t]hat the Authority utilize the Acme Construction Company of Cochran, Georgia," and Gould Barrett seconded the motion. Braxton Blalock, Tarbutton, and Barrett voted in favor of the motion, but Jim Compton requested he be recorded as being opposed on the grounds that he did not believe that Acme "had sufficient equipment or qualified personnel to assure an immediate beginning or a prompt completion of work." Unlike the other JIA members, Compton had researched the Acme Company and learned that Jimmy Dykes owned the company. Despite Compton's opposition, the JIA awarded the paving bid to Acme.[4] Within a few months, Dykes would take advantage of many questionable opportunities on the island.

Besides his strong ties to Herman Talmadge and Marvin Griffin, Dykes also had a connection to State Highway Department Director James "Jim" Gillis and to JIA chair D. B. Blalock, who owned two businesses that sold road paving equipment. His association with these important political figures helped Dykes to control much of the island, both directly and indirectly. Once the Jekyll Creek Bridge was completed, Dykes's influence on the island grew rapidly. By the end of 1955, he had acquired exclusive leases on paving, building supplies, hotel properties, concessions, general contracting, and the only gas station on the island. In fairness to Dykes, he was often the only bidder, but since he lived on the island, he clearly had an advantage in that he often had prior notification of each call for bids, which usually gave interested parties only two weeks to submit their bid. From the time he acquired the lease of the island's first business, the Bonded Building and Supply Company, he had the additional financial advantage of having crew and materials already on the island. For a time, Dykes had a monopoly on construction and contracting business on Jekyll.

Marvin Griffin, who became governor of Georgia in 1955, announced that he wanted Cherokee Cottage to become the summer executive mansion. He later denied the statement. Throughout his governorship, he vacillated in his support (or lack thereof) for Jekyll Island. (Courtesy of Hargrett Rare Book and Manuscript Library, University Libraries, University of Georgia, Athens, Ga.)

Shortly after Marvin Griffin won his gubernatorial bid in 1954, he announced that he wanted to have a summer governor's residence, the "little executive mansion," on Jekyll Island. Cherokee Cottage was the intended location. On May 5, 1955, the governor's wife, Mary Elizabeth Griffin, requested $6,891 to cover orders with an interior decorator for the renovation of Cherokee, with additional orders of $2,510 for such items as draperies, wallpaper, and carpet for the house. Griffin and his wife were also in the process of redesigning the governor's mansion in Atlanta, known as the Prado. The same day she placed the orders, twenty-five pieces of furniture—including chests, mirrors, tables, desks, hat racks, washstands, a love seat, and a Chippendale chair—were taken from the cottages and the Jekyll Island Club and presumably sent to the Prado. On May 8, a JIA board member indicated that he had been advised that Mrs. Griffin requested the orders be handled on an emergency purchase basis.

When Governor Griffin was asked about the renovation of Cherokee Cottage, he flatly denied that his wife had anything to do with the purchase orders, claiming that "Mrs. Griffin has never requested that purchases be made for any house on Jekyll Island, emergency or otherwise, and has no intention of doing so."[5] Despite his earlier comments, he would later vigorously deny that he had wanted a summer executive mansion on Jekyll. Perhaps Governor Griffin was not aware of his wife's actions, or maybe he realized that the sumptuous Prado, as well as a proposed summer mansion, might not play well with his rural voters. Even though a considerable amount of time and money had gone into the house on Jekyll, the governor and his wife never lived in it.

Cherokee Cottage had been in good enough condition in 1953 to be used by a big party of state officials and authority members. However, during a remodeling effort three years later, William McMath, the authority's construction superintendent, who was also connected to Dykes, had all of the cottage's light and plumbing fixtures removed and had the plaster ripped off the walls of several rooms. The former island superintendent, Hoke Smith, said the house had needed "only a small amount of paint and remodeling. Now it would be a major job to fix it."[6] A 1956 legislative committee recommended $17,800 for refurbishing the cottage.

In the meantime, a group of investors from Bleckley County formed the Jekyll Island Development Corporation, which appears to have included subsidiary companies, among them the Bonded Building and Supply Company and the Jekyll Hotel Corporation. The investors, all from Cochran, included Leo L. Phillips, J. Auburn Webb, and H. McWhorter. The authority inquired about Dykes's connections with the company, and Dykes assured the JIA that he had none. In late 1955, the authority leased the Jekyll Island Clubhouse to the newly established Jekyll Island Development Corporation. After the lease was granted, it was revealed that not only was Dykes a principal stockholder, but he also was designated as the operator of the clubhouse. Somehow, these misrepresentations were overlooked, possibly because of Dykes's political connections—or perhaps Dykes had important paving resources on the island at a time when they desperately needed more road development. Blalock, the JIA chair, insisted that "it was two months before we ever had any inkling that Jimmy was connected to it," but it appears that Blalock himself also benefited financially from Dykes's operation.[7] A 1955 audit showed that Blalock's firm had sold more than $85,000 worth of roadbuilding machinery, and much of that money went to Dykes. The audit also revealed that Dykes was in arrears with his leased properties. Even after the discovery of these conflicts of interest and lease violations, the authority negotiated an additional $218,000 in paving contracts with Dykes and his brother-in-law and allowed him to open the Jekyll Insurance Corporation, which dealt in real estate and cottage rentals on the island.

These questionable dealings did not go unnoticed. Jim Compton, who oversaw JIA purchases, began to question requisitions and invoices related to Dykes. On June 17, 1955, he sent a letter to Blalock complaining about the state of accounts: "I am opposed to the very sloppy way in which materials and equipment are being ordered. . . . I don't think anyone can tell what has been ordered, what it cost, and who authorized the [purchases]. I do not care to be involved in the controversy which is very likely to arise over the placing and payments of these orders."[8]

Six weeks later, on July 30, Compton stunned his fellow board members by resigning, ostensibly for reasons "hav[ing] to do with my business and my health." *The Brunswick News* claimed that "informed circles both here and in Atlanta [believe] that Mr. Compton resigned because of the increasing political deals being made in Jekyll's operation."[9] In his June 17 letter to Blalock, Compton begged him not to let "any one individual or group get control of all the island's best facilities, as has been the tendency during the past eight to ten months, for it will hurt the further development of the island and bring great criticism down on the authority."[10]

His words were prophetic, as within a few weeks of Compton's resignation, the state's Legislative Economy Committee launched an investigation of the Jekyll Island Authority. Somehow, most of the political deals and troubles surrounding Dykes were somewhat muted until September 1955, when the committee began an inquiry about paint purchases at Jekyll Island. The JIA had purchased 3,600 gallons of paint for the Jekyll Club, but 1,000 gallons of it had disappeared. The committee called on the State Purchasing Department to produce records on paint purchased at Jekyll Island, but they could not recover the invoices. Senator Blalock told the committee he was not familiar with many of the detailed operations on the island, and he acknowledged, "I think some of that paint got away."[11]

Blalock admitted that the authority had been lax about collecting Dykes's rent. The hearings also revealed that the paint was stored at Dykes's Bonded Building and Supply Company, but Dykes had never paid any rent for his leased property. Gould Barrett explained that Dykes had been in dispute with the JIA about whether an additional wing of the warehouse was part of the lease, and he assured the committee that rent should be coming in shortly. The committee also inquired about Blalock's machinery firm, which had sold road equipment to the state for use at Jekyll Island for $85,000. Blalock denied any wrongdoing and brushed off the questions by saying, "If any of you have any idea that my firm has overcharged Jekyll items, I'll be glad to refund the money this afternoon."[12]

The Legislative Economy Committee's controversial hearings resulted in a seventy-eight-page report released on December 10, 1955, in which the committee argued for dissolving the JIA and for turning island management over to the State Parks Department or selling the island altogether. Boiled down from five months of study and some stormy hearings, the report wasted few words in presenting and explaining the committee's conclusions. The committee severely criticized the authority for ignoring ethics, keeping sloppy financial bookkeeping records, failing to properly develop the island, and allowing the concentration of leases. The committee recommended not only the abolition of the Jekyll Island State Park Authority but also the withholding of additional state funds for Jekyll and the prevention of long-term leases.[13] The committee's report was released amid an avalanche of criticism from politicians and journalists directed at the high prices at Jekyll Island and the authority's policy of leasing residential lots. Throughout the mid-1950s, many people complained about the cost of accommodations at Jekyll and urged the authority to build low-cost housing and motels so that the average family could afford to spend their summer vacation there. Perhaps more importantly, the residential leasing policy came under heavy scrutiny after lessees had difficulties securing mortgage loans on leased property. Asserting that the leasing policy inhibited development of the island, some legislators viewed it as "out of step with the way America does things by putting the state in competition with private developers." Governor Griffin seemed to agree, proclaiming that "I am a free enterprise man myself. . . . I'm inclined to believe that if those lots were sold in fee simple, it would bring two or three million dollars back into the treasury."[14]

From the time he was elected governor in 1955, Griffin viewed Jekyll Island as a perpetual problem, repeatedly calling it a "white elephant," and he wavered constantly on the issue of what should be done with Jekyll. An article in *The Atlanta Constitution* on January 10, 1956, reported that the governor had told state legislators to sell Jekyll Island "if we can get back the money the state has spent developing it." In remarks to reporters afterward, he added, "I would like to swap Jekyll Island for a science center for the University of Georgia or an atomic reactor."[15] However, his indecision was on display two days later in an article in *The Brunswick News*, which noted that "Governor Griffin this afternoon released a statement reversing his declaration Monday that Jekyll Island should be sold outright"; instead, he now "called for [the] sale of lots on the island and made no mention of disposing of the property as a whole."[16]

In view of the governor's most recent position, the Jekyll Island Committee of the Georgia Legislature, chaired by Rep. Robert L. Scoggin, persuaded the governor in February 1956 to provide additional funds to make improvements on the island. The committee called for the state to appropriate funds in the amount of $397,731, most of it earmarked for properties leased by Jimmy Dykes. The committee did not advocate the cancellation of Dykes's leases, since Dykes had spent $100,000 on repairs to the Jekyll Island Hotel and planned to spend another $150,000 before the end of the year.

However, beginning in July 1956, shortly after the opening of the $10 million bridge across the Turtle River that finally linked the Jekyll causeway to Brunswick, a tidal wave of criticism once again crashed onto Jekyll Island. A series of articles in *The Atlanta Constitution* in late July charged the JIA with corruption and exposed how Dykes had gained control of just about every facility on the state-owned island, including three hotel buildings, beach houses, and a building supply company. In addition, the articles revealed that Dykes was selling beer on Jekyll without a license. The revelations infuriated Governor Griffin, and *The Brunswick News* reported that he "renewed a proposal to sell at least most of the island, which he referred to [once again] as 'this white elephant.'"[17] Griffin also halted any further spending for Jekyll

Construction of the Sidney Lanier Bridge across the Turtle River was finally completed in 1956. The bridge linked the Jekyll Island Causeway to the mainland, making travel to Jekyll far more convenient. (Courtesy of Mosaic, Jekyll Island Museum)

Island improvements, holding back the remaining $180,000 of the appropriation he had approved earlier.[18]

Such reversals were no longer a surprise. There had been rumors in Atlanta for months that the Griffin administration still wanted to sell Jekyll to developers, and Griffin had concluded some years earlier that Jekyll Island was an expensive failure. He claimed that he had "opposed the state purchase of Jekyll Island as impractical for I did not believe then, and I do not believe now, that the state government should be in the beach resort business. It is obvious that private enterprise is the only suitable agency by which the island can be properly developed."[19] Former Governor M. E. Thompson, who had purchased the island for the people of Georgia, was furious about the situation. He charged "illegalities and shenanigans" in connection to Dykes's leases and demanded that those leases be cancelled.[20]

The series of negative articles in *The Atlanta Constitution* began by documenting how Dykes had gained control of just about every facility on the state-owned island, including three hotel buildings, beach houses, a building supply firm, a service station, and several servants' cottages, as well as having an exclusive paving contract for the island. Some local people had started calling it "Dykes Island."[21] The second story in the series connected Dykes to Talmadge and Griffin and reminded readers about Dykes's belligerent role in the three governors controversy.[22] The third article focused on Dykes's associates, including Leo Phillips and William McMath, who had recently made it clear that they were joint stockholders in Jimmy Dykes's various enterprises on Jekyll, including the Bonded Building and Supply Company and the Jekyll Hotel Corporation. They leased the garage on the island to house the Bonded Building and Supply Company. Thanks to their unique arrangement, the supply firm's sales picked up almost immediately. Records showed six purchase requisitions totaling $4,038.52 for sales transactions between the Jekyll Island Authority and the supply firm. An additional $1,626 in transactions occurred between April 27 and December 19, 1955. McMath, in his role as construction superintendent, signed off on most of the requisitions, making him both the buyer and the seller. Dykes and his employees had begun to buy supplies from their own corporation through strange transactions that could not be documented. McMath quit the authority job after Governor Griffin issued an executive order banning sales to the state by state employees.[23]

A fourth article recounted the story of Governor Griffin and what the JIA (perhaps at the request of the governor) had designated as the "little executive mansion." The last article in the *Constitution*'s series brought attention to Laurence S. Miller, an architect-engineer who was hired in 1954 for $35 a day. A year later, he was made a full-time JIA employee with a salary of $600 a month. A few months after that, he accepted a lucrative contract in lieu of salary, receiving $8,991 for his architectural services. When Dykes finally received the $250,000 in frozen funds from Governor Griffin to "update" the Jekyll Island Hotel, he brought in Miller as a contract builder, offering up to $40,000 to be spent on hotel repairs, which left Dykes with $210,000. For a time, Miller was working for both the authority and Dykes. On May 6, 1956, the JIA leased the marina to Jekyll Island Marina, Inc., headed by Laurence Miller, who turned it over to his son, L. S. Miller Jr. Miller's son was also paid $2,310 for architectural services, which bought up the issue of nepotism.[24]

These negative articles led to the formation of new legislative committees. Dykes had his defenders, starting with Rep. Scoggin, who argued that Dykes had received no special favors: "Every hotel man in Georgia was not just invited but was urged to bid on the property. Many of the resort hotel operators all over the country were approached and all deemed the risk was too great or lacked the resources to take the gamble. The present lessee [Dykes] is gambling, although the state is not." State senator and JIA board member Gould Barrett said, "Newspapers are victims of some smart politicians that have started a whispering campaign for no damn reason. I hope you gentlemen won't be sucked in by a bunch of people who are trying to make a fool out of the members of the authority and make suckers of you. I'm sorry to be so brutally frank, but that's the way I feel."[25] The most direct defense came from Dykes himself in a letter he released to the press on August 30, 1956: "It seems in the past several weeks that some newspapers have made every effort to convince the people of the state of Georgia that I have used political influence to secure certain properties at Jekyll Island. They also inferred that this property was not properly advertised in order that other Georgians could have the opportunity to bid on concessions on which my firms were high bidders. . . . If they can make a better deal or even one just as good, I'll get out. But if they can't, I want to get down to the business of making a real resort out of the island."[26]

There also was some severe criticism, not just of Dykes but of the state of Jekyll Island and the JIA. M. E. Thompson was now running for the U.S. Senate against his old gubernatorial opponent Herman Talmadge, and Thompson had much to say about the corruption and cronyism at Jekyll: "I knew in 1948 what should have been done with Jekyll Island. It should have been developed as a public park for the benefit of all of the people of Georgia. Since Talmadge took it over and turned it over to the politically powerful, it is in such a mess until I do not know what can be done about it. This I do know: At least one of the Golden Isles has been turned over to the people for which its purpose was not intended. The Talmadge-Griffin regime are responsible for [the] shattering of a dream which I had for the people of Georgia."[27]

In the wake of such publicity, tourists flocked to the island "to see what the ruckus was all about."[28] Overall, they were pleasantly surprised by what they found. One visitor from Atlanta commented that he "went down [to Jekyll] expecting, from newspaper reports, to find a jumble of inefficiency and beer joints, but I found neither. . . . In fact, I have never seen a more beautiful, natural or better-run place."[29] In a letter to the editor of *The Atlanta Journal and Constitution*, Mr. and Mrs. Roland C. Drozeski said, "Whatever the price

While politicians squabbled over legislation concerning Jekyll Island, summer tourists were enjoying themselves there. (Courtesy of Mosaic, Jekyll Island Museum)

paid for it back in 1947, the people of Georgia got a real bargain, in which tourists from all over the nation will eventually share."[30]

After years of negative publicity, there were still strong sentiments within the legislature and across the state for shaking up the Jekyll Island Authority or selling the island. Griffin appointed Fred Aldred of Summerville to the authority's board, but the remaining board members were confused as to whom the governor wanted as JIA chair, especially after the sudden resignations of Blalock and Tarbutton, who claimed that they did not have time for the authority.[31] A few weeks later, Griffin appointed Mike Benton as the acting chair, with W. T. "Deke" Giles, Earl Edwards, Fred Aldred, and Gould Barrett as board members.

The crisis over Jekyll Island subsided in the following months, but nevertheless, when Griffin gave his State of the State speech on January 16, 1957, he called Jekyll "a perennial problem" and reiterated the idea that "the state has no business running a beach resort."[32] He declared that if the approximate cost could be recouped, "the wisest course the state could follow would be to divest itself of this property."[33] Griffin claimed that syndicates from Chicago and Miami had each made an offer of $4,500,000 for Jekyll. The governor also said he would not approve Jekyll expenditures unless they were needed to protect what the state had invested.[34]

Two days later, Griffin appointed a new legislative committee to review a plan to sell Jekyll Island. An outline of the new plan for disposing of the island had been presented to the governor by a group of ten investors who wanted to buy Jekyll. But the JIA chair declared that the state-owned island was "worth a cool twenty million" and that he would not sell at any price. Committee members included Reps. Downing Musgrove of Clinch County, Lester Souter of Macon, Robert Scoggin of Floyd County, J. Ebb Duncan of Carroll County, and Robert Stevens of Clarke County and Senators James Gould of Brunswick and F. Everett Williams of Statesboro. The governor's choices for the committee were curious, as most of them were publicly in favor of keeping Jekyll Island.[35]

Within a few days, there was an outpouring of concern from the "average citizens" of Georgia, who seemed to feel that Jekyll Island was their own property. Ray Whittle said that "the sentiment has crystalized all over the state to not sell it at any price." *The Atlanta Journal and Constitution* gave over its number one editorial space to the issue, saying that "Jekyll indeed is a gem and a nugget and a pile of uranium to boot. It also is a public trust." State Senator James Gould, who was quoted in the editorial, came home to a flood of telephone calls from all over the state, all of them favorable to the state's retention of the island. Peyton Hawes, the Senate floor leader for the Griffin administration, claimed that the administration would not snap up the first solution to what he called "the Jekyll problem."[36]

Over the next few months, the Griffin administration struggled to find a better way to control the Jekyll Island Authority. The state auditor, B. E. Thrasher, joined the sharp criticism of Griffin's recommendations for selling lots. He also warned that the administration was making Jekyll "a real estate development." In addition, Thrasher suggested that the administration of the island should be removed from political maneuvering and that the resort should be developed "for the 'average' Georgia family." He added, "Before they can make any long-range plans, they're going to have to stabilize the situation down there."[37]

All of this was taking place while politicians were deliberating the creation of a new Jekyll Island Authority. Fred Aldred, now chair of the JIA, was opposed to naming any state officials to the authority. He also objected to the sale of lots. Around one-fourth of the six hundred available lots were leased by that time, but more than one hundred leases had been cancelled, which Aldred said was "largely . . . a result of threats to sell the island." He acknowledged that the authority had made mistakes, the biggest being its failure to have a single contractor carry out all the work. Aldred remarked, "I haven't seen eye to eye with him [Jimmy Dykes] by any stretch of the imagination," but he added that Dykes was a "puller and pusher" who "gets a good job done."[38]

Dykes's problems still lingered in the press and in the legislature, and a group of representatives wanted to investigate him and his leases. Rep. Jack Murr charged that "there have been fantastic political maneuvers which gave Jimmy Dykes an empire furnished by state funds." Rep. Edgar Blalock, a member of the 1955 Legislative Economy Committee, remarked that "we heard all of the rumors and went to the bottom of it, but the committee could find nothing wrong." D. B. Blalock told the committee that he would like to see an investigation. Dykes then appeared in the House to "answer any questions anybody wants to ask about Jekyll Island," but House Speaker Marvin Moate ruled it would be out of order for Dykes to speak from the House floor since he was no longer a member of the legislature. Before leaving the House, Dykes told the press that he was "losing $1,500 each week at Jekyll."[39]

Within a few weeks, a compromise emerged that finally rejected once and for all the notion of selling Jekyll Island and created a new and reconstituted authority, this one made up of high-ranking political officials, including the secretary of state, the public service commissioner, the state auditor, the attorney general, and the director of the Department of State Parks. But the issue of selling versus leasing lots was still undecided. Unlike the previous JIA, which had been authorized to lease lots but not to sell them, under the new law the authority was empowered to do both. Some members of the newly appointed authority, however, were at odds concerning the issue. Thrasher was adamantly opposed to the sale of lots, which he made clear even before Governor Griffin signed the bill: "They better get somebody else as chairman because I won't sign any deed." The attorney general, Eugene Cook, who also was a member of the new JIA board, countered, indicating that he favored

Eugene Cook favored selling lots on Jekyll Island instead of leasing them. (Courtesy of the Office of the Attorney General of Georgia)

the sale of lots to give investors "the dignity and stability of an estate title."[40] Both Thrasher and Ben Fortson believed that if Jekyll was going to live up to the promise of it being a resort for all Georgians, then the state must maintain the leasing system and finance the construction of motels and other inexpensive accommodations, rather than turn them over to private investors. Thrasher and Fortson finally won out, for when the authority members undertook a legal study of the leasing system at Jekyll, they concluded that they could not break the leases "without bringing them [the lessees] to court," which they did not want to do. As a result, they opted not to exercise their right to sell lots.[41]

Within three days after the new JIA took control, B. E. Thrasher, concerned as both a committee member and the state auditor, announced that Jimmy Dykes, who still held many of the island's leases (including those of the Jekyll Island Hotel, the Sans Souci apartments, the Crane Hotel, the tennis court, picnic areas, and bathhouses), was once again in arrears with his rent, in the amount of $7,492. Given the situation, Thrasher decided to crack down on the loose administration at Jekyll Island and initiated new procedures, including temporarily freezing all transactions, banning purchases with fewer than two bids, preventing any purchases in excess of twenty-five dollars without approval, allowing no advertising without approval, and halting the free use of any facility. The ban on free facilities was prompted by a report that a house with a maid in the historic district was being used by authority members and friends. Thrasher also tightened up on the use of gasoline and oil as well as on telephone calls and telegraphs.[42]

Still under Griffin's freeze for Jekyll, Thrasher said, "We got a lot of property but no money."[43] Clearly, these new restrictions were mostly directed at Dykes. Thrasher also confronted James Asher, the island manager, regarding charges of nepotism concerning Asher's wife, who was receiving $200 a month as a secretary. Ben Fortson, who had been named chair of the new JIA, halted any transactions connected to leasing or selling lots and agreed to employ Judge A. J. Hartley, an assistant attorney general, to review present leases.

Fully established in March 1957, the reconstructed Jekyll Island Authority ushered in a prolonged period of rapid development and political stability.[44] The recently appointed members had specific ideas about how to develop Jekyll. Chair Ben Fortson observed that, "[a]lthough the rest of the island is beautiful, people mostly come to Jekyll to go to the beach." Thrasher commented, "I like the idea at Daytona Beach, with its great expanses of attractive motels and small apartments. . . . I lean that way for Jekyll—make it a place where all Georgia can go to play and rest, rather than turn the island over to a relatively few homeowners."[45]

By late June 1957, Governor Griffin had a more favorable perspective on Jekyll Island. Taking advantage of the governor's new attitude, the authority asked for $250,000 for capital improvements, including the development of additional lots and the installation of a fire protection system in the old Jekyll club, as well requesting as another $500,000 for an annual budget. Griffin responded, "Let's count the eggs first. . . . Let's say we make it a quarter of a million dollars and later on see what else we can do. . . . [L]et's do what is necessary to provide facilities for the citizens of Georgia and get all the tourists we can get."[46] His more positive position, reflected in his loosening of the purse strings and his admonition that "[w]e've gone too far not to finish up the job," encouraged the authority members to pass a resolution on September 9, 1957, wherein they indicated that, with the governor's help, the JIA aimed to turn Jekyll into "one of the finest recreational resort islands on the Atlantic coast."[47]

The new authority accelerated the beach area development, and within two years, Jekyll's beachfront featured a shopping center, two motels, concession stands, a two-mile boardwalk, acres of paved parking lots, two bathhouses, a miniature golf course, and several new homes. The authority also leased properties for a campground, an amusement park, a convention center, and a brick clubhouse. By the summer of 1958, the rapid development would stimulate the interest of private enterprise in leasing land for new facilities, including the development of a ninety-six-unit motel with all rooms facing the ocean. Established motels were also in the process of expanding. Additionally, the JIA announced bids for the building of a massive recreation center with a

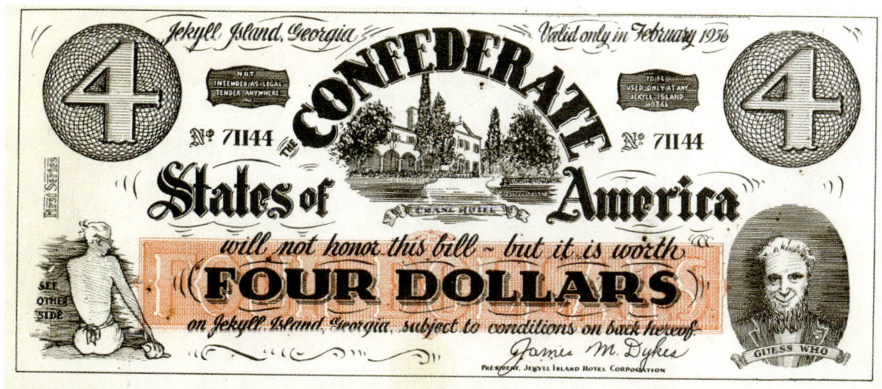

Jimmy Dykes, identified here as president of the Jekyll Island Hotel Corporation, held among his enterprises the leases to the Jekyll Island Hotel, the Sans Souci apartments, and the Crane Hotel, the last of which is featured at the center of this signed four-dollar coupon, which could be used at any of his establishments. (Courtesy of Mosaic, Jekyll Island Museum)

The late 1950s saw the addition of many more concessions to Jekyll Island, among them this shopping center, which was demolished during the island's recent revitalization. (Courtesy of Mosaic, Jekyll Island Museum)

Two modernist bathhouses were built in the late 1950s. (Courtesy of Mosaic, Jekyll Island Museum)

150-foot indoor swimming pool, a bowling alley, a skating rink, and a dance pavilion. These developments all took place within the framework of Andre Steiner's original master plan, which the new authority pledged to follow.[48]

Suddenly, there were positive feelings around the new Jekyll administration, the new modernistic bathhouses, a new shopping center, and the prospect of an attractive air-conditioned convention hall. Looking ahead, Ben Fortson made it clear that "[i]t's going to take capital improvements of about $5 million to get this thing moving."[49] Jack Nelson of *The Atlanta Journal-Constitution* wrote an article about the successes of Jekyll Island State Park. In the article, entitled "Jekyll—A Golden Elephant," Nelson notes that two years earlier Governor Griffin had called Jekyll a "white elephant," but according to Fortson, "Without the governor's help, we would have been stymied. He has let us run the island and develop it without interference. . . . [H]e has cooperated and made funds available for the needed improvements." The former JIA members were appointees who met once a month but could not devote the time necessary for rapid and efficient development on the island. The new authority members, on the other hand, met every week, and because they were all important officials in the state, they had easy access to the governor.[50]

Last, the JIA moved to address the issue of Jimmy Dykes, who had been an embarrassment for several years. The authority ordered an examination of his leases and found in him in default on several provisions, including nonpayment of rent and the failure to have proper amounts of insurance. He paid his back rents, which amounted to $10,082, but the JIA still brought legal action to strip him of his leases. However, Dykes fought back and won his case in the courts. Still under pressure, Dykes finally signed a quit claim deed on January 22, 1960, relinquishing all his businesses at Jekyll. He went on to win another state senate term from 1961 to 1962. By the end of 1963, he had severed all ties with Jekyll Island. Dykes considered a possible gubernatorial run in 1966 but decided against it.

On December 27, 1966, Jimmy Dykes shot himself with a .22-caliber pistol in a restroom near his main office in Cochran. Several of his employees heard the shot. The sheriff, Gus Giddens, said there was no note and indicated that he knew of no motive other than that Dykes had been depressed. Dykes left behind his wife and seven children.[51] Despite all the controversy surrounding Jimmy Dykes, he was an important person who created much of the island's infrastructure during that critical early period of Jekyll Island State Park.

The St. Andrews Beach Pavilion was the first structure made available to African American visitors to Jekyll Island. The "Colored Beach House" (with attached picnic pavilion) opened in September 1955. (Courtesy of the Coastal Georgia Historical Society)

SEPARATE & UNEQUAL

6

From the opening of Jekyll Island State Park in 1947, Black citizens throughout Georgia and beyond made it clear they wanted a stake on the island. By 1955, the Jekyll Island Authority had approved a plan for five hundred lots for white lessees, but Andre Steiner's original master plan did not include developments for African Americans. It was apparent that the authority was deliberately deferring construction at the south end of the island, where the JIA planned to uphold Jim Crow laws by creating a Black district, St. Andrews. The JIA's vision was to cater primarily to white lessees and visitors on the north half of the island, which at that time was considered the most desirable part of Jekyll; it was close to the historic district, the golf courses, and eventually the most developed amenities of the island, including the fishing pier, the business area, restaurants, stores, and other amusements.

In September 1947, before the state park opened, local Black leaders and businessmen in Brunswick made it clear that "negroes are just as much interested in the development of the resort as whites." The authority also received letters "from the negro leaders of Savannah inquiring about the status of a negro development on Jekyll Island." The JIA responded that, "[i]n the formulation of the plans of development for Jekyll Island, the Authority has given careful consideration to the needs of the negro citizens of Georgia."[1] But when Jekyll Island State Park opened to the public on a limited basis on March 5, 1948, Black people were not allowed. When the dedication of the Turtle River Bridge (later renamed the Sidney Lanier Bridge) was held, Black people were not invited. After the official opening of the park, Black people were not welcome. Development at the south end did not begin for nearly eleven more months. Without support from the segregationist Governor Marvin Griffin, it was difficult to find the money for St. Andrews development, and the authority had to build a paved road to the remote south end of the island and prepare lots for facilities. The first development was the St. Andrews Beach Pavilion. L. L. Phillips, an associate of Jimmy Dykes, was allocated $25,000 for the construction. Phillips scaled down the project so that the final cost was only $8,658. On September 24, 1955, a ceremony was dedicated to the formal opening of the beach pavilion.

Jim Bacote was in the fourth grade when he first visited the St. Andrews

At its opening, St. Andrews Beach was the only public beach accessible to African Americans in the state of Georgia. (Courtesy of Mosaic, Jekyll Island Museum)

area of Jekyll Island in 1957. He had vivid memories of enjoying St. Andrews with his family and friends and his classmates at Risley School in Brunswick: "It was very exciting . . . and it became a ritual, a Sunday afternoon ritual for many, many families. St. Andrews was the only [public] beach in Georgia that was accessible for Black people." Later, he and his friends camped out at St. Andrews as Cub Scouts and Boy Scouts: "We were thrilled. Even though it was second class, we were thrilled just to have someplace to go."[2]

The inequality of white and Black facilities on the island would be underscored after Governor Griffin traveled to Canada for a hunting excursion in Manitoba in late October 1958. While he was in Canada, a major accident occurred at the Springhill mine in Nova Scotia on October 23, 1958. Indeed, it was the most severe underground seismic event in North American mining history, and it was the first international event to be covered live on television. Seventy miners died instantly; within a few hours, some seventy survivors had found their way out, but ninety-nine miners were still trapped below. Many of those miners were rescued within a few days, but a group of twelve miners and a separate group of seven miners remained trapped. After five days of trying to reach them, rescuers finally made contact with the group of twelve, who were soon brought to the surface. But the other group was still trapped 400 feet underground behind a 160-foot rockfall.

During that desperate and dangerous time, one of the still-trapped miners, Maurice Ruddick, sustained the group's morale by singing songs such as "Bye Bye Love" and "Don't Be Cruel" in the dark, stifling heat. Ruddick, whose leg was injured in the accident, later said, "I got along pretty good at first, but later the singing got harder. . . . My voice cracked because I was so dry." One of his acquaintances remarked, "If it wasn't for Maurice, they'd all have been dead."[3] On the ninth day after the collapse, rescuers at last made contact with Ruddick's group. People around the world were glued to their televisions as the last seven miners were brought to the surface one by one.[4]

In the aftermath of the rescue, some of the "miracle miners" appeared on *The Ed Sullivan Show*. Another survivor became a spokesperson for the soft drink 7 Up, because while he was trapped and after his rescue, he asked repeatedly for a 7 Up. Upon learning of the rescue of the first twelve miners, Governor Griffin's aide Sam Caldwell sensed an opportunity to publicize Jekyll Island and rushed into negotiations to bring the rescued miners and their families to Jekyll. The governor was upset about the expected cost of hosting the miners, especially after the second group of seven miners was found, adding to the potential expense. Because he wanted to capitalize on the publicity surrounding the event and also save money, Griffin was unwilling to postpone the miners' visit until all of them were well enough to travel; thus the date set for them to arrive was November 18.

Twelve miners from the two groups, including Maurice Ruddick, accepted the invitation to bring their families for a free vacation at Jekyll Island. This created an awkward and embarrassing situation for Griffin, an ardent segregationist, as Caldwell had not realized that one of the miners, Ruddick, was Black. It was a dilemma for the governor's office. After much deliberation about the matter, the governor informed Ruddick that he was welcome to participate in the Jekyll visit, but only on a segregated basis. Ruddick commented, "There's nothing I'd like to do better. But I wonder if this fellow realized that I have twelve kids." In another gaffe, Griffin claimed that "[w]e have facilities available at Jekyll Island for colored people," when in fact there was only the foundation for a Black motel, and the concession stand was closed for the winter. Ruddick stated, "Maybe I'd better write to this governor and see just what this is all about."[5]

By that point, many of Ruddick's miner friends had decided they would refuse to go without him, but Ruddick and his wife, Norma, chose to accept the governor's half-hearted invitation, because Ruddick knew his colleagues needed a well-deserved beach vacation. So he, his wife, and four of their children went to Jekyll Island. They were not permitted to visit the developed

The only housing made available to Maurice Ruddick and his family when Governor Marvin Griffin invited them to visit Jekyll Island was a trailer, while the white miners stayed in island motels. At far left in this photo is Earl Hill, who organized the first integrated golf tournament on Jekyll Island; Maurice Ruddick is second from left. (Courtesy of Carl Mydans, *LIFE* picture collection, Shutterstock)

Maurice Ruddick, who was considered a hero of the Springhill mine disaster in Cumberland County, Nova Scotia, walks with his family on the beach at Jekyll Island, accompanied by a policeman for their protection. (Courtesy of Carl Mydans, *LIFE* picture collection, Shutterstock)

part of the island, and they did not see his friends during their free week at Jekyll. But Ruddick viewed the experience as "a chance to open some people's eyes."[6]

To accommodate Ruddick and his family, Sam Caldwell was obliged to rent three trailers and have a roadway bulldozed to the beach area at the south end of the island, where the Ruddicks would be housed. One of the trailers was for the Ruddick family; another was for the president of Savannah State College and his wife, whom the governor had persuaded to come to keep the Ruddicks company. A third trailer with a kitchen was provided for a cook to prepare meals for the Black visitors.[7] While the governor marginalized Ruddick and his family, the African American community in Brunswick showered the Ruddicks with love and attention. Jim Bacote recalled that Ruddick "couldn't be with all of the wonderful programming that the community had for the white miners."[8] So Governor Griffin appointed Genoa Martin, the manager of Selden Park in Brunswick, to set up a special party at the park. Martin arranged a fishing trip for Ruddick and his family. He also asked local African American fraternal and social organizations to help by chipping in for the Ruddicks' entertainment. Bacote remembered the support of the Black community and how everyone "came out, all of the local talent, the churches, people were dressed up and everything. It was very festive and happy . . . virtually everybody was there." In retrospect, Bacote thought, "I guess the Black family probably learned a lesson in race relations that they were unfamiliar with."[9]

After the miners and their families returned to Nova Scotia, the press asked Ruddick about his visit to Jekyll; he said he was treated hospitably everywhere he went, but he was "not pleased with anything that keeps people apart—it is something out of the past. I wasn't allowed to visit my Springhill friends although they could come to see us."[10] In the end, Maurice Ruddick had the last laugh. In February 1959, *The Toronto Telegram* polled its readers to determine Canada's Citizen of the Year for 1958, and Ruddick won the honor, pulling in 51 percent of the vote against twenty other nominees.[11] By contrast, Governor Marvin Griffin was investigated by a Fulton County grand jury over corruption allegations in 1960, after he had left office, but he ultimately was not indicted. The Griffin administration was rife with cronyism, misconduct, and wrongdoing, and several members of the administration, including Griffin's brother, were found guilty of crimes. Indeed, Robert Dubay wrote that "the Griffin administration is fully deserving of its reputation as one of the most corrupt, amoral, mismanaged, and inefficient administrations in Georgia history."[12]

After the dedication of the St. Andrews Beach Pavilion in September 1955, it took a few more years for the JIA to consider more development on the south end of the island. In the spring of 1956, a group of Black businessmen and local leaders formed the St. Andrews Beach Corporation to raise capital to obtain a lease for a motel site in the St. Andrews area. The Jekyll Island

The Dolphin Club and Motor Hotel opened in 1959. (Courtesy of Mosaic, Jekyll Island Museum)

Authority had to cosign the loan for the motel site, and the St. Andrews Beach Corporation began construction in October 1958. There was still only a concrete foundation for the motel at the time of the miners' visit in late November, but the Dolphin Club and Motor Hotel was in operation by August 1959. Maurice Ruddick traveled to Jekyll once again in late July 1959 to attend the Dolphin's opening, having been invited by the owners.[13] Shortly after, there was squabbling among the members of the corporation, and they defaulted on their mortgage payments. In response, the JIA took possession of the motel property.

Within a few months, an African American entrepreneur named Dave E. Jackson, of Adel, Georgia, came into the picture. Jackson, a cattle and grain farmer who supplied grain to the Purina Company, was a millionaire and an investor who sat on the boards of the Farmers Merchant Bank in Adel and the Citizens Trust Bank of Atlanta, even though—according to his business consultant, Dr. W. Ray Hill, whose family had worked for the Jekyll Island Club for many years before the state era—Jackson had only a third-grade education. It just happened that Jackson was seeking an investment property so his sister could operate her own business. Hill approached the authority to see if arrangements could be made for Jackson to lease the Dolphin property. Judge A. J. Hartley was the main person to work with Hill during the negotiations. Thanks in part to financial backing from the credit union of the Georgia Teachers and Education Association, a Black teachers association, the authority granted Jackson the lease to the property in December 1960.[14]

The Dolphin Club and Motor Hotel became a family business under Jackson. His sister Annabelle Robinson was the manager of the hotel, and another sister, Betty Chandler, was the assistant manager. James Chandler, his nephew, oversaw the lounge and restaurant. The hotel had fifty-eight units. For a time, the Dolphin Club was hailed as one of the best facilities for American African visitors in Georgia. The club featured a restaurant, a leather-padded bar, and a dance venue. Bacote recalled that "[t]he Dolphin Club was some kind of nice. It was mostly glass . . . it was two-story, and it had a little patio up top. . . . It was a lot of fun. It used to be so packed in there because with the hotel and the club, . . . we were like 14, 15, 16, and you can get drinks. I mean it wasn't legal, but who cared." He also remembered that "they had slot machines. . . . I guess they didn't care, you know, Jekyll Island Authority, they didn't care what the heck was going on, as long as these Negroes stayed down on their own end of the island!"[15] Between 1959 and 1966, some notable bands performed at the Dolphin Club on Friday and Saturday nights. At first, most of the musical acts were local groups, including the Swinging Turbans and the Doves. But starting in 1961, Charlie Cross, a promoter on the so-called Chitlin' Circuit, provided musicians and bands for Black-owned nightclubs throughout the South, and for a while the Dolphin Club was a regular stop for musicians such as B. B. King, Percy Sledge, Millie Jackson, and Clarence Carter.[16]

The Dolphin Motor Hotel was said to be one of the best tourist facilities for African Americans in Georgia at the time. (Courtesy of Mosaic, Jekyll Island Museum)

The St. Andrews subdivision was an area in which building lots were made available to African Americans. (Courtesy of Mosaic, Jekyll Island Museum)

Only a few homes were built in or around the St. Andrews subdivision. According to Ray Hill, who worked on the island from 1963 to 1965, the first house completed on the south end was that of Dr. James Clinton Wilkes, a Brunswick dentist, and his wife, Josephine. Constructed in 1962, the Wilkes's home stood just beyond the main subdivision. The second house, and the first one actually built within the St. Andrews subdivision, was that of Genoa and Mamie Martin. Mr. Martin was a community-minded person and an entertainment promoter in addition to being the manager of Selden Park in Brunswick.[17] Joseph Henry and Lillian Armstrong constructed the next house, which was completed in 1964. Mr. Armstrong had previously worked for the Jekyll Island Club as a houseman at Indian Mound. When asked why he built his house on Jekyll, he replied, "My wife decided she wanted to live on Jekyll Island."[18] In February 1959, the authority promised there would be apartments at St. Andrews, but they were never built.[19] Whether due to lack of promotion, lack of investment, lack of equal facilities, lack of development, or lack of interest, the St. Andrews development, aside from the Dolphin Club, rarely drew large crowds of Black visitors, and the plan for a separate residential and commercial district never materialized.[20]

Ernest Vandiver, governor of Georgia from 1959 to 1963, threatened to sell off all Georgia state parks if segregation could not be maintained. Attorney General Eugene Cook, an authority board member, stated that, rather than integrate, "I would be firmly in favor of closing the public facilities."[21] These racist policies were clearly in evidence on Jekyll Island, where the authority upheld Jim Crow laws by providing inferior facilities to Black visitors. For instance, in 1961 the authority opened Aquarama, a large indoor pool within a dramatic, architecturally modernist structure, for white people. Two years later, the JIA announced that it planned to spend $75,000 to add a pool for African American visitors.[22] The result was a small pool in a building that resembled a tin metal box. Dr. James C. Wilkes, one of the more prominent Black professionals in Brunswick, wanted to hold the annual convention of the Black Dental Association of Georgia on Jekyll Island. Since there was no place on Jekyll for Black citizens to meet, Wilkes argued for the authority to build a convention hall for African Americans at St. Andrews. Jim Bacote said, "It seemed like it was built almost overnight. . . . So that's the 'separate but equal' version of the Aquarama and the tin St. Andrews Auditorium. It was a joke." To make matters worse, the St. Andrews Auditorium did not have air conditioning, so when people inside the auditorium danced, they sweltered in the heat; according to Bacote, at least one person died there of heat stroke.[23]

The first public stirrings to desegregate Jekyll Island came in May 1960, after the NAACP announced its plans to integrate public beaches along the southern U.S. coast. Eugene Cook responded by issuing a prepared statement calling on the governor to declare martial law if integration was attempted at Jekyll Island. Other members of the authority, namely Ben Fortson and Thrasher, did not support Cook's proposed course of action. Thrasher publicly stated that the JIA probably would not close the resort and that he, for one, did not want to.[24] In an August 1, 1962, letter to Rev. Julius C. Hope, leader of the Zion Baptist Church in Brunswick and local NAACP chief, Fortson stated that "a meeting during the month of August would be extremely difficult," but he indicated that he would bring the matter to the attention of the full authority. Hope received no further response from Fortson.[25]

The issue came up again in March 1963, when the biracial Georgia Council on Human Relations asked the authority to voluntarily desegregate Jekyll

LEFT The Aquarama, which housed an indoor swimming pool for whites only, was opened in 1961. (Courtesy of Mosaic, Jekyll Island Museum)

RIGHT A metal structure housed a swimming pool for African Americans. (Courtesy of Mosaic, Jekyll Island Museum)

Governor Carl Sanders was in office when the NAACP brought legal action against the Jekyll Island governing board, demanding the integration of island facilities. (Courtesy of the United States Senate)

Island or else face court action.[26] Fortson responded that "a majority of white people won't accept integration," and "as custodians of the island, we must do what is best for the majority of people." Nonetheless, he promised to confer with other authority officials before taking any action. A few days later, NAACP leaders from Savannah and Brunswick tested the segregated facilities on Jekyll Island, visiting the amusement park, beach houses, cafeteria, indoor swimming pool, picnic areas, motels, and golf courses. A spokesperson announced, "We were denied entrance to all these places except the drugstore, where two of our group ate lunch at the counter."[27]

As a result, in September 1963, state and local NAACP leaders filed a class action suit against the Jekyll Island Authority, making the case that segregated facilities violated the Fourteenth Amendment rights of Black citizens. The new governor, Carl Sanders, asserted that he would fight the suit. Although he had campaigned as a segregationist, he was regarded as a moderate on the race issue. He once said, "I'm a segregationist but not a damn fool." Despite his position on civil rights, he made it clear that "we are going to obey the laws, we are not going to resist Federal court orders, and we are not going to close schools."[28]

On September 24, 1963, the NAACP plaintiffs brought a civil action, asking for a declaratory judgment against the Jekyll Island Authority. Among the plaintiffs were W. W. Law of Savannah and Reverend Hope. Their lawyer was Vernon Jordan, a celebrated civil rights attorney who went on to have a

Vernon Jordan was the lawyer for the NAACP when it brought a civil action against the Jekyll Island Authority demanding an end to segregation of the island. (Courtesy of Library of Congress)

very successful law career. The coordinator of the desegregation program was Constance Baker Motley, who later became a federal judge. Among the witnesses concerning the segregated facilities were younger African Americans such as Leroy Mac, Ollis Douglas, and Jim Bacote. Bacote recalled that when it was his turn to testify, he was very nervous. In retrospect, Bacote realized that it was all orchestrated, but when Jordan asked, "Why did you attempt to use the bathing facilities?" Bacote responded, "Because my daddy works at the Pulp plant. And he pays taxes, and this is a state facility." The declaratory judgment did not come until seven months after the hearing. The federal district judge ordered the JIA to desegregate all state-operated facilities, and in a later decree, he declared that all future leases "must require that the lessees operate without discrimination as to race or color."[29]

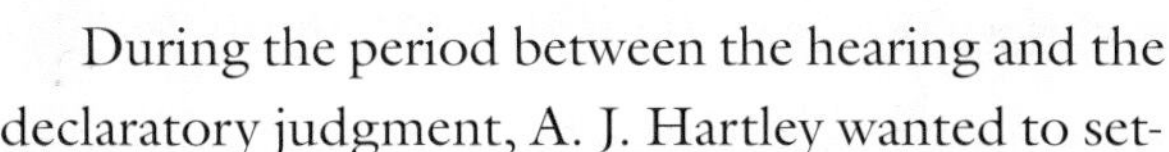

Judge A. J. Hartley sought ways to make the process of desegregation peaceful on the island. (Courtesy of Mosaic, Jekyll Island Museum)

During the period between the hearing and the declaratory judgment, A. J. Hartley wanted to settle the problems at Jekyll Island, especially the segregation issue. Ray Hill had made a positive impression on Hartley when they worked together in 1960 to obtain the lease for the Dolphin motel for Dave Jackson. Hartley also talked to several members of Glynn County's African American community, all of whom recommended Hill. And so Hartley hired Hill to be a peacemaker for Jekyll Island, though Hill's title would be "foreman." Hill said, "I accepted the job because I wanted Jekyll Island integrated, but I knew that the community of color would have to compromise on the demands they were making and be patient."[30] Hartley had retired as an assistant attorney general in September 1960 and had begun working daily at Jekyll Island. He later was named executive secretary of the JIA. According to Hill, "the crazy fringe group . . . wanted to oust Judge Hartley before he hired me as a peacemaker."[31]

Some members of the authority wanted to desegregate the island, but there were also powerful segregationists on the JIA board. According to Ray Hill, Ben Fortson was a liberal who wanted desegregation if it could be accomplished peacefully. Hartley was for desegregation, but he knew he had to be careful. As the executive secretary of the authority, he knew that some JIA members were more politically powerful at the state level than he was. He had already had a conflict in 1960 that brought forth a group calling for his ouster, and he had had to deal with Eugene Cook, the state's attorney general, and former Governor Ernest Vandiver, both of whom were adamantly segregationist.[32]

In the aftermath of the declaratory judgment against the JIA, the national, state, and local elections were heating up in Brunswick. Rev. Julius Hope, who was running for a city council seat, held mass meetings at the Zion Baptist Church every Tuesday and Thursday night to fire up the community. By this time, nine local Black students, including James Wilkes's son, had integrated formerly all-white schools. On Election Day in November 1964, a majority of Brunswick's white voters favored Republican presidential candidate Barry Goldwater, and with the help of the White Citizens Council, William Frank Holzendorf won the city council seat with a six-hundred-vote majority, defeating Reverend Hope.

Shortly after the elections, the National Educational Television network spotlighted the issue of integration in Brunswick in an hour-long episode of its series *At Issue*. By this time, the city had a voluntary school desegregation plan and had integrated beaches, bowling alleys, tennis courts, public parks, and a skating rink, though rather than integrate the municipal swimming pool, they had closed it earlier in 1964. The *At Issue* episode, titled "Quiet Conflict," was televised in 1965 and featured interviews with Reverend Hope, the Brunswick mayor, the White Citizens Council, members of the local biracial committee of the Georgia Council on Human Relations, and prominent Black leaders in the community. The program depicted Brunswick as a city in which local leaders embraced a cooperative change that came early and quickly, and it projected that change as a model for the South.[33]

Hill originally told Hartley that he would stay at Jekyll Island for a year, but he worked there for nearly three years. In late April 1965, someone placed a snake in his car, which was the last straw for Hill; he was ready to leave, but Judge Hartley asked him what the JIA should do to replace him. Reverend Hope was still agitating, and the situation had not been resolved. Hill later recalled, "I told the judge to hire the reverend's younger brother, Freddie, to take my place. I knew that if the judge talked to him, Freddie would probably take the job, and Reverend Hope would ease up on his baby brother. . . . Reverend Hope took it hard and moved on to Macon."[34]

Following the ruling, Jekyll Island integrated peacefully and quietly. As most Black visitors began using recreation facilities elsewhere on the island, occupancy plummeted at the Dolphin motel, forcing it to close in 1966. The authority later converted the motel into a facility for youth groups. The people who remember the St. Andrews area in the 1950s and '60s still have vivid, happy memories, and some dwell on what they lost. Sandra, Genoa Martin's daughter, said, "I like the little roughness of Jekyll, you know, the little naturalness of it. And when you see these big old hotels and things coming up like that, so big and tall you can't even see the sun . . . it just kind of hurts me a little bit."[35] Jim Bacote remarked, "With us being able to go in the Aquarama, we didn't want to go down there [to St. Andrews] anymore. . . . I always wondered just how good the integration notion was. We had a hotel, we had service stations, we had a lot of Black businesses, but after that we started going to all the other businesses. Even then, some of them did not want you."[36] Nevertheless, in the long run integration has proven to be successful on the island. Today, hotels and other businesses are open and welcoming to Black as well as white customers, and the authority has made increasing efforts to attract more Black visitors and to interpret the history of African Americans on the island.

This sign represents one of the first promotional efforts to lure passing tourists to Jekyll Island. (Courtesy of Mosaic, Jekyll Island Museum)

EXPANDING TOURISM & DEVELOPMENT

7

On an early summer day in 1962, Bruyn Deneroy and his wife were driving through Georgia on their way to Florida. Keenly aware that certain South Georgia towns were notorious for speed traps, the couple from Newburgh, New York, was staying well within the speed limit. Suddenly, the flashing lights and siren of a Brunswick police car beckoned them to pull over. Deneroy could hardly believe it, but he grudgingly pulled the car over to the side of U.S. Highway 17. When the police officer approached the car, he looked at them and asked, "You folks on vacation?" Hoping it would make a difference, Deneroy confirmed that they were indeed tourists, and the officer responded, "Will y'all come along with me?" The Deneroys wondered if the patrol car was escorting them to city hall or jail, but instead they pulled up in front of the Chamber of Commerce building, where a committee of local boosters greeted them warmly. "How'd you like to spend the night with us?" one of them asked. Still not sure what was going on, Deneroy asked cautiously, "Where, in jail?" The men burst into laughter and finally told them that they were in the midst of a major campaign to promote Jekyll Island. To boost word-of-mouth publicity, they were hauling in out-of-state motorists and offering them a free overnight stay on Jekyll Island.[1]

Throughout the 1960s, the Jekyll Island Authority partnered with the Glynn County Commission to advertise and promote "Fabulous Jekyll Island" in the hope of diverting tourists en route to Florida. Governor Ernest Vandiver pledged that his administration would "leave no stones unturned" in promoting tourism in a state that he claimed had more tourist attractions than any other state. He complained that Georgia had "sat idly back" as tourists passed through on the way to Florida. Vandiver wanted to attract "these passers-through" to become "stay-awhilers," to ensure that the state would receive its rightful share of tourist dollars. As a result, his administration conducted the state's first large-scale survey to determine the strengths and weaknesses of its tourism promotions. He also created a tourist division of the Georgia Department of Commerce, which led to the first comprehensive tourism promotion campaign, placing advertisements in national magazines as well as in state and regional publications. The Department of Commerce began the first outdoor advertising program by putting up almost a thousand billboards throughout Georgia and

Governor Ernest Vandiver was determined to make Jekyll Island a popular tourist attraction. (Courtesy of S. Ernest Vandiver Papers, Richard B. Russell Library for Political Research and Studies, University of Georgia Libraries, Athens, Ga.)

the surrounding states publicizing Georgia's tourist attractions. Vandiver's administration also built the first welcome stations for tourists and worked to improve travel on U.S. 17, then a major coastal highway. No previous Georgia governor had invested in tourism in the state.[2]

Vandiver knew that Jekyll Island State Park was the premier tourist destination on the Georgia coast. To encourage increased visitation to the state-owned Jekyll Island, his administration paid off the debt for the Jekyll Creek toll bridge connecting the island to the mainland, as well as that of the Sidney Lanier Bridge, which crossed the Turtle River into Brunswick. Vandiver asked for $1,218,000 for the legislature's Jekyll Island Committee to spur more development and new attractions, including the eighteen-hole Oleander golf course, the $1.2 million Aquarama with its almost Olympic-sized indoor swimming pool, and an exhibition hall.[3]

Throughout the 1960s and early 1970s, the main leaders of the Jekyll Island Authority were Ben Fortson, chair of the JIA board of directors and Georgia's secretary of state; Horace Caldwell, state parks director; and A. J. Hartley, who resigned as assistant state attorney general to take the newly created job of executive secretary of the Jekyll Island Authority.[4] These three elderly men and their staff struggled under enormous challenges, which included promoting Jekyll Island State Park, building a modern infrastructure on a fragile island, creating several recreational amenities, maintaining the island's landscaping and historic resources, providing public safety, and advocating for the allocation of state funds.

In the early 1960s, there were difficult issues concerning crime on the island, including two murders. The manager of the Jekyll marina, Captain Howard Doughty, who was having financial difficulties, had recently undergone mental treatment and had talked of suicide. On January 4, 1960, he repeatedly struck his wife, Catherine, with an antique candlestick holder, killing her. According to Jekyll policeman Clarence Ellis, Catherine Doughty had previously reported that her husband had asked her to join him in "a watery grave."[5] After the murder, Howard Doughty jumped into the cold marsh and drowned. His body was found six days later. In 1966 there was another horrific murder/suicide that resembled the Doughty murder. James Joseph Daly, a homeowner on the island since 1960, shot his wife, Ruth, with multiple bullets at about 1:40 a.m. She lived long enough to tell the police that he shot her. Less than two and a half hours later, Daly hanged himself with his belt at the Brunswick jail.[6]

Frequent crimes were a problem on Jekyll, in part because many criminals were aware that houses on the island were often unoccupied, especially in the winter. In February 1961, there was a two-week spike in burglaries, thefts,

Ben Fortson (at center) and Horace Caldwell (at right) present a certificate of appreciation from the State of Georgia to Tallu Fish, who established the first museum at Jekyll Island in the Rockefeller Cottage (Indian Mound) in 1954. (Courtesy of Mosaic, Jekyll Island Museum)

Matilda Denegal Hill, whose family had a long association with Jekyll Island during the club era and who worked for Tallu Fish at the fledgling Jekyll Island Museum, sits on a Red Bug (an electric "cyclecar" that club members once used to travel around the island) on the porch of Indian Mound. (Courtesy of Mosaic, Jekyll Island Museum)

Peppermint Land, a beachfront amusement park, was one of the victims of the spike in burglary on Jekyll in February 1961. (Courtesy of Mosaic, Jekyll Island Museum)

and stolen cars, and a go-cart was stolen from Peppermint Land, a beachside amusement park then on Jekyll. The police finally captured the thieves: three juveniles and a twenty-year-old.[7] At Jekyll's Wanderer Motel in 1962, a guest entrusted an employee named William Marshall to place $1,500 overnight in the motel's vault. The following morning, Marshall suddenly resigned, stealing the guest's $1,500 and another $200 in motel funds. Marshall drove to Kentucky, where he was arrested in Beattyville, and he later pleaded guilty to a charge of embezzlement in the Superior Court of Georgia.[8] In other incidents, a Jekyll service station was burglarized, as was the Jekyll Island Golf Club. Only a few weeks later, burglars raided and ransacked the Jekyll marina, stealing equipment, money, and even an outboard motor.

Another lingering problem was the presence of convict laborers on the island. Most of the workers building the golf courses, clearing lots, and landscaping were convicts. On October 3, 1960, Burley Turner, a twenty-four-year-old convict serving a robbery sentence, eluded the Wayne County guards, who did not notice he was missing for thirty minutes. Burley had been working over a widespread area near the golf links. Guards were concerned that he might shelter in empty houses and cottages, but searches with helicopters and bloodhounds failed to find him.[9] Three months later, Turner, still wearing his prison uniform, emerged from the Jekyll dump, where he was taken into custody without a struggle. Bloodhounds had previously led officers to the dump, but they failed to find him. He later told authorities that he had hidden beneath piles of corrugated boxes, and troopers were only feet away from him on several occasions.[10] Six months later, Turner once again tried to escape, this time with another prisoner, William DuBois, but both were injured by a guard's gunshots.[11] Two years later, in January 1963, a pair of convicts fled a golf course work detail, but after eluding searchers all night, they were flushed from the woods on the north end of Beachwood Drive near Tyler Lane.[12]

Only a few weeks later, in a joint House-Senate appropriations committee meeting, State Corrections Director Jack Forrester announced that the JIA had not paid for prison labor in over eight years. The Associated Press in Atlanta reported that the total arrears would be $2,500,000. Asked why the money had not been not paid, Forrester said, "[T]here seems to be a general agreement that one department cannot collect money from another department."[13] There were other convict escapes on the island over the next two years. On the afternoon of November 16, 1965, three "extremely dangerous inmates" escaped from a work gang on Jekyll Island, stole a pickup truck, and were armed with a pistol and a shotgun. They had a twenty-five-minute advantage over their pursuers because they locked up the foreman and two guards. They crossed Jekyll Creek and drove toward Waynesville. After a cold, wet night, the fugitives were finally captured in an African American church.[14] The last known convict escapee on Jekyll Island was Robert Lee Huffman, who was working with a thirteen-man detail. When the guard turned his back, Huffman slipped into the brush. He stole a car and was last seen in Brunswick, and it appears he was never apprehended.[15]

Aside from dealing with crime on the island, the JIA also struggled to maintain a reliable drawbridge. Because the causeway was the primary way to get on and off the island, a major problem occurred whenever one of the bridges used to reach the island malfunctioned. On April 25, 1960, a breakdown of the Sidney Lanier Bridge stopped all cargo ships and all traffic on U.S. 17 for five days. Only a few months later, the Jekyll Creek Bridge failed, delaying Jekyll workers and stranding many Jekyll residents for at least five hours.[16] Six days after that, workers and residents were blocked for about two hours.[17] Twelve days later, the Jekyll Creek Bridge was still closed. The local press in Brunswick commented that the drawbridge was "a regular source of trouble for auto and boat traffic over failures in its lift mechanism."[18] More than a month later, the JIA started a major overhaul of the lift's electrical and mechanical equipment so the bridge could be lifted 10,000 times a year.[19] In late July, another lift jam blocked island traffic for six hours, and car vacationers lined up for many miles. The Wanderer Motel resorted to airlifts to bring in maids.[20] Even though the bridge had been completely rebuilt a year earlier, the most extended breakdown in the troublesome history of the Jekyll Creek Bridge occurred on June 2, 1965, when a six-inch steel shaft at the top of the structure snapped with the sound of a shotgun report while the span was being raised to permit a boat's passage. What could have been a serious accident turned into an inconvenience to motorists on both sides. When they realized that it would be at least a ten-hour wait, some people left their cars, and others on the island side of the bridge decided to stay on Jekyll for another night.[21]

The Jekyll Creek drawbridge would remain a problem until it was finally replaced in 1996 by a higher bridge that allowed small boats to pass underneath, thus eliminating the need for a drawbridge. The new bridge was dedicated as the M. E. Thompson Bridge, making it the only structure on the island to recognize the governor who acquired Jekyll for the state of Georgia.

Another infrastructure problem was the handling of sewage on the island. Prior to the 1960s, the Jekyll homes used septic drain fields and tanks that commonly clogged up and emitted smelly, unhealthy odors. The initial push for sanitation sewers and water distribution came from Rep. Charlie Gowen, who offered a bill to give the Jekyll Island Authority power to issue self-liquidating revenue certificates for an island-wide sewer system.[22] After the authority accepted final bids for the proposed sewer works, they selected the low bid from the Osborne Firm. To pay for the new system, the JIA obtained a federal grant for $250,000 and advocated for $450,000 in funds from the Georgia legislature. In September 1961, the authority announced that the Jekyll sewage system would serve all the populated areas on the island, though some homeowners still chose to use septic fields and tanks, which would prove problematic in the 1970s.[23]

Just after midnight on September 10, 1964, Hurricane Dora passed close enough to Jekyll to cause substantial shoreline erosion and damage to homes and hotels, as well as to large trees and limbs. The outcome could have been much worse: At one point Dora was recorded as having 140-mile-per-hour winds, but the storm weakened to a Category 2 hurricane, and by the next morning it had been downgraded to a tropical depression. In the aftermath of Dora, Peppermint Land Amusement Park, which had been built about 1956, lay in ruins; the park's Ferris wheel had toppled to the ground early in the storm, and some other rides were damaged.[24] Harvey R. Smith, Peppermint Land's owner, wanted to revive the amusement park, but he claimed that A. J. Hartley was harassing him and charging too much for the lease. In an earlier meeting, Hartley and Smith had started yelling at each other. In the end, the lease was not renewed, and Smith soon left Jekyll Island.[25]

Throughout the 1960s, one of the most contentious issues on Jekyll was the subject of alcoholic beverages. Although Brunswick and Glynn County were "wet" in 1961, most people assumed that beer and alcohol were forbidden in state parks. Solicitor General Jack Ballenger was open to approving liquor licenses for Jekyll, but Governor Vandiver refused. In May 1961, local police raided four Jekyll motels, and the motels' owners were jailed.[26] In the aftermath of the raids, Attorney General Arthur Bolton proclaimed that he didn't know of a law that "prohibits liquor on state property." The South Georgia Methodist Conference adopted a unanimous resolution calling on the governor and the authority to stop the sale of alcoholic beverages on Jekyll. Dr. Louis D. Newton and other prominent ministers pointed out that "Gov. Vandiver flatly stated that no alcoholic beverages would be sold" on Jekyll during his administration and stated their intention to take their fight to Revenue Commissioner Dixon

Oxford and Attorney General Eugene Cook, who was also a member of the JIA. Cook had recently rendered an opinion that the sale of alcoholic beverages on Jekyll was legal, using as an example Atlanta's Henry Grady Hotel, which was, like the Jekyll establishments, on state property.[27] Following Cook's statement, the Glynn County Commission promptly began granting liquor licenses to Jekyll motels. Governor Carl Sanders, however, ordered the state revenue commissioner to deny the necessary state liquor licenses to Jekyll businesses to save Jekyll Island from "the blight of liquor." Newton, who had devoted much of his ministry to the Methodist community, urged local churches to try to stop the use of alcoholic beverages on Jekyll Island.[28] A few weeks later, during the island's Fourth of July celebrations, state agents once again raided most of the motels and hotels on Jekyll. Owners paid a fine and kept their bars open. Over the next several years there would be more raids, several attempts to ban liquor, more confusion about liquor licenses, and more promises from politicians to stop the sale of liquor on Jekyll. The controversy finally came to an end in April 1971 with a local referendum in which Jekyll citizens voted 223 to 96 to allow liquor on the island.[29]

Hurricane Dora swept through Jekyll Island on September 10, 1964, causing much damage, including the virtual demolition of Peppermint Land, the beachfront amusement park, which was never rebuilt. (Courtesy of Mosaic, Jekyll Island Museum)

Another significant controversy arose from the perception that some politicians had favorable access to leases and development opportunities on Jekyll. The presence of current and former politicians on the Jekyll Island Authority board created the appearance of conflicts of interest, particularly when some of those politicians directly or indirectly funded the authority. And the JIA may have demonstrated favoritism to certain political figures for leases and for lucrative projects on the island. For instance, in the last days of Governor Vandiver's term in early 1963, Vandiver arranged with the JIA to lease a lot on the island. State legislator Iris Blitch and her husband easily secured a home lot. A. J. Hartley had already attained a home on the island in 1961. Nevertheless, Fortson claimed that all authority leases and lots were granted on a first-come, first-served basis.

Despite Fortson's claim, a former employee named John Mann quoted Hartley as saying that beachfront lots were held "open for our friends."[30] Mann, who had been the cleaning superintendent for the authority but had left when his annual salary was cut from almost $11,000 to $5,000, made the assertion about Hartley during a subsequent complaint by the employee who had replaced him, E. L. Rogers. Rogers was dismissed from his job on Jekyll Island after a physical altercation with Hartley in 1963; Rogers subsequently brought a harassment claim against the authority, seeking back pay and damages for what he considered an illegal and malicious firing.[31]

Fortson insisted that only a few politicians leased lots on Jekyll, but in reality, numerous political figures had already built homes or secured residential lots, including Comptroller Jimmy Bentley; State Rep. Frank Twitty; former mayor of Macon Ed Wilson; former state legislator Francis Shurling; Paul Stone, a former member of the state board of education; assistant adjutant general and former board of education member Larry Morris; State Rep. Jimmy D. NeSmith, who had a twelve-month option for a bank on Jekyll; State Rep. Pierre Howard of Decatur; and Marvin Moate, Speaker of the Georgia House of Representatives.[32]

Despite their denials, Fortson and Hartley continued to favor selected members of the Georgia government who wanted leases and opportunities for lucrative developments on the island. For instance, Larry Morris, an All-American Georgia Tech football player who went on to play eleven years in the NFL and later became a member of the Georgia House of Representatives, publicly announced that he was building a 132-unit motel on Jekyll called the Sand Dollar. The project was mostly financed with a loan from the Teachers Retirement System of Georgia. The authority quickly approved the motel, which became a controversial development on the island because it was less than one hundred feet from the beach.

By 1972, there were more than six hundred homesites, and the JIA was continuing to show favoritism in granting leases and lots. For example, State Senator Hugh Gillis and his mother received a ten-year lease on apartments, but the JIA denied a proposal for a $5 million cooperative development promoted by a St. Simons developer.[33] State Auditor Ernest Davis, who was a member of the JIA, secured a choice lot in an area in which there were not supposed to be any more lots. He released the lot only after exposure of the facts.[34]

Starting in 1970, Mike Egan, a respected Republican in the Georgia Assembly, along with Democrat Reid Harris, pushed for laws that would precisely define tidal salt marshes and high land in the Coastal Marshlands Protection Act (CMPA).[35] The next year, Egan made distinctions between "marshes" and "land area" with respect to the law limiting development on Jekyll Island. This was reinforced through the passage of legislation to require the creation of a master plan for Jekyll Island and by reducing the percentage of the island's area that was eligible for development.

Horace Caldwell, who served as the JIA's executive director from 1967 to 1972, was responsible for one of the first controversies concerning the CMPA. In 1972, the JIA had decided to fill twenty-five acres of salt marsh to build a parking lot near the North Clam Creek picnic area. An article in *The Atlanta Constitution* opened with this sentence: "The first large scale violator of the new Georgia Marshlands Protection Act apparently is the state itself." Following complaints, Caldwell stated that they had "already received all the permits we need from all agencies of the federal and state governments." He claimed that the U.S. Army Corps of Engineers had approved the filling of the marsh area

The fishing pier was built at the north end of the island while Horace Caldwell was executive director of the JIA. (Courtesy of Mosaic, Jekyll Island Museum)

and that a state agency had issued a permit, though he could not remember *which* agency did so.[36]

It was not the only controversy about facilities at the island's north end. In 1968, Caldwell decided to build a large fishing pier and concessions there. Funds in the amount of $383,000 were allocated for the construction project. Salvaged cars were to be secured to the pilings under the pier.[37] Almost immediately after the project's completion, complaints came from fishermen that it was difficult to fish there because of the swift currents. People did not like the pier's location or design. Although the pier was intended for fishing and crabbing, even today as many people come to the north end for the spectacular sunsets as come for the fishing.

The fishing pier area today is a favorite place on the island for viewing the spectacular Jekyll sunsets. (Photo by the author)

By the early to mid-1970s, serious concerns had arisen about overdevelopment on the island. Residents were worried about violations of the law limiting development to one-third of the island, the neglect of Jekyll's ecology and natural habitats, and the fragility of the coastal marshes. Indeed, the 1970s were possibly the most challenging era in the history of the state park. While Caldwell still served as executive director, A. J. Hartley, the JIA's executive secretary, resigned his position after suffering a second heart attack in 1970. In 1972 Ben Fortson resigned as JIA board chair after fifteen years in the position, though he continued to be a JIA board member. After an extensive period of stability throughout the 1960s, it appeared that Jekyll Island was poised to struggle in the 1970s.[38]

After Jimmy Carter became governor of Georgia in 1971, he expressed dissatisfaction with the way Jekyll Island was being run. (Shutterstock)

8

"WHAT'S WRONG AT JEKYLL ISLAND?"

The first indication of trouble in the new decade started with the 1970 election of Governor Jimmy Carter, who made it clear that by July 1, 1971, Jekyll Island State Park would have to begin paying all its own operating expenses. The state would continue to subsidize capital improvements but not the day-to-day operations. Governor Carter's private memos reveal his disappointed perceptions of the Jekyll Island Authority. On December 1, 1972, Carter commented in a memo: "There are several things which I don't like of [sic] the Authority, but I've refrained from injecting myself into it." Instead, he urged Mike Egan, a respected Republican Assembly member from Savannah, to shake up Horace Caldwell about the appearance of overdevelopment on Jekyll. Egan subsequently sent a letter to Caldwell on February 2, 1971, about future developments on Jekyll. He wrote that he had consulted with Ernie Davis, a member of the JIA, who had indicated that "considerably less than 35% [of the island] is now under actual or planned development."[1] Egan also reminded Caldwell that he had proposed a bill that would not allow more than one-third of the high land to be developed.

Mike Egan of Savannah (right), a Republican member of the Georgia House of Representatives, worked with Democrat Reid Harris in helping to pass the Coastal Marshlands Protection Act. He is talking here with Rep. George Busbee, who became governor of Georgia in 1975. (Courtesy of Georgia Info, Digital Library of Georgia)

The Super Slide, one of the early facilities for entertaining visitors to the island, was considered by some to be a blight on the landscape. (Courtesy of Mosaic, Jekyll Island Museum)

Starting in early 1972, multiple articles from all over Georgia criticized the management of Jekyll Island. On January 18, Bob Harrell of *The Atlanta Constitution* wrote an editorial about his recent visit to Jekyll in which he lamented that the changes there had "dispossessed 'my' Jekyll Island." He condemned the Super Slide as a monstrous blight, decried the dredging that was dumped in the marshes, and suggested that they should change the name of Beachview Drive, since were no views of the beach.[2] On June 21, the *Waycross Journal-Herald* suggested that Jekyll was going downhill due to corrupted legislators.[3] On May 27, the *Wayne County Press* recommended that a moratorium be declared on future development on Jekyll Island; while the JIA claimed that only 19 percent of the land had been developed, the *Wayne County Press*, like many others across the state, disagreed: "Take into consideration the island's roads, parking lots, disposal plants, water towers, golf links, beachfront development, apartments, Aquarama, large convention center, and several motels." Total developments on Jekyll were clearly nearing 35 percent of the land, according to the paper—"a far cry from the development that was on the island when the State of Georgia purchased the isle."[4]

Another unflattering article in May 1972 spotlighted what appeared be a rush for development on Jekyll before a new Robert and Company land-use plan could be implemented. Various enterprises were competing for rights of refusal on properties. In 1969, a company named Georgia Factors, Inc., sent a three-thousand-dollar check to the JIA for the right of refusal on a property on which it proposed to build a motel. A year later, the company sent plans for the motel, but the authority took no action because it wanted three sets of plans, and after another year the JIA forfeited the check. In the meantime, Senator Jack Henderson and Rep. Howard Atherton, both of Marietta, stepped in with a three-thousand-dollar check for the same parcel, on which they planned to build an upscale 176-unit apartment complex. The article also uncovered the infuriating practice of holding two or three leases for future use. Records indicated that officials of a savings and loan firm in Brunswick were holding several leases. Two contractors and several real estate brokers were doing the same thing. Horace Caldwell, the authority's executive director, had two houses on the island. One lease was with his brother-in-law, Downing Musgrove, who was a member of the State Highway Board, and the other home was in his wife's name. Senator Henderson had two commercial lots in addition to his Jekyll residence. Senator Gillis had two residential lots, one for him and another for his mother.[5]

Perhaps the most striking article was Margaret Shannon's long exposé in *The Atlanta Constitution* spotlighting the problems at Jekyll Island State Park.[6] One challenge for the authority was the reaction of approximately a thousand year-round residents who were deeply concerned about the changes on the island. At that time Caldwell was the most visible figure on the island, and his vision for Jekyll was a combination of free enterprise and state money. Many of the island's citizens had a very different point of view on the ongoing developments at Jekyll. One of their leaders was Si Fryer, a retired assistant commissioner of the U.S. Bureau of Indian Affairs and the president of the Coastal Georgia Audubon Society. From his perspective, the Super Slide, which Caldwell initiated in September 1970, was an awakening for the residents, most of whom hated the slide. Even Caldwell conceded that it was a costly $40,000 mistake.[7] Then the authority stunned the citizens of the island when it announced that a "sea circus" was to be constructed on the beach. Circus officials announced that the Jekyll Island Authority would allow the circus's oceanarium to temporarily dump its filter backwash water into the Jekyll sewer mains. Within a few days, R. S. "Rock" Howard, the director of the Environmental Protection Division of the state's Department of Natural Resources, said, "We told them some time ago they couldn't discharge into the ocean. We don't want their waste being dumped into recreational water. . . . They're not going to get that permit. The federal courts have ordered the Corps of Engineers not to issue any more of those."[8]

Although the sea circus never came to be, the controversy around it emboldened Jekyll citizens to speak out against the JIA. The authority had already made other costly mistakes, including the $3.5 million marina that could not be used—the banks of Jekyll Creek kept sliding back in, so they tried to do dredging on top of dredging. Another disappointment was the $500,000 fishing pier constructed at the northwest end of the island; the view was beautiful, but the current was very swift, making it difficult to fish.[9]

Aside from the two eighteen-hole golf courses, the historic nine-hole Great Dunes course, and another proposed eighteen-hole golf course, Pine Lakes, perhaps the most environmentally destructive development was the amphitheater. Its story began in 1968 when Reid Harris, a member of the Georgia General Assembly, secured an appropriation of $500,000 for an amphitheater on Jekyll Island. "It was one of those political trades," said Caldwell. In 1972, workers started digging a massive hole in the ground to make a pile of dirt thirty-six feet high to put up the tiers. The project destroyed several acres of forest, and there were concerns that the parking areas would damage more of the forest.[10]

Criticism of the Jekyll Island Authority from the press and from powerful legislators forced Ben Wiggins, the JIA chair, to halt all development on the island. He said he was "adamant" about keeping the majority of the island in its natural state. After receiving a letter from Rep. Michael Egan asking that no more commitments or improvements of any sort be made on the island until after the 1973 session of the legislature, Wiggins announced that the authority would comply with the request. Egan had received a copy of a memorandum from the state's attorney general, Arthur Bolton, stating that

The Jekyll Island Amphitheater, which opened in 1972, was popular with island visitors but was environmentally destructive. The first production in the amphitheater was *Drumbeats in Georgia*, a historical drama written by Paul Green. (Courtesy of Mosaic, Jekyll Island Museum)

The adapted interior of the casino built by club member Edwin Gould, which was used for several years as an auditorium, thus providing an indoor alternative to the Jekyll Island Amphitheater. The Allman Brothers performed at the Gould Auditorium on June 2, 1972. (Courtesy of Mosaic, Jekyll Island Museum)

it "is legally permissible for the Authority to develop and improve the entire land area of Jekyll Island." Egan had drafted legislation in 1971 "to limit the Authority's power to improve and develop the island to 35 percent of the ground beyond the high water mark," and the legislation had passed overwhelmingly in the House and the Senate and been signed by Governor Jimmy Carter. Egan was dismayed that there still seemed to be no limitations whatsoever on the authority's power to develop and improve the island. Egan said, "I want the limits set out by law—as I think the intentions of the 1971 legislature indicated—so that no future commission could change it."[11]

In the aftermath of the unfavorable articles about the JIA, Governor Carter and Joe Tanner, the commissioner of the state's Department of Natural Resources, were considering a bill for Jekyll Island beach restoration. On November 1, 1972, Governor Carter wrote a memorandum in which he expressed his disapproval of the management of Jekyll Island: "My impression is that the Authority has been more concerned with development than with the quality of the island, dunes, beach, and open space." In a stunning comment, he added that "forty-six percent of the high ground is developed or authorized (contrary to state law) and the fishing pier and the marina were a waste of money. I feel terrible every time I fly over the island. What is going on there? What are future plans? Who is now in charge?"[12]

To make matters worse for Jekyll Island, on November 7, 1972, a tragic accident occurred at the Sidney Lanier Bridge. The SS *African Neptune*, an eleven-thousand-ton freighter, was moving rapidly down the Turtle River because of a fast-dropping tide when the ship smashed into the center span of the Lanier Bridge. The collision destroyed three of the bridge's pillars, and six cars on the bridge were sent plunging into the river, killing eleven passengers, including a two-year-old and a three-year-old. Traffic to and from Jekyll was temporarily impeded by the crash, and cars were rerouted via Georgia Highway 50. It would be several months before the bridge reopened.[13]

On November 28, 1972, Governor Carter responded to a letter from Horace Caldwell requesting funds for various projects and improvements on Jekyll Island. Carter wrote, "I really appreciate your fine letter about Jekyll. The truth of the matter is that we simply do not have $9,340,000 to spend on the island. In fact, the total expenditure for capital improvements for the entire park system will be $1,900,000. The list of projects is certainly well considered, and all are worthy. Steps should be pursued, in my opinion, to guarantee that Jekyll is self-supporting." He indicated that if there was a "continuing hope of massive state grants," they were not likely to happen. He added, "There are several things which I don't like about the administration of the Authority, but I've refrained from injecting myself into it. However, I have a deep interest in the island as one of Georgia's finest treasures, and certainly have nothing but appreciation for your dedication to its proper use."[14] A few weeks later, in late 1972, Caldwell retired. Since he had a house on the island, he became an unofficial one-man Jekyll Island welcoming committee.

Governor Carter continued to refuse and veto appropriations for Jekyll Island, putting the Jekyll Island Authority in the worst financial crisis of the park's history. In early June 1974, Jekyll Island was $15 million behind in its budget needs and was soon to be in violation of certain health standards, according to the island's operations director, R. C. Anderson. The authority halted work on the marina, stopped restoration efforts, and pulled funds for a new campground. Over the previous two years, Carter had repeatedly denied funding for capital and operation expenses for the JIA. Anderson said, "Carter's office just doesn't understand Jekyll Island." State Senator Roscoe Dean blamed the appropriations losses on Carter's vindictiveness toward him for opposing some administrative bills. At stake were funds for the island's sewage system, a beach erosion plan, and an ambulance.[15] A week later, Rock Howard, director of the state's Environmental Protection Division, claimed that the island's drinking water system and sewage treatment were being operated illegally, without state approval, and indicated that his office was prepared "to take whatever action is necessary to correct these things, or close it [the island] down." According to Howard, his office had been asking since 1972

The EPA refused to certify the island's drinking water due to the lack of suitable sanitary treatment equipment, which had caused sewer problems. This was the pumping station. (Courtesy of Mosaic, Jekyll Island Museum)

EPA Chief Hits Jekyll Inaction

By FREDERICK ALLEN

A headline from *The Atlanta Constitution* on June 18, 1972, notes that the EPA had refused to certify the island's water.

for regular tests to be run on Jekyll Island's water supply; however, he said, "We haven't had any kind of response. They haven't performed the tests [we] requested." As a result, the EPA had refused to certify the island's drinking water. Howard also pointed out that Jekyll's incinerators were poorly operated and its sewage treatment plant was "overloaded." Meanwhile, Ray Hill, who was now vice president and general manager of the Georgia Hotel-Motel Association, said that the closing of Jekyll Island "would be a complete disaster to the motel-hotel industry."[16]

Three days later, in mid-June, JIA chair Ben Wiggins tried to assure the public that there was nothing wrong with Jekyll's water and that it was all a misunderstanding. Wiggins said, "[T]here's no need to shut Jekyll Island down. . . . There's just a bad rumor that got out that's regrettable." He insisted that "[t]he water is very pure down there, purer than a lot of other places you hear about." Wiggins reported that Robert C. Anderson, the new director of the island, had "a very pleasant meeting" with state EPA officials in which he explained that the island was getting a new sewage treatment plant and that the misunderstanding was resolved.[17]

Within a few days, Rock Howard hit back by saying that there were "potentially dangerous" health conditions on Jekyll, and he renewed his threat to take legal action to force the JIA to comply with EPA directives. He vigorously disputed Wiggin's comments that it was a misunderstanding that had been resolved, asserting that there was "no misunderstanding about it. They want to compromise and we can't compromise. We've got to get everything cleared up. . . . They are violating several acts of the state law." Howard also cautioned that visitors at Jekyll who swam, fished, or went boating or otherwise had "intimate contact with the water" could be in danger. He advised that "[t]hey shouldn't go swimming in Jekyll Creek or anywhere near the sewage

Governor George Busbee refused to adequately fund the JIA, offering only $25,000 to help pay for clearing up the sanitation problem. (Courtesy of Georgia Archives)

treatment plant . . . where they've been dumping raw sewage."[18] The next day, *The Atlanta Constitution* published another article about Jekyll's water quality and about reports of raw sewage.

There was every reason to be concerned, as this was not the first time Jekyll had had such problems. Back in the era of the Jekyll Island Club, a half-dozen club members died of typhoid fever, an outbreak that was traced back to sewage being dumped too near the oyster beds.[19] Glynn County, including Brunswick and St. Simons, had deep wells drawing from the same freshwater aquifer, but Jekyll Island had the only system that did not use chlorination on its wells. Howard demanded that the state-owned system add chlorination at Jekyll. Within a few weeks of that change being implemented, the purification of the island's water met state standards.[20]

However, the larger problem for Jekyll Island continued to be the serious lack of funds. During this period, the nation was struggling with high inflation and a stagnant economy. After four years of denied state appropriations and no authorization for tolls on the island, the authority requested $4.6 million in funds for the year 1975, but the new governor, George Busbee, offered only $25,000. He commented, "[I]n this time of economic hard times, I don't think it's fair to ask the taxpayers of the state to pay for sewer service for those who live on the island." Ben Wiggins and Ernest Davis begged for another $350,000 just to keep the park clean.[21]

Despite what one reporter described as "a record fall season for tourists on the island," the mortgage contracts for two popular beachfront motels, the Corsair and the Carriage Inn, were terminated in December 1976. The motels were forced to shut down after the authority cut off their water for failure to pay $2,000 in water bills. Both motels were judged to be in a "run-down" condition. A member of the authority estimated that refurbishing the motels would cost at least $200,000. Since the JIA did not have the funds to fix them up, its only option was to negotiate an arrangement with another buyer, but no one wanted to invest during a period of high inflation.[22] The authority had supported a bill to bail out distressed motels on Jekyll Island earlier in the year. Both the House and the Senate passed the bill, which would have allowed owners to convert the motels into condominiums and sell units to private individuals, but Governor Busbee vetoed it. He feared that most of the motels would be converted and sold, leaving the average Georgian with no place to spend the night at Jekyll. Busbee remarked that "[t]he State bought Jekyll Island with the expressed intention of making it a vacation facility for the average Georgian. Allowing motels to convert to condominiums would tend to make Jekyll Island into an exclusive resort for the rich."[23]

More than a year later, the Corsair Motel and the Carriage Inn were still closed, and the JIA had taken over negotiating with prospective buyers after an earlier agreement fell through. William M. Nixon, the recently elected chair of the authority, said, "I don't know whether they thought they just couldn't live with our terms. They just said they wanted to withdraw." In the meantime, the costs of improvements were soaring. Estimates for renovation costs had rapidly climbed to $250,000 for the Carriage Inn and $700,000 for the Corsair.[24]

By 1977, there had been a notable drop in the number of tourists at Jekyll Island. Disturbed by the island's declining popularity as a tourist destination, a state house subcommittee traveled to Jekyll on a fact-finding mission. The House Subcommittee on Tourist Relations, chaired by Rep. Lauren "Bubba" McDonald Jr., toured the Georgia coast and met with the island's promotional and tourism development officials.[25]

Following Busbee's veto of the motel bailout bill in April 1976, the JIA denied Larry Morris permission to convert his financially troubled motel on the island to condominiums. Morris owed $2.5 million on a $2.6 million loan from the Georgia Teachers' Retirement Fund. Morris also owed a second mortgage of $1.5 million, as well as owing $19,000 to the authority for rental fees. On top of this, the JIA was still trying to find new management for the Corsair Motel and the Carriage Inn.[26] Given all the problems the JIA faced, the future of Jekyll Island was uncertain.

In retrospect, the authority had made several bad decisions that were irreversible. For instance, over the previous eighteen years, the JIA had twice used bulldozers to flatten sand dunes, which protect the coastline, so that people could more easily see the ocean from their car, home, motel, or seaside cottage. The issues surrounding the construction of the marina, the fishing pier, and the amphitheater, along with inaccurate estimates of the number of groups that would want to use the convention center, seemed to add up to mismanagement. In 1977, a special panel of legislators began questioning whether Georgia's twenty-six quasi-public authorities had been properly managing their responsibilities, with some lawmakers arguing that the authorities could be better handled by regular state agencies; the Jekyll Island Authority demanded most of the committee's time. During the committee's hearings, it became apparent that Ben Fortson, Ben Wiggins, and Ernest Davis were making the authority's decisions, including those that led to the construction of the controversial marina, the fishing pier, the convention center, the Aquarama, and the amphitheater. Newer authority members resented the criticism coming their way for actions taken before they became members. Joe Tanner, commissioner of the Department of Natural Resources and a JIA member who had long been critical of the authority, at least privately, told the legislative panel that "[t]he history of the Jekyll Island Authority has been one of mismanagement. . . . The authority makes too many decisions with too little information."[27]

After several years of mismanagement, the Jekyll Island Authority suffered from a chronic lack of funds. The new executive director, Robert Case, who was hired in December 1978, acknowledged that "Jekyll is struggling to get

One of the greatest mistakes made during early state ownership of Jekyll Island was bulldozing the dunes to provide a better view of the ocean to homeowners and beachgoers. (Courtesy of Mosaic, Jekyll Island Museum)

money." However, he was optimistic that three new motels would open and that the Corsair and the Carriage Inn would be refurbished and would reopen by early spring.[28] Rep. John Greer of Atlanta proposed a fifty-cent entrance fee for the park; there also had been talk of imposing a toll to raise the $250,000 needed to pay for picking up litter on the island. However, various officials expressed doubts about the legality of using tollway funds or a fee to enter Jekyll as operating revenue. And in an interview, State Senator Don Ballard, chair of the Senate Committee on Industry, Trade, and Tourism, said that a plan to charge a toll to reach the island "is about squelched."[29] It would be another fifteen years before an entry fee was established.

In the early 1980s, Jekyll administrators and residents struggled to realize a new and unique identity for the island. Many of the year-round residents were retired, and they favored preserving Jekyll's wilderness areas, protecting the wildlife, and encouraging visitors to enjoy the beach. However, the Jekyll Island Authority believed that Jekyll needed to be developed and promoted as a first-class resort, with amenities, amusements, and entertainment facilities to attract upper-income families. Case, the authority's executive director, saw "no conflict between the state park concept and the resort concept." But the residents did not agree. Lorraine Dusenbury, who had recently served as chair of the Glynn County Commission, said, "I definitely see a conflict developing." She pointed out that "signs on the island now refer to Jekyll Island Resort, not to Jekyll Island State Park." Joe Kaylor, president of the Jekyll Island Citizens Association, had seen sections of the new Robert and Company master plan that in his view looked "more like a promotional plan than a land-use plan." Case, however, contended that Jekyll Island was "on the threshold of jumping out into the world as a competitive resort." These two perspectives seemed to be in complete conflict. Dusenbury, perhaps, stated it most clearly: "[W]e've reached the point where a conscious decision has to be made on whether to have a resort here, or a state park, or both."[30]

After so many years of negligence, misconduct, and unprofessionalism on Jekyll Island, however, it seemed that things were beginning to improve, at least in terms of strengthening it as a resort. Robert Case, who helped to reorganize how the authority governed the island, appeared to be a strong hire. He had been a successful resort manager for Howard Hughes and had effectively produced resort developments in Las Vegas, Florida, the Bahamas, and Hilton Head. He quickly improved food service on Jekyll and converted the Sand Dollar into the Jekyll Island Inn, a first-class motel. He also refurbished the Corsair and the Carriage Inn nearly two years after the motels were shut down.[31]

Less than two years after he was hired, Robert Case stepped down in the face of a sexual harassment charge. An authority member said the complaint was "basically groundless." Nevertheless, the board reluctantly asked for Case's resignation, concluding that "it would be in his best interest if Case pursued some other opportunity." Bill Shipp of *The Atlanta Constitution* wrote, "If the complete latter-day history of state-owned Jekyll Island is ever written, it will be a tragic saga of a ruined environment, political corruption, mismanagement and plain stealing."[32] Little did he know that Jekyll Island was on the verge of a major revival in its historic district that would propel a revitalization of the entire island.

The African American community known as Red Row, constructed during the Jekyll Island Club era, was demolished in the early years of state ownership of Jekyll. (Courtesy of Mosaic, Jekyll Island Museum)

9 SAVING THE HISTORIC DISTRICT

When the State of Georgia acquired Jekyll, the most challenging resources on the island were the historic remains of the Jekyll Island Club, which included the Jekyll Island Clubhouse, the annex, the Sans Souci, the cottages, and several other structures. Unfortunately, most of the members of the Jekyll Island Authority in the 1950s did not believe in spending time or money on historical resources, mainly because the authority promoted Jekyll Island as a beach park. As a result, the JIA opted to demolish important historic structures, including Red Row, the Pulitzer-Albright Cottage, and the Brown Cottage. Red Row was the Black community on Jekyll Island during the club era. Once the state purchased Jekyll, African Americans were no longer welcome on the island until the creation of the St. Andrews area on the south end. After more than six decades, the tight-knit community of African Americans who had worked for the Jekyll Island Club had been forced to resettle. Many former employees moved to Brunswick or to nearby communities such as Fancy Bluff, Dover's Bluff, Honey Creek, and Brookman.[1]

The Pulitzer-Albright Cottage, built for Joseph Pulitzer in 1897, was still standing in 1947, but in 1951 a small fire damaged the interior. With no funds for restoration, the authority decided to demolish the structure.[2] The cottage of Bayard Brown, never used by its owner, was still standing in 1948, but by 1949 it had been demolished.

With no state funds for restoration and preservation, the historic district languished in the semitropical climate, in which buildings needed nearly year-round protection from pests, humidity, and vandalism. Many Jekyll officials did not recognize the significance of the historic structures. Indeed, State Auditor B. E. Thrasher remarked that the hotel and cottages were "a rathole to throw money down the drain." Fortunately, that viewpoint did not prevail among most members of the authority. In the mid- to late 1960s, the JIA finally realized the importance of historic preservation, and A. J. Hartley and Horace Caldwell advocated for funds to restore the historic district. As early as 1963, Hartley envisioned the restored historic district as "a sort of little Williamsburg," referring to Colonial Williamsburg, the historic site and open-air museum in Virginia.[3]

Despite the criticism of the Jekyll Island Authority in the 1960s, the JIA

The Jekyll Island home built for Joseph Pulitzer and later owned by John J. Albright was torn down during the summer of 1951 after a small fire damaged the structure, since no funds were available for restoration. (Courtesy of Mosaic, Jekyll Island Museum)

A. J. Hartley (left), executive secretary of the Jekyll Island Authority, was the first person to suggest the importance of Jekyll's historic district. He believed it could become "a sort of little Williamsburg." (Courtesy of Mosaic, Jekyll Island Museum)

successfully carried project ideas into the 1970s and 1980s. For instance, an archaeological study at the ruins around the Horton residence recovered hundreds of fragments, glass bottles, Native American pottery, musket flints, brass buttons, and a "one-halve cannon shot."[4] A month later, the JIA employed J. Everette Fauber Jr., who previously had worked at Colonial Williamsburg. His feasibility study for the village restoration led to a two-year contract for Fauber to draft preliminary plans for restoring what they called the "millionaires village." Caldwell commented that he "didn't think the project would attract many visitors to the island." By December 1965, Fauber's preservation work had begun, and newspapers reported that the "entire village" was being restored at a cost of $50,000.[5]

Within a few months, Fauber hired the famed Clermont Lee as the histor-

In the 1960s the JIA began to show interest in preserving the historical aspects of Jekyll Island and did an archaeological study at the ruins of the Horton House at the north end of the island. (Courtesy of Mosaic, Jekyll Island Museum)

ical landscaping expert for the project. After two years, Fauber delivered to the JIA a six-page report of his work at Jekyll, which focused on Faith Chapel and the Rockefeller Cottage (also known as Indian Mound). Fauber wrote to Caldwell that "[t]his can be the all-important 'groundbreaking' step to initialize a catalytic action, which we all hope will terminate in the eventual restoration of the Jekyll Island Club Village as one of the most interesting and appealing open-air museums in the nation." His report pointed out that there was scant documentary evidence for the structures, and they needed more contact with the Rockefeller family. He also had planned the restoration of other cottages, focusing especially on the Maurice Cottage. At the end of the report, Fauber calculated that the restoration costs for Faith Chapel, the Rockefeller Cottage, and the Maurice Cottage and the associated professional fees would total $1,272,885, considerably higher than the original estimate. Although the JIA could not spend that amount of money, Fauber's plans for the concept of the "millionaires village" would contribute to the restoration and preservation of the historic district over the next two decades.[6]

Approximately two years later, the JIA hired Roger K. Beedle as its first full-time preservationist. Beedle had a long practice as an engineer for Dupont before he retired in 1962 and moved to Jekyll Island. When he accepted the position at Jekyll in November 1968, his stationery listed him as "Roger K. Beedle, Consulting Engineer," but he was not a preservationist. However, Beedle assisted with documenting the historic district's buildings and sought

The Jekyll Island Authority hired J. Everette Fauber Jr. to draft preliminary plans for restoring the historic district. He in turn hired Clermont Lee (shown here), a landscape architect from Savannah, to assist in the project. (© Don Hardigree—USA TODAY NETWORK)

OPPOSITE The JIA moved its offices into Villa Marianna in 1969. The authority's offices are no longer located in one of Jekyll's historic homes. (Courtesy of Mosaic, Jekyll Island Museum)

to restore many of the structures. He kept a diary in which he commented on what was happening on the island. On July 28, 1969, Beedle wrote, "These houses are rapidly deteriorating mostly due to leaky roofs and termite damage and should be repaired as soon as possible."[7] Caldwell asked him to estimate the cost of restoring the Crane House, hoping the authority could move its offices out of the shopping center and into one of the cottages. Beedle wrote in his diary that "[t]he JIA liked Caldwell's idea of moving the Authority to the Crane House but the [legislators] decided the JIA would take the Gould House."[8]

One of the main obstacles to getting the restoration work done was the lack of skilled workers. At various times, Beedle, writing in his diary, complained about his situation: "I stopped the roofing job on Rockefeller House because of the incompetent workman." Clermont Lee spent several days finalizing the landscaping in 1970; when Beedle received her final site plan, he wrote, "[L]ots of work involved. Don't believe JIA people will get it done very soon." His frustration with Caldwell boiled over on July 22, 1971, when he wrote, "Submitted my resignation. . . . I could no longer abide the incompetence and casual disregard of carefully prepared plans. I will never again put my name on any document having to do with the Jekyll Island Authority."[9] After five months with no restoration, Caldwell asked Beedle to take over again, and within a few days, Caldwell himself resigned.

Beedle next turned his efforts to preparing the dormitory for the actors and actresses of the drama *Drumbeats in Georgia*, which opened at the new Jekyll Island Amphitheater in the summer of 1973. On September 5, 1973, Beedle wrote, "Green and I caught two of the *Drumbeats* cast making off with half a truckload of furniture and had them arrested, but [Officer] Anderson would not prosecute, so they went free much to my disgust."[10] A few days later, Beedle wrote, "We are still finding out about the items that have been stolen. Now

The JIA considered demolishing the historic Jekyll Island Clubhouse because it had fallen into such disrepair. (Courtesy of Vance Hughes)

it appears that most of the dishes and the silverware belonging to the club [have] disappeared."[11] He also had constant problems with break-ins and "serious threats concerning 'rip-offs'" in some of the houses in what they called the Old Village.

Beedle's work was crucial in the 1970s for sustaining numerous buildings in the historic district. Without much money, and during a period of high inflation, he sustained the Rockefeller Cottage, Faith Chapel, the Frank Gould Cottage, Mistletoe, Goodyear Cottage, and Crane Cottage (which was partially restored). The restoration of Villa Ospo was essentially completed, but during the summers of 1972 and 1973 it was used as headquarters for the theatrical production of *Drumbeats in Georgia*. According to Beedle, "It was a financial disaster," because the large parties in Villa Ospo ruined his restoration work. He also stabilized Macy Cottage, Hollybourne Cottage, the Sans Souci, and the Jekyll Island Club by repairing their roofs and painting their exteriors. About the clubhouse, Beedle wrote, "At present, it appears doubtful that the Jekyll Island Club will be used again." Indeed, the JIA decided that the decaying Queen Anne hotel was a liability. In 1969, the hotel's operations began to wind down, and in 1971 the authority decided to close the Jekyll Island Hotel and the annex.

The following year, the Jekyll Island Authority hired the accounting firm Harris, Kerr, Forster and Company of Atlanta to develop a feasibility study for restoring the clubhouse, but the firm's conclusions were quite negative, and its assessment was brutally revealing. The firm did not view the project as "feasible from an economic standpoint," pointing out that the clubhouse "has deteriorated substantially in the intervening 30 years" since the Jekyll Island Club closed in 1942 and "its condition is very poor."

The study mentioned falling ceilings on the third and fourth floors and structural defects created by water damage from a leaky roof, as well as "deficiencies in plumbing and electrical systems." With no one interested in taking on the expense of leasing the structure and making the necessary repairs, the authority had little choice but to simply close the building, maintain the exterior to a limited extent by replacing the roof and refitting doors and windows, and leave it to deteriorate as the object of vandals for the next fourteen years. At the end of so many years of neglect, the clubhouse was in a serious state of disrepair. If not for a fortuitous and quite remarkable series of events in the early to mid-1980s, the historic Jekyll Island Clubhouse would have been demolished.[12]

In 1983, two old friends from Calhoun, Georgia, who had recently reconnected at a high school reunion climbed into the clubhouse through an unlocked window and fell in love with the decrepit structure. Larry Evans was an architect who had long been interested in historic preservation. Vance Hughes, Evans's former classmate, was an environmental lawyer who worked for the Natural Resources Division of the U.S. Department of Justice in Washington, D.C. The two men pondered what it would take in terms of time and money to restore the crumbling building. They contemplated the idea for more than a year until they met again the following spring at their twentieth high school reunion in Calhoun. At that reunion, they decided it had to be now or never.[13]

Not long thereafter, Evans and Hughes approached George Chambliss, then the executive director of the Jekyll Island Authority, with their idea of restoring the old clubhouse for use as a hotel, which Chambliss met with enthusiasm. Only a year or two earlier, the authority had been involved in discussions about such a renewal. The JIA had even asked State Senator Bill Littlefield to introduce a bill in the legislature that would allow the Brunswick–Glynn County Development Authority to issue tax-exempt bonds for projects on Jekyll in the hope that a developer who would be eligible for such bond issues might step forward.

Evans and Hughes could fulfill that hope, but they would have to develop a feasible plan to present to the Jekyll Island Authority. Chambliss informed them that the JIA would have to issue a request for proposals. According to John McTier, who had been elected chair of the Jekyll Island Authority the previous summer, the board had already decided that something had to be done, or else the JIA was going to be faced with the prospect of having to demolish the clubhouse, which had been added to the National Register of Historic Places in 1972.

A young architect, Larry Evans (at right), and his lawyer friend, Vance Hughes (at left), decided to take on the mammoth project of restoring the clubhouse to historic preservation standards for use as a modern hotel. (Courtesy of Vance Hughes)

Ultimately both Hughes and Evans left their current jobs, which allowed them to devote more time to the project; though they continued their work professionally as an independent architect and a lawyer, they took an extraordinary risk for something they believed in, a dream they hoped to fulfill. At the time, the old clubhouse, particularly the interior, was in terrible condition. Nearly one hundred years old, the building had been almost completely neglected for well over a decade. Restoring it to usable condition would inevitably require a huge amount of money and care. But the two men believed that it was well worth preserving and that it should not come to the same end as the magnificent Oglethorpe Hotel, a Brunswick landmark that opened for its inaugural season in 1888, the same year as the Jekyll Island Club, but was torn down in 1958 to make room for two undistinguished structures.

Evans and Hughes knew it would take many hours of labor to develop tentative plans and draw up the proposal. They formed a company called the Circle Development Corporation and began work on a development program that included a conceptual architectural plan and construction cost estimates, as well as funding estimates for running the hotel. In January 1985, they hired the Philadelphia accounting firm of Laventhol and Horwath to conduct a market study and prepare financial projections for the restored property.

The full renovation of the clubhouse, the annex, and the Sans Souci was to result in 144 guest rooms, eight meeting rooms, a ballroom, and a full-service restaurant and lounge, as well as a landscaped pool and health and tennis facilities. The stated goal of the renovation proposal was to return the old clubhouse to its "full grandeur" and "to expand the markets available to Jekyll Island by providing first class accommodations to upper income guests who previously have not visited the island."

In anticipation of the restoration project, the authority contracted with the architectural firm of John Tuten, of which Larry Evans was still an associate at the time, to complete the base drawings of the Jekyll Island Clubhouse, the annex, and the Sans Souci for a $5,000 fee. The contract stipulated that the drawings would be given to Taylor-Ward Consultants, which would complete the conceptual engineering work and any engineering-related items. With the results in hand, the authority issued the request for proposals (RFP). At the JIA meeting on January 31, 1985, Chambliss announced that six developers had thus far requested copies of the RFP and that their proposals were due on February 14. By the time of the authority's meeting on February 22, the field had been winnowed down to two applicants: Winn Development Company of Boston and the Circle Development Corporation of Brunswick. The board members were impressed by the thoroughness of the Circle Development Corporation's proposal and were convinced Evans and Hughes really cared about the project. The only problem was that the two men did not have sufficient funds for completion, which called for almost $20 million. They had only a short time to come up with the money, and they had little time to work out the details. Considering all that, the restoration of the Jekyll Island Club seems somewhat of a miracle.

The local bonds initially did not pan out, in part because local people did not show any enthusiasm. Luckily, another friend from Calhoun, a man named George Daves who was a lawyer with the U.S. Department of Housing and Urban Development (HUD), called Evans and Hughes with a suggestion. "If [Daves] had not been proactive it would have never happened," said Hughes.

Daves's idea was a long shot with an unlikely partner. He recommended that they take their proposal to Leon Weiner, a developer from Delaware who specialized in low-cost housing rather than luxury hotels. Weiner had been called "the conscience of the housing industry," but Daves sensed that Weiner wanted to branch out into development areas, having recently financed a hotel in Connecticut. Evans and Hughes made a quick trip to the offices of Leon N. Weiner & Associates in Delaware, where they met the larger-than-life man who would become their benefactor. After an impressive and enthusiastic presentation by Evans and Hughes, Weiner decided to visit Jekyll Island. During the winter of 1984–85, Weiner and several of his associates, including David Curtis and Meg Sowell, who were major players in the project, came to Georgia to look at the dilapidated hotel. "We did one of those things you're not supposed to do" as an investor, said Curtis—"we fell in love with the real estate."[14]

The Delaware developer Leon Weiner visited Jekyll Island, "fell in love" with the old clubhouse, and agreed to help with funding. (Courtesy of David Curtis)

Now they were interested, but before making a commitment, the Weiner & Associates group decided to pay a visit to the well-known Hilton Head developer Charles Fraser to ask his opinion. Fraser was not enthusiastic and told the Weiner group that they couldn't possibly make a go of an upscale hotel on Jekyll Island, which he viewed as a "blue-collar island." Fraser assured them it would fail. "I knew right then and there we needed to buckle our seat belts," said Curtis, "because that was like throwing down the gauntlet in front of Leon. He liked a challenge. . . . The combination of immediately being mesmerized by the property and then the thrill of the challenge of the famous resort developer telling Leon it couldn't be done successfully was enough to get us very interested."[15]

With full funding plans assembled, negotiations were concluded with the Jekyll Island Authority for a lease of fifty-five years, with no payments for the first two years, except for the lease of $100,000. Then for the next five years, the authority would receive 3 percent of the hotel's gross income. After that, the hotel would be required to pay the authority 3.5 percent of its gross income. In addition to their leasing the Jekyll Island Club, the adjacent annex, and the Sans Souci, lessees had authorization to construct a beach pavilion and to lease the indoor tennis court for ten years. Their only immediate outlay of money was a $50,000 security deposit.

Examining their options, the investors decided on a three-pronged approach to raising the necessary funding. They needed to find a $10 million letter of credit to secure a loan obtained through the industrial development bond. But that would not be enough to pay for a $20 million project. They would need to raise almost $8 million from individual investors, which would still leave a $2 million gap.

The City of Brunswick came to their aid with an urban development action grant (UDAG) from HUD. Roosevelt Harris, who was at that time Brunswick's director of downtown development but who later served as city manager,

Leon Weiner (center) signs the contract for the restoration of the Jekyll Island Clubhouse with John McTier (left) and Governor Joe Frank Harris (right). (Courtesy of John McTier)

Roosevelt Harris, director of downtown development in Brunswick at the time, helped obtain a $2 million federal grant to support the club restoration project. (Photo by the author)

wrote a grant proposal to support the project in which he contended that the hotel's revitalization would provide jobs for the city of Brunswick. When the resulting $2 million grant was approved on June 15, 1985, it was the largest small city grant in the nation's history up to that time. The money that the federal government granted to the City of Brunswick was in turn loaned to the Jekyll Island Hotel's developers, with an agreement that they not only would provide jobs but also would pay interest on the loan. In the end, the city would recoup the entire amount. It was an excellent investment of time and energy on the part of Harris.

Calling themselves Jekyll Development Associates, LP, the general partners in the enterprise were Leon Weiner, Weiner's friend Samuel Primack, and Primack's son-in-law, Joseph May, along with Vance Hughes and Larry Evans. Weiner and Primack had worked together on the board of the National Association of Home Builders while Weiner was president of the association. These five men would form the ownership core. David Curtis's job was to find additional individual investors to raise $7.75 million through limited partnerships sold as 50 units of $155,000 each.

David Curtis worked with Leon Weiner in raising funds for the Jekyll Island Clubhouse project. He went on to be involved in the building of four new hotels on Jekyll. (Courtesy of David Curtis)

Curtis brought prospective investors to Georgia to see the old hotel, which definitely "did not look like it does today," he noted in 2011. His efforts to sign up investors required a keen imagination and caused the thirty-year-old Curtis a lot of "sleepless nights." Nevertheless, he was successful in putting together a group of seventy-six limited partners who would share the units. These limited partners came from a wide array of backgrounds and included future governor of Virginia George Allen and members of the rock group ZZ Top. Their primary incentive was a 25 percent tax credit for the rehabilitation of historic income-producing properties established by the 1981 Economic Tax Act. However, as the project was moving along, Congress passed another bill, the 1986 Tax Recovery Act, that would dramatically alter the provisions of the earlier legislation, reducing the tax credit to only 20 percent and allowing credits solely for passive income. To ensure that investors would reap the benefits they had been promised, the pressure was on to complete the project and open the hotel before the new law went into effect on January 1, 1987.

However, the final piece of the funding puzzle was not yet in place. The investors still had to find a bank willing to provide the necessary letter of credit. Local banks seemed to lack faith in the project. Finally, Weiner approached the Banque Indosuez in Paris, which agreed to back the project with the necessary letter of credit. In the end, the papers were signed on December 23, 1985.

With all financing in place, the restoration of the historic clubhouse building could finally begin. Then came a critical race against the calendar. By the time contracts had been signed with Blosam Construction, a Jacksonville firm, Evans and Hughes realized they had slightly less than a year to complete the mammoth project before December 31, 1986. Much of the work involved undoing modifications made in the 1950s and 1960s. Larry Evans was on the

The Jekyll Island Clubhouse was in run-down condition both inside and out before restoration. (Courtesy of Vance Hughes)

Once funding was in place, restoration of the old clubhouse began. One of the challenges was undoing the "improvements" that had been made during the state era. (Courtesy of Vance Hughes)

The restoration included rebuilding the porte cochere and the original staircase in the lobby. (Courtesy of Vance Hughes)

site virtually every day, solving problems and making decisions about the historic structure. The primary goal of the restoration was to "recreate the hotel in all its glory." Although Evans preserved everything he possibly could and faithfully followed then-current historic preservation standards, he decided on several innovations to make the hotel more attractive and more workable. For example, the basement area, which had been only a generous crawl space, was dug out an additional two and a half feet or so to make room for staff offices, shops, and other modern necessities. Evans also developed a courtyard veranda system. At the same time the hotel was being restored, the Sans Souci, which had once housed apartments for J. P. Morgan, William Rockefeller, and Henry Hyde, was converted into a modern hotel facility.[16]

In the last few months of 1986, work on both structures continued furiously. Three hundred workmen were on the job at a single time, and as the months grew shorter, the crew was compelled to work ten hours a day and seven days a week to meet the deadline. Evans recalled that the construction workers took so much pride in their work that "they would bring their families to see the site on Sundays."[17] The fruits of the labor of all of those involved are evident today in the beautifully restored hotel and grounds.

On December 29, 1986—just in time to meet the tax deadline—the Jekyll Island Club Hotel opened its doors for its first paying guests. The soft opening was an important step for the hotel to make sure that everything was ready and in place before its grand opening in late March. These early guests

The Sans Souci, whose occupants once included the likes of J. P. Morgan and William Rockefeller, was restored to add additional hotel rooms. (Photo by the author)

The restored hotel was once again magnificent. (Photo by the author)

were largely family members and friends of those involved in the project—a forgiving group, according to David Curtis, "to make sure that we weren't going to stumble all over ourselves."[18]

Fairly early in the process, the owners had hired a hotel management company called MHM to manage the property, bringing in the man who would become the hotel's general manager, Kevin Runner, in March 1986. The intense labor of the previous year continued into 1987 with work to address "punch list" items and the landscaping of the hotel grounds. The official grand opening of the Jekyll Island Club Hotel–A Radisson Resort took place on March 31, 1987, with Governor Joe Frank Harris, the general partners, and various other dignitaries in attendance.[19]

The rehabilitated structures of the Jekyll Island Clubhouse, the annex, and the Sans Souci were a triumph, and the excellence of the newly restored hotel was widely recognized. In 1987 the project won the Award of Excellence from the National Commercial Builders Council of the National Association of

Home Builders as the Best Historical Commercial Rehabilitation Project over $3 million. That same year it also won a Grand Award at the Builders' Choice Design and Planning Awards, an award from the Georgia Trust of Historic Preservation, and an American Institute of Architects Preservation Award. The renovation of the clubhouse demonstrated a successful public-private partnership and inspired the JIA to revitalize other parts of the historic district, namely Crane Cottage, Cherokee Cottage, and the Morgan Tennis Court.

On March 31, 1987, the grand opening of the Jekyll Island Club Hotel–A Radisson Resort took place with Governor Joe Frank Harris, the general partners, and various other dignitaries in attendance. (Left to right in foreground: Kevin Runner, Leon Weiner [at podium], and Governor Harris.) (Courtesy of the Jekyll Island Club Resort)

Nine years later, the owners of the Jekyll Island Club Hotel began negotiations with the authority to undertake an expansion that would add sixty-seven rooms to the hotel. On October 9, 1996, a proposal for an addition designed by Saxelbye Architects of Jacksonville was presented to the authority. However, the authority scrapped the plan after learning that construction of the addition could bring about the loss of the district's National Historic Landmark status and any tax breaks that came with it.

Mark Edwards, the State of Georgia's historic preservation officer, recommended that the hotel owners work with architects who specialize in historic preservation. One of those on the suggested list was Tom Dalia of Smith Dalia Architects of Atlanta. Dalia agreed to take on the project and presented a new design proposal on March 27, 1997, that would embrace the Crane Cottage garden. Several other designs followed, but the proposed addition remained problematic since, as Edwards pointed out, it still had a "high potential of disturbing significant archaeological deposits dating from the prehistoric period to the early part of this century," which was a factor in the historic district's National Historic Landmark status. Eventually, the idea of an addition was abandoned altogether.

At the same time, negotiations were underway for the state and the Jekyll Island Club Hotel to work together in restoring Crane Cottage and Cherokee Cottage so they could be used as additional facilities by the hotel. This proposition was far less problematic, and the "adaptive reuse" of the cottages quickly met with a favorable reception. Architect Tom Dalia, who had originally been hired to plan the now-scrapped addition to the hotel, thought that "[s]ince the buildings were set up for families and guests, the hotel requirements fit like a glove."[20]

Both historic structures were sorely in need of renovation. Crane Cot-

In 1997, plans were underway to restore Crane Cottage (shown here) and Cherokee Cottage, which would add twenty-three additional rooms to the hotel's capacity. (Photo by the author)

tage, constructed in 1917 and designed by well-known architect David Adler and his associate Henry Dangler, had been built for the family of plumbing magnate Richard Teller Crane. The cottage contained twenty bedrooms and seventeen bathrooms. According to Warren Murphey, then the director of operations for the Jekyll Island Authority, "[A] well-intentioned effort to save it many years ago . . . made it worse." A thick coating of special paint had been applied to the exterior of the cottage to keep out moisture. However, moisture still found its way in, and the water-repellent paint kept it in, causing the bricks to break down. In addition, the front doors were cracked and weather-beaten, wrought iron balconies and fixtures were "badly rusted and broken," and the mortar had loosened, among other problems.[21] Similar issues existed at Cherokee Cottage, which by the 1990s was in dire need of restoration. The exterior was cracked, letting moisture penetrate the walls and nourish termites. Cherokee would require considerable adaptation, especially compared to Crane, as six bedrooms and seven servants' rooms would have to be converted into ten hotel rooms.

The adaptation of the cottages would provide only twenty-three additional guest rooms to the hotel. Nevertheless, the extension of the public-private partnership between the Jekyll Island Club Hotel and the Jekyll Island Authority to add these two cottages to the hotel's inventory proved to be a successful approach. Although the Jekyll Island Authority was required to be self-supporting, Governor Zell Miller proposed in his 1997 budget that $1.725 million be allocated for the historic district, mostly for the Crane Cottage and Cherokee Cottage renovations, while the Jekyll Island Club Hotel would fund $1.1 million and had agreed to absorb any expenses that exceeded the proposed budget.

The restored and repurposed Morgan Center opened in November 2010. (Courtesy of Judson McCranie)

The results were stunning. Smith Dalia Architects won a Design Award of Merit from AIA Georgia. Likewise, the Georgia Trust for Historic Preservation presented an Excellence in Rehabilitation Award to the Jekyll Island Club Hotel for the work on Crane and Cherokee.

One more addition to the hotel's facilities was the refurbished Morgan Center. Built in 1929, the Morgan Tennis Court was named for J. P. Morgan Jr., the club's president at that time. The indoor facility survived into the state era, and the JIA had used it to house convict laborers for a short time in the late 1940s. The building was subsequently used again as a tennis venue for decades until the JIA closed it in 2001. By that time, the facility's skylights were leaking, and termites had done significant damage to the structure's timbers. During the 1997 negotiations around restoring the Crane and Cherokee Cottages, the authority had informally agreed to take possession of the Morgan Tennis Court and share the costs of the facility's restoration with Jekyll Landmark Associates. Ten years later, the JIA formalized this arrangement by agreeing to pay half the projected $3 million cost of renovating the structure as a meeting facility. When the Morgan Center opened in November 2010, Jekyll Landmark Associates had invested $2.3 million and the JIA had spent $1.5 million in an adaptive reuse program to create a new facility to accommodate 350 people.

From the 1970s to 2010, the revitalization of Jekyll Island's historic district proved to be a major achievement that brought in new visitors and inspired a regeneration across the island. But those restoration efforts, important as they were, did not end the controversies.

One of the first issues Chambliss addressed was to prevent shrimp boats like this one from using the Jekyll dock. (Shutterstock)

CONTROVERSY & PROTEST

In the summer of 1950, a sixteen-year-old student at Valdosta Junior College in South Georgia was hitchhiking back to school. An older man pulled over to give him a lift to town. When the student climbed into the passenger seat, he vaguely recollected the man but was not quite sure who he was. As they pulled back onto the road, the man introduced himself as M. E. Thompson, former governor of Georgia (1947–1948). As Thompson drove down the road, he started talking about Jekyll Island. The young student "knew about Jekyll almost all my life but hadn't been there yet." When Thompson dropped him off at the college, he asked, "What's your name again?" "My name is John McTier." This accidental encounter between Thompson and McTier was a happenstance for the Jekyll Island Authority that resonated for decades.[1]

After earning his juris doctor at Emory University School of Law in Atlanta, John McTier practiced law in Valdosta before joining an Atlanta law firm, where he worked for several years. He went on to be the business manager for Emory University before returning to Valdosta in 1966. In 1981 Governor George Busbee appointed John McTier to replace a JIA member who had been elected to the state supreme court. McTier did not know Busbee, and he "wasn't seeking anything," he said, but "if they want me, I'll do it."

At that time, Sam Williams was chair of the JIA and state commissioner of natural resources. Robert Case had recently resigned as executive director, and the board had started a search for appropriate candidates to fill the position. At the beginning of the search, there were ninety-six applicants. The board eventually narrowed that down to two, one of whom was a staffer who worked for a gubernatorial candidate in the upcoming elections. The other candidate was George Chambliss. He had an impressive portfolio, with several years of directing parks in Georgia, as well as having been assistant director of recreation in Dallas, Texas. According to McTier, the majority of the Jekyll Island Authority preferred Chambliss because "he had more experience, and they wanted someone not connected to politics and with no strings attached." When Chambliss accepted the position, one of his first tasks was to create a vision statement: "The Jekyll Island Authority acknowledges its power to beautify, improve, and render self-sufficiency of the park to its facilities for the people of average income, and to advertise its beauties to the world."[2]

George Chambliss became executive director of the JIA in 1981. (Courtesy of Mosaic, Jekyll Island Museum)

To help make that vision a reality, the authority had already hired a firm called Hammer, Siler, George and Associates to create a comprehensive plan for the island. In late May 1982, the consultants held a public hearing at which they presented four broad themes to pursue for the next decade. First, they called for renovation of the "millionaires village"; that objective would be partially fulfilled by the hotel restoration that Larry Evans and Vance Hughes would soon undertake. The authority and the planning firm believed that restoring the historic "village" would attract tourists, invigorate that part of the island, and provide more resources for historic preservation. Second, the consultants pointed out the need for increased recreational opportunities, such as additional bike trails and other outdoor amenities. Their third suggestion was that the state park should develop more vibrant ecological and environmental educational programs for children and adults. The fourth and last of their recommendations involved the need for financial self-sufficiency, which was a goal that had seemed beyond the authority's reach for the first thirty-five years of state ownership. It would also prove to be the most controversial aspect of their proposal. They recommended the addition of more housing (twenty-five new housing units per year), which would provide a significant new source of income, as would the possible construction of two more motels over the next five years. Another fundraising concept was to charge an entrance fee for the island. That idea met with overwhelming support.[3] The

JIA established an initial daily "parking fee" of $3, but the fee has risen over the years to $10, with an annual parking pass available for $100.

The consultants' study kickstarted the hiring of certain specialized employees, such as Thom Rhodes, who was to serve as the new director of the authority's Museum and Historic Preservation Division, with the goal of developing long-range plans for the historic structures and professional interpretive programs.[4] He in turn hired Pam Meister as the museum's curator and Warren Murphey to aid in efforts to restore the various cottages that had once belonged to members of the Jekyll Island Club.

Among the other issues that Chambliss addressed was the Jekyll Wharf, which at that time was used exclusively by shrimpers. The JIA board decided to repurpose the wharf and restore its pilings for public use and transient boats. Many tourists, citizens, and shrimpers did not like the idea and resisted such change, but it would ultimately turn the pier into a popular spot. Additionally, the authority upgraded the bike paths throughout the island and made rental bicycles accessible and affordable. Next, it decided to upgrade the campground, which had been badly run for years, making major improvements that included better showers and sanitation, clean water, and safety enhancements. As these efforts were set in motion, they would mark a turning point in the island's state-era history.

In 1983, John McTier became chair of the JIA. He and Chambliss worked well together, embracing most of the consultants' advice with enthusiasm. They saw it as a time for renewal on Jekyll Island and began with actions such as demolishing the iconic Aquarama, which had in the past thirty years deteriorated to the point of becoming a dangerous hazard.[5] After many years of criticism of the JIA, it appeared that the new authority management had become more professional, doing studies and gathering facts before acting. An example of the board's previous failure to take considered action occurred a decade earlier during a dredging project on the intercoastal waterway. Those in charge had apparently not realized that, because of the causeway construction completed twenty-five years before, the river currents had changed, and with the dredging, the channel filled with silt. As a result, the authority was compelled to abandon the $1 million project. Such waste led to the reorganization of the JIA to include more specialized and knowledgeable people appointed by the governor. Within a few years, the only state official who remained on the board was the director of natural resources.

One aspect of the consultants' proposal did not go over well. The recommendation to add more residential development and more hotels to the island was rejected by the JIA. Instead, McTier and Chambliss, in consultation with a task force that included island residents, hotel owners, historic preservationists, environmentalists, and the Georgia Department of Natural Resources, collaborated with the University of Georgia Institute of Community and Area Development to alter the plan. Their changes met with a positive response.

Summer Waves, approved during the Chambliss administration, would become one of the most popular facilities on the island. (Courtesy of Mosaic, Jekyll Island Museum)

One island resident and member of the Coastal Georgia Audubon Society, Lorraine Dusenbury, expressed her reaction thusly: "I like the plan because it bans all further beachfront development." According to the new plan, the two motels on the north end and residences on the south end could not be rebuilt if they were destroyed by a storm.[6]

Overall, however, the JIA embraced the ideas proposed by the consulting company, which the authority hoped would help address the perception both of the consultants and of island visitors that Jekyll was dull and sterile.[7] Indeed, many visitors felt that the island had an "asphalt image" because of the many concrete parking areas and roads throughout the island. Chambliss had acknowledged this perception of Jekyll: "We want to get rid of the concrete-asphalt image of the island. . . . We are trying to diversify activities so it's not just golf and tennis." The authority approved more recreational activities, such as an electric cable-ski system known as the Ski Rixen, and started negotiations for the establishment of a large water park. Although many residents detested the idea of a big water park on the island, Summer Waves would eventually become one of the most important facilities to generate revenue for a self-sufficient island.[8]

Despite the successes, there were still myriad problems with the island's infrastructure. On March 23, 1985, another Jekyll Creek Bridge malfunction stranded hundreds of employees and vacationers on both sides of the drawbridge. The Georgia Department of Transportation indicated that it was difficult to project how long it would take to repair the bridge, but they estimated about ten days. Within a few hours, the authority had arranged for a ferry, the *Island Queen*, which could carry a maximum of 140 passengers. It would take four trips and five hours to transport over a thousand people.[9]

That incident would not end the problems with the bridges leading to Jekyll Island. Two years later, on May 3, 1987, the Polish freighter *Ziemia Bialostocka* struck the Sidney Lanier Bridge connecting Brunswick to Jekyll Island. A temporary repair was made, but eventually the state built a new suspension bridge that would allow large freighters to pass underneath without the necessity of a drawbridge.

Despite such setbacks, the progress at Jekyll continued. Chambliss followed through on several more projects, including the construction of an inshore artificial reef at the Jekyll pier to enhance recreational fishing in that area. During a board retreat in late April 1990, the JIA received word of the creation of the Jekyll Island Museum Associates, a new organization composed of citizens who proposed to help with fundraising, grants, donations, and gifts to boost and support the fledgling Jekyll Island Museum. Over the years the members of the group have made many contributions, volunteering

This photo taken in April 2001 shows the new Sidney Lanier suspension bridge being constructed alongside the old drawbridge. (Courtesy of Bob Webster)

The cleaning of the Maitland Armstrong window in Faith Chapel was one of the projects funded by the Friends of Historic Jekyll Island. (Courtesy of Judson McCranie)

their time for various projects, and footing the bill for the restoration of the tombstones in the DuBignon Cemetery and of the windows at Faith Chapel. Today the group is known as the Friends of Historic Jekyll Island, and its stated mission is "to assist with the preservation and interpretation of Jekyll Island's natural and historical heritage."

The JIA board's discussions included potential plans for such things as beach renourishment and consistent signage. In the meantime, the authority continued to hold open meetings to allow residents to have a voice. McTier commented, "We had continual issues with the [Jekyll Island] Citizens Association, who felt they were treated terribly. They objected to the parking fees. We used what money we had on the citizens, but the citizens still came to every meeting griping about something. It was interesting."[10] On the other hand, Governor Zell Miller had openly applauded the work of Chambliss and the authority over the previous several years. The governor was also good friends with John McTier at the time.

In early January 1995, the JIA decided to complete a long-awaited oceanside golf course by expanding the historic nine-hole Great Dunes course to eighteen holes. According to McTier, the expansion of the golf course was fully approved in late 1994. The JIA minutes from December 1994 show that both the authority and many of the residents supported the new golf links. McTier said, "We had the provisions to build a new nine holes, and we had the approval to move forward." In mid-January 1995, the surveyors started the process in the area where it had been approved. But as McTier later observed, "George Chambliss made a terrible mistake." The engineers and surveyors approached Chambliss and explained that they could not survey the golf course amid all the vegetation; they indicated that they needed to clear some areas so they could see the boundary line. Chambliss consulted with someone in Glynn County and called a state official to ask permission to use a small bulldozer to clear some of the boundary lines, and he was told that it would be okay, but he did not obtain permits. When the surveyors resumed work, a local citizen, Jean Poleszak, witnessed the bulldozer and confronted Chambliss to see if he had permits. Within a few hours, an Atlanta lawyer who represented several environmental groups called Governor Miller, who in turn lambasted Chambliss. The JIA had now incurred the wrath of environmental regulators and conservation groups by bulldozing land before obtaining the necessary permits. To make matters worse, the new holes would have encroached directly on thirty acres designated by the JIA master plan as a natural conservation area.[11]

Zell Miller, who became governor of Georgia in 1991, was initially pleased with the work of George Chambliss and the JIA. The Jekyll Island Citizens Association, however, was critical of some of the authority's actions. (Courtesy of the United States Senate)

Governor Miller sent a directive to McTier that Chambliss should be removed as executive director immediately. McTier spoke with Miller at length about it, saying later that he told the governor "that's not the thing to do. George didn't do anything wrong. We had approval to do it, and it was not

A major attraction at Jekyll Island is its four beautiful golf courses, including the historic Great Dunes course, Oleander, Pine Lakes, and Indian Mound. (Courtesy of the Jekyll Island Authority)

permanent, but Zell wouldn't hear it because he was listening to very powerful people." Miller said, "George has to go." McTier took this to the authority board, and they sided with Chambliss. McTier called the governor and told him, "You don't have the votes. We are not going to fire him." Miller mulled over the situation and called McTier back that same day, saying, "I'm going to appoint some additional people to the Authority to get those votes." McTier told him, "You can't do that."[12]

However, over the next few days, it became clear that Miller wasn't going to bend. The authority met with Chambliss and told him that it was not going to work out for him to stay. They set up a resignation package, and Chambliss agreed that "it would be hell down the road based on all this turmoil." Thus, Chambliss formally resigned on January 13, 1995. McTier called the governor with the news: "George is going to leave." Miller said, "Good." McTier then told him, "You can accept my resignation also." A few weeks later Caroline Stradley, a longtime JIA member, also resigned because she thought Miller "had treated Chambliss unfairly."[13]

In the aftermath of the resignations, several articles, editorials, and letters to the editor provided differing perspectives. After working with George Chambliss for fifteen years, John McTier respected him and commented, "Based on my personal knowledge of the history of the island, since it was acquired by the state of Georgia, it is my opinion that Mr. Chambliss is by far the best executive director the authority has ever had." He praised Chambliss's accomplishments, which included the restoration and stabilization of the thirty buildings in the historic district, the $20 million restoration of the Jekyll Island Clubhouse, a $5 million renovation of the convention center, the $4 million Summer Waves water park, and an award-winning tennis center. Chambliss said, "I am proud to say that not one dime of state money has been used on Jekyll since 1983."[14]

Becky Shoreland of the Georgia Conservancy expressed another opinion: "We've had a lot of concern about the leadership there—making a decision that would lead to bulldozing without permits. It's just unconscionable." Explaining the perspective of the Citizens Association, Jean Poleszak said, "We want the development stopped and the authority to admit it has a park to care for."[15] Another issue was that Chambliss had earlier suggested that golf courses should be counted as wildlife habitat, which did not align with the ideas of legislators and citizens. Not all the citizens, however, were pleased by the ousting of Chambliss. One of the letters to the editor, written by a resident of twelve years, contended that "Mr. Chambliss procured a top hotel company, and he took it over and made it a jewel. Chambliss brought pride and progress to the island."[16]

Perhaps the most thoughtful and balanced editorial came from *The Atlanta Constitution*. The editorial suggested that Chambliss's leadership was a critical watershed in Jekyll's long history. The editors noted that the island's infrastructure and economy were in far better shape than when Chambliss came on the scene in 1981. They acknowledged that Chambliss deserved a large share of the credit for facilitating the dynamic improvements while working under a mandate for the JIA to be a self-supporting entity, but they questioned his attitude toward preserving the ecologically fragile island from overdevelopment. The editorial concluded that "[t]he same hardheaded business instincts that allowed him to reinvigorate the island's finances also led him to dismiss environmental concerns too easily and to sometimes run roughshod over the island's residents."[17]

It was partially in reaction to that last problem that island residents had banded together during Chambliss's tenure as executive director and formed the Jekyll Island Citizens Association in 1985. The organization kept its members informed about authority meetings, proposals, and actions. And as an organized group, its members were able to speak with a stronger voice, which would become increasingly important in the years to come. The objections and opinions of the association would go on to have significant impact on some of the decisions made by the Jekyll Island Authority.

Following Chambliss's departure, Governor Miller appointed James Bradley as the acting executive director, and the authority resumed meeting on February 13, 1995. Members elected Charles Jenkins as the board's chair and decided, after all the brouhaha, that any expansion of the Great Dunes golf course would be postponed, pending the implementation of the new 1996 master plan. In the April board meeting, James Bradley announced that Warren Murphey was the new director of the JIA's Museums and Historic Preservation Division and that he would operate Jekyll's National Historic Landmark District. By this time, it had become customary at the end of board meetings for citizens to speak of their concerns, complaints, and ideas. The residents who attended the February 13, 1995, meeting had suggestions for the upcoming master plan. Their concerns included the need for funds for the historic district and questions about the 35 percent/65 percent rule. They also wanted support for the Jekyll Island Citizens Resource Council so that they could communicate directly with Governor Miller. Over several meetings, one of the main discussion topics was the loggerhead turtle protection program. In most cases, the citizens were making suggestions to improve the island and to notify the authority about what they were seeing and experiencing on the island that needed attention.

In 1996, both residents and visitors began to complain about a new "deer fence" encompassing the entire historic district that was built to keep deer from feasting on the plants and flowers in the area. In *Jekyll's Golden Islander* in May 1996, a woman named Gertrude Drew complained that "the fence won't define the District: it will serve to be a barrier to keep people out." She claimed as well that "the fence will be an eyesore. I vote for NO FENCE!" Another resident complained that the fence would block the view: "It is hard

The JIA's construction of a fence around the historic district to prevent deer from eating the plants caused another controversy. (Photo by the author)

Georgia Governor Roy Barnes presents a proclamation to the Jekyll Island Authority on July 27, 2001, commemorating the restoration of Crane and Cherokee Cottages for use by the Jekyll Island Club Hotel. (Left to right: Tom Lewis, chair of the Jekyll Island Authority; Governor Barnes; Kevin Runner, general manager of the Jekyll Island Club Hotel; and Bill Donohue, executive director of the Jekyll Island Authority.) (Courtesy of the Jekyll Island Club Resort)

to find anyone in favor of a fence around the north end of the District. . . . A five-foot fence would completely block the view for all drivers."[18] Some of the negative comments were a bit mean-spirited. For instance, in a September issue of *Jekyll's Golden Islander*, a visitor wrote, "I have visited Jekyll on several occasions and found it to be a lovely island. I have just visited again, and I was affronted with a horrible sign of an ugly fence being put up at the Historic District. Who was the dipstick who thought that up??? No one who lived on the island would have wanted that monstrosity to greet the people who visit the island. If I lived there, I'd be furious at the destruction of a peaceful scene."[19] Nevertheless, the deer fence remains to this day, and now few people even notice it.

On August 7, 1995, Bill Donohue joined the JIA as the representative for the state director of natural resources. Over the next two years, he participated in many deliberations with the authority. During that time, board member Lonice Barrett was chairing the search for a new executive director and was interviewing candidates. After almost two years, the unanimous vote was to hire Donohue, who had impressive credentials. Born in New Jersey, Donohue graduated from Cornell University with degrees in hospitality management and hotel administration.

He later took a position with Georgia State Parks. At the time he accepted the Jekyll job, he was the executive director of the North Georgia Mountains Authority.[20]

Once Donohue accepted the JIA executive director position, his first goal was to build a team of local business leaders, hotel and restaurant owners, and other off-island groups. He was eager to bring in new physical construction, additional funding for new programming, product improvement, and more development on the island, including a new convention hotel and another twenty-seven homes. The main issues were modernizing existing hotels and upgrading the campground and golf facilities. Donohue was working together with island employees, residents, and legislators to accomplish these goals.[21]

According to the planners, more emphasis was needed on improving the island's marketing, enhancing current amenities, and providing a new interpretation of the environmental and historic assets of the island. In response to recommendations for the 1996 master plan, Donohue approved more than $1 million in funds for a museum visitors center, improvements to the DuBignon Cottage, campground amenities, trail rides on Jekyll Island, kayaking, and additional special projects over three years. Additionally, he embraced the private sector with the state government and citizens to create a strategic process to fund and deliver projects. Island residents were ready to help and created a task force known as Jekyll Island Creative, which developed a partnership with the Burroughs-Molette Elementary School to develop a modern playground for children.

Despite such occasional cooperation, when the authority sought to impose fire fees on residents to raise funds, the Jekyll Island Citizens Association was ready to fight, and it took the JIA to court to stop the measure. The citizens lost: On January 8, 1996, the Georgia Supreme Court issued a unanimous decision allowing the fire fees. Jean Poleszak, then-president of the association and an outspoken Jekyll resident, said, "We are very disappointed. We have gone back to square one."[22]

It was also under Donohue's administration that the proposed expansion of the Jekyll Island Clubhouse, which would have involved adding another wing to accommodate more guests, became an issue. That project was abandoned after the JIA learned that the plan, if enacted, could cause the historic district to lose its National Historic Landmark status. Donohue's support for and efforts on behalf of the sea turtle project would be more successful, eventually resulting in the creation of the popular Georgia Sea Turtle Center.

In the year 2000, Jekyll's controversies would extend beyond the island itself and into the local political environment. The state had begun to allow counties to collect a 1 percent sales tax known as a SPLOST (special purpose local option sales tax). That year, for the first time, the JIA sought to receive a portion of the local sales tax. However, the leaders of Glynn County and Brunswick were not eager to share the $14 million that the JIA had requested

OPPOSITE Improvements to bicycle paths were among the Jekyll Island projects included in the Glynn County SPLOST 2022 funding. (Photo by the author)

for projects on Jekyll Island. Glynn County commissioners accused the JIA of blindsiding them and implied that the authority's efforts were a form of extortion. They were bitterly opposed to sharing the tax proceeds, even though Jekyll Island residents paid the tax like other Glynn County residents.[23]

Settling the issue required the intervention of Georgia House members who six months later introduced a bill that would compel Glynn County to share a portion of the SPLOST revenue. Once again, leaders of the Citizens Association supported the authority, urging Jekyll residents to vote for the new SPLOST IV in the upcoming referendum so that the Jekyll Island Authority might garner at least $3.3 million for Jekyll projects, including water improvement and additional infrastructure.[24]

The bill instantly drew criticism from Brunswick officials and Glynn County commissioners, who suggested that the legislation would require taxpayers to prop up an inefficient state park. They called it a bailout. Brunswick Mayor Brad Brown said, "We're going to have a fight," and County Commissioner Fred Tullos commented, "Why they would want to give special treatment to this unelected authority to spend taxpayers' money is beyond me." Clearly, partisan politics were in the mix. However, Brown said the city and the county had included Jekyll Island representatives in recent meetings, and they agreed to reimburse Jekyll Island only $50,000 for bike paths. Donohue contended that Glynn County's attitude was "You're getting everything you deserve and we're not going to discuss it."[25]

On November 2, 2001, two Brunswick commissioners filed a suit in Glynn County Superior Court to halt the collection of the special purpose local option sales tax because it included funding for Jekyll Island. City Commissioner Ken Plyman and an associate contended that the county could not legally give the authority $3 million of the sales tax revenue, because the JIA was "not authorized to do water and sewer projects. The law doesn't allow it, not with this money." The plaintiffs claimed that there was no record of a vote by the JIA board to approve such expenditures there. Although Donohue had been meeting with city and county officials, he could not act, nor could he sign any contracts until after the state attorney general approved them.[26]

Following earlier attempts to share the local tax revenues, coastal lawmakers wanted to create a study committee to overcome the disputes that arose from Jekyll's unique status as a state-owned island. Homeowners paid the state rent on long-term leases, but they also paid property taxes to Glynn County. Senator Tommie Williams acknowledged the confusion caused by paying taxes on leased land: "The people who live on the island don't feel like they're getting services for the tax they pay."[27] In the end, the Georgia Supreme Court dismissed the Plyman lawsuit, finally settling the SPLOST IV issue. In a unanimous decision, the court upheld the Glynn County Superior Court ruling that the Plyman suit had been filed forty-two days too late to seek an injunction to stop the collection of the special purpose sales tax. As a result,

In 2002, Sonny Perdue was elected as the first Republican governor of Georgia since Reconstruction. (United States Department of Agriculture)

Jekyll Island began to receive a portion of the SPLOST proceeds, which has proved to be a great help to the island. In 2022 the Glynn County SPLOST allotted $3,287,000 for improvements to Jekyll Island's bike trails, beach access points, drainage, and roads.

An even more serious issue was looming for Jekyll citizens, who were beginning to worry whether they would be able to hold onto the land beneath their feet. The authority's lease was set to expire in 2049, as were the leases of the island's homeowners. There seemed to be plenty of time to clarify the situation. Nevertheless, Tice Eyler, president of the Citizens Association, expressed residents' concern that "we're going to reach a point where banks aren't going to loan money." Donohue understood their concern very well and assured them that "corrective legislation" had already been proposed, but the legislature was holding it until the next legislative session in January 2003. Everyone was nervous about the date, but Donohue predicted that the bill would pass and that the authority's lease would extend another fifty years.[28] Still, many residents had already begun to worry about what would happen if the authority's charter (and their leases) should expire.

In the 2002 gubernatorial race in Georgia, Roy Barnes lost to Sonny Perdue, who became the state's first Republican governor since Reconstruction. In such a hyperpoliticized climate, Perdue asked all eighty heads of state agencies, including Bill Donohue, to offer their resignations. Unfortunately, members of the legislature's Jekyll Island Study Committee had never met with residents and other stakeholders because they were focused on their own elections. Then, following the election of the new governor, the committee's mandate ended in December 2002, and the entire study was abandoned. Meanwhile, Donohue had reapplied for his position and was awaiting Perdue's decision.[29] In fact, it took another six months, until June 2003, for Sonny Perdue to announce his reappointment of Donohue as the executive director of the Jekyll Island Authority.

It was a time of uncertainty for Jekyll, as things were beginning to change. For example, 2005 would be the last year for the island's outdoor amphitheater, which had been constructed in the early 1970s. Many residents and visitors had enjoyed the plays and musicals presented there. Florida State University produced shows at the amphitheater until 1983, followed briefly by the University of Georgia. Valdosta State University had the longest run at the amphitheater; in 1989 the school's theater department signed a contract to stage productions each summer, but the 2004 season would be its last on the island.

While some things were ending, new ones were beginning. The new Jekyll Island Foundation, which had begun its fundraising efforts in 1999, was working to fund a sea turtle center. The authority collaborated with the foundation to raise more than $2 million for the project. Together they sponsored a Family Weekend event that proved to be a lucrative fundraiser and an important occasion to advocate for and bring visibility to the forthcoming sea turtle center. The event would prove to be an important step in drawing new visitors to the island. Mark Dodd, the sea turtle program coordinator for the Georgia Department of Natural Resources, pointed out that it had been "a dismal year for Georgia sea turtles." Only 365 nests had been counted statewide, including 25 on Jekyll, making it "the worst nesting year on record." Scientists had not determined why there were so few nests, but they were concerned.[30]

In 2005, Terry Norton, who would become the turtle center's director and staff veterinarian, published a study that underscored the fact that sea turtles were officially "endangered" as a result of coastal development and hazards such as injuries from boats and fishing nets, the ingestion of ocean debris, and the overharvesting of turtle eggs. The new Georgia Sea Turtle Center,

The Georgia Sea Turtle Center, founded in 2007, is one of the most popular attractions for families visiting Jekyll Island. (Photo by the author)

This photo shows the first turtle release in 2009. Dr. Terry Norton, second from left, was instrumental in the founding of the Georgia Sea Turtle Center and served as its director and veterinarian until March 1, 2023. (Courtesy of the McCash Collection)

which opened in 2007, would seek to remedy the situation, and it did. In 2024, for example, 5,312 hatchlings emerged from 153 nests.

While the sea turtle center was a successful undertaking, the island overall had begun to look rather shabby in recent years. Decades of wear and tear on the motels and hotels were evident, and conventions had become less frequent because of the island's outdated facilities. The Georgia Rotary Clubs had held their annual convention on Jekyll Island for some forty years, but complaints about the accommodations had increased in recent years, and in 2003 the Rotarians went elsewhere. The water park temporarily shut down in 2006 because of a cracked basin in the wave pool. Even the number of rounds played on the island's golf courses had declined dramatically, with income from green fees dropping by $750,000 from the previous decade.

As facilities on the island declined, political appointees were beginning to call for the building of luxury hotels and million-dollar homes, and developers were pressing to build more stylish developments. One development team proposed to create a "high-end luxury" community where soccer fields and the 4-H center were presently located. Another proposal called for the construction of two thousand new homes and condominiums ranging in price from $350,000 to more than a million dollars. Ed Boshears, a former state senator and a JIA board member, agreed that the island needed new hotels and an updated convention center. But he warned against making it more expensive than most people could afford. Citizens also worried that Jekyll Island would price out the average family. As Frank Mirasola, a retired island resident, observed, "There are so few of these places left, why can't this be kept for the people? Not everybody can afford a $500,000 condo."[31]

Nevertheless, improvements to the island's amenities were clearly needed. The JIA decided to put out a request for proposals to begin the updates. It was clear that Jekyll was going to be transformed, for better or worse. Even before that transformation was formally underway, residents, politicians, activists, developers, board members, visitors, and environmental groups were all closely following the process. It would become a controversial issue throughout the state of Georgia and would bring out both the best and worst of revitalization before it was over.

The unspoiled south end beach was the best spot on the island for flocks of sea birds to congregate. Residents fought to keep the beach in its natural state. (Photo by the author)

THE PERILS OF REVITALIZATION

11

One of the most serious altercations over the future of Jekyll Island during the state era began in 2006, as the Jekyll Island Authority completed a study of options to revitalize the island. In a JIA board meeting chaired by Richard Wood on October 16, 2006, suggestions included adding new businesses and more condos, demolishing and/or rebuilding dilapidated buildings, extending the lease life of the island, hiring a master developer, moving the soccer complex and the Georgia 4-H club sites to another location, and seeking legislation to "eliminate the tax dollars now going to Glynn County."[1]

Governor Sonny Perdue, on the other hand, reviewed studies made by private consultants from the real estate development perspective. Their proposals called for building hotels and condominiums on the south end of the island and opening a plat that had not been used during the Jim Crow era. JIA Executive Director Bill Donohue also floated the idea of a golf course/condominium development at public meetings of the JIA.[2]

One of the most pressing issues under consideration was the extension of the JIA's lease on the island beyond its original expiration date of 2049. Few developers would be interested in making long-term commitments until that matter was resolved. On January 8, 2007, the JIA met in public session in the Georgia Department of Natural Resources boardroom in Atlanta. JIA Chair Richard Wood presented four options concerning the lease: (1) leave the status quo unchanged until 2049; (2) extend the lease and life of the authority and the staff operations and redevelopment; (3) extend the lease and life of the authority *and* contract with a private sector partner to redevelop and manage the commercial aspects of the island; or (4) sell or convert to fee simple. Governor Perdue was opposed to options 1 and 4. In roundtable discussions, a consensus emerged that the Jekyll Island Authority should select a private sector revitalization partner who would operate under the direction, oversight, and vision of the JIA board.[3]

To the displeasure of Jekyll residents, further development at the island's south end was on the table. They began reaching out to conservation allies and media outlets, including newspapers and radio and television stations, to express their opposition. On the day of the Atlanta meeting, more than fifty members of the Jekyll Island Citizens Association (JICA) rented a bus and traveled to Atlanta to protest and to urge the governor to prevent any further south end development. The Citizens Association also hired a lobbyist at a cost of $3,000 to represent it during the legislative session. Although JICA members strongly opposed south end development, they favored that part of House Bill 214 that would extend the JIA's lease on the island to 2089, or an additional forty years, a measure needed to secure the financial means to improve or sell Jekyll's aging hotels and homes. The controversy concerning the south end also led to a stir of opposition from the Georgia Conservancy. In an interview on Georgia Public Radio on March 23, 2007, Jill Johnson, a lobbyist for the conservancy, commented, "Why do we have to extend leases now? What's the rush? The current leases last until 2049." Her comments concerned both citizens and the JIA, who feared that the conservancy might block passage of HB 214 altogether.[4] That did not happen, however. The House did in fact pass the bill to extend the lease, though without any protections whatsoever for the island's south end. Still, before the bill could become law, it had to be passed by the state senate.[5]

Meanwhile, over several months of 2007, the JIA was moving forward

Developers began to compete for Jekyll Island development rights. (Political cartoon by Samuel C. Rawls, better known as "Scrawls"; courtesy of Janet Rawls)

The wide expanse of the south end beach with its adjoining undeveloped land area was eyed avidly by developers. (Photo by the author)

The strip mall at Jekyll, built in the 1950s, was outdated by the first decade of the twenty-first century. (Courtesy of Mosaic, Jekyll Island Museum)

in its search for a revitalization partner. The three big private developers in contention were E. Wade Shealy Jr., the developer of the Hampton Plantation near Savannah; Mercer Reynolds, who built the posh Reynolds Plantation in Greensboro, Georgia; and Trammell Crow, one of the nation's largest commercial developers, which was interested only in acquiring and demolishing the Buccaneer Motel and rebuilding the site with 300 rooms and 120 condos.

But the big prize was winning the contract to redevelop the rest of the island. Both the Shealy proposal and the proposal from Reynolds's Linger Longer Communities recommended demolishing the Jekyll strip mall and the outdated convention center and building a new convention center and shopping area, as well as new hotels and condominiums. Shealy proposed the construction of 1,500 condos starting at a selling price of $1 million per unit, 192 houses selling for upwards of $1 million each, and 200 golf course houses starting at a price of $500,000 apiece. He also wanted to remove the Jekyll Island Airport to build a residential area and to relocate the soccer complex and Georgia 4-H and University of Georgia Extension, which had provided youth programs on Jekyll Island since 1983. The idea behind moving the 4-H complex was to create room to build a South End Village with $4 million beachfront homes, condos, a small hotel, shops, and restaurants. Mercer Reynolds offered as well to convert one of Jekyll Island's three 18-hole golf courses into a private membership course.

In the meantime, the JIA had its own redevelopment ideas, which aligned to a great extent with the plans of some of the developers. The JIA's plan consisted of a new convention center, a new and improved shopping area, and new hotels, as well as rebuilding the 4-H center on the south end of the island and removing the soccer complex so that developers could be ready to build on the south end. All of this had been under discussion even before the General Assembly started its deliberations.[6]

Citizens worried that Jekyll Island was being overpowered by influential people in state government and private developers, who were proposing not only to revitalize the island but also to enhance its appeal to the wealthy. For instance, House Speaker Glenn Richardson said, "It's a multimillion, maybe a billion-dollar asset sitting there owned by the state and it's just not producing." He supported a range of new hotels but clearly preferred the more extravagant end of the spectrum: "Can you imagine if a Ritz-Carlton or Four Seasons or something like that, a Saint Regis came in there, and each one of them took one of the [golf] courses, developed the villas around them and a hotel beach?" Glenn continued, "It would be a fantastic source of revenue for the state of Georgia and a good place for the people of Georgia to go."[7]

On March 29, during a State Institutions and Property Committee meeting, Rep. Ron Stephens (R-Savannah) sought to underscore what he saw as a pressing need to refurbish the island. Amid a debate on the House floor over passage of HB 214, Stephens declared that "Jekyll is no longer the jewel that it was. It's an absolute dump, ladies and gentlemen, with fleas and cockroaches." His testament was ultimately echoed in the preamble to the House's version of HB 214, albeit expressed in less strident language: "[T]he General Assembly further finds that the deteriorating conditions of public and commercial facilities is of great interest to the legislature and to the public, and by significantly extending an existing authority of the island's property, the state will hereby help to secure and encourage future investments and provide a basis for long-term revitalization of the island."[8]

The House passed HB 214 by a vote of 130–35, but outspoken Jekyll Island resident Jean Poleszak called the bill "horrendous" for its lack of legislative detail. Although the legislation extended the island lease and clarified the fact that the authority was not obliged to pay Glynn County taxes, Poleszak said, "It does not protect the island. We've had a lot of people say, 'Trust us. We'll take care of the island.' I don't want to take that chance."[9] Both environmentalists and Jekyll residents were angry and disappointed that the final legislation did not contain any safeguards against overdevelopment. It did not restrict developers from adding hundreds of upscale houses, condos, shops, and restaurants. The bill also left out language that would preserve both Jekyll's pristine south end and the island's affordability for "people of average income."[10] Art Hurt, a member of the Atlanta Audubon Society, commented, "This is not and should not be Daytona Beach or Hilton Head. Jekyll Island should not be used as a bonanza for real estate developers."[11]

After the House passed the bill without adding the hoped-for protections sought by environmentalists and citizens, those concerned turned their sights toward the Senate, hoping to win the battle there. Neill Herring, an environmental lobbyist, commented, "The refusal to protect the one place that people care the most about, means that they don't intend to protect it. We intend to lobby the Senate really hard, and we don't believe that the Senate is going to be as unfriendly as the House."[12]

As the bill moved to the Senate, even some lawmakers worried that a plan to revamp the island's outdated infrastructure could lead to overdevelopment and undermine the status of the island as an affordable vacation destination for middle-class Georgians, with some expressing particular concern about development on the south end, which was an important site for both nesting sea turtles and the 4-H center. For example, Rep. Debbie Buckner (D-Junction City) commented, "I have a fear that this bill has some safeguards and some good things, but I'm really concerned about the south end of the island and whether or not it will be protected with this bill." Senator Jeff Chapman (R-Brunswick) raised yet another issue. Although he supported extension of the JIA's lease on the island and most of the citizens' demands, he did not want any additional homeowners' leases, remarking that "the residential aspect of it is something that I don't believe is healthy." While he felt the state must honor the current leases, which would expire in 2049, he believed that they should take another look at allowing people to live in a state park.[13]

State Senator Jeff Chapman (R-Brunswick) was active throughout the development debates. From the outset, he was opposed to any new residential development. (Courtesy of Jeff Chapman)

A few weeks later, the Senate Natural Resources and Environment Committee heard from island residents, developers, environmentalists, and state officials about HB 214 and extending the Jekyll Island lease. During that meeting, Senator Chapman vowed to amend the bill to prohibit development on the south end: "We should want to protect and enjoy, not simply develop, the state-owned park." In an interview, he acknowledged that "[w]e need long-term protection of that asset, that pearl we call Jekyll." Chapman's stance drew strong opposition from his fellow Republicans.[14]

The controversy was heated and sparked interest as far away as California and New York. A story in the *Los Angeles Times* about the possibilities that faced Jekyll Island noted that "Coastal Georgia, which has for decades been protected by strict environmental laws, is one of the last battlegrounds for development on the Eastern Seaboard: The shorelines of Florida and South Carolina have already been heavily developed with condominiums and hotels." The article pointed out the value of Georgia's 1970 Coastal Marshlands Protection Act, which saved the marshes as "a nursery for significant wildlife species and a buffer against flooding and erosion," and praised Georgia for avoiding "the scattershot construction" to be found up and down the southern Atlantic coast.[15] An article in *The New York Times* quoted Chris DeScherer, a lawyer at the Southern Environmental Law Center in Atlanta, who suggested there was pressure on the JIA to further develop the island: "Developers have figured this out, and there's almost a gold-rush mentality."[16]

On April 20, 2007, Georgia state senators voted 32–12 in favor of amendments to HB 214 that would address most of the concerns that had been expressed, such as protection of the unspoiled south end of the island, sending a clear message to developers that that part of the island was off-limits. They also voted unanimously to extend the lease of the JIA, which in turn opened the possibility that the island's 632 residential leaseholders might also extend their leases. While Chapman had considered proposing an amendment to the bill that would prohibit any additional year-round residents, it was a potential deal killer for developers. Frank Mirasola, an island resident, seemed pleased with the amendments, commenting that "[w]e—the citizens' association, preservationists and other people—appealed to their conscience and they responded." But Georgia Conservancy lobbyist Jill Johnson was still wary: "It's far, far, far from over and we have to keep the pressure on to make sure the south end is protected."[17]

Jekyll Island officials were less enthusiastic. JIA chair Ben Porter, who was open to the possibility of south end development, reacted to the vote with muted optimism: "We hope that the final legislation will give the authority the opportunity to do what's best for Jekyll Island and the people of Georgia," which he described as "moderate development, improvements and revitalization."[18] He made it clear that he didn't "want any restrictions [on] the direction and future of the island. Micromanagement is never good because you can't see the future."[19] Bill Donohue, executive director of the Jekyll Island Authority, agreed, commenting, "I would prefer that we not be limited in any particular area north, south, east or west, and find out what's the best use of the island."[20]

After weeks of deliberations, the problem of how to make Jekyll more attractive to developers without destroying one of the most unspoiled public beaches along the Atlantic Ocean was still unsolved, but clearly something needed to be done. Rep. Terry Barnard (R-Glenville), chair of the House State Institutions and Property Committee, described Jekyll as a dilapidated dump and "a travesty."[21] Only a few days later, a journalist writing in the *Statesboro Herald* issued an even harsher judgment of the island and the way it had been run: "Jekyll Island is probably the most abused, misused and exploited piece of real estate ever owned by the state of Georgia. Much of the 60-year-long assault on Jekyll's precious resources has been conducted right under the collective noses of the Jekyll Island Authority and often at its behest."[22]

Finally, after months of squabbling over where and what kind of development would be allowed, a deal for the future of the island emerged. In a small room in the basement of the capitol, a group of lobbyists met with Senator Jeff Chapman and island officials. It was what one journalist called an "odd meeting," with reporters, lobbyists, and members of the public allowed to observe "a conversation that would usually be held behind closed doors."[23] The House-Senate conference committee was trying to find a compromise between the competing versions of House Bill 214. Chapman was still concerned that revitalization could bring an influx of new residents. While he had previously voiced qualms even about allowing the residents who already lived on Jekyll Island to reside in a state park, he was determined that unrestrained growth of the island's population was not an option.

By this time, it seemed too late for any new deals. Then Joe Tanner, formerly the natural resources commissioner and now a lobbyist for one of the interested developers, joined the discussion. He and Chapman went back and forth, until Tanner proposed a new idea, as recounted by a reporter for *The Florida Times-Union*: "Would the authority's executive director . . . be willing to agree to put a limit on the number of residents into the new master plan being developed for the island? That would allow lawmakers, who have veto power over the master plan, to reject any increase in the island's population. Yet, the appointed authority, which has day-to-day responsibility for management of the island, would still have the first say on that aspect of development, as pro-development legislators have insisted."[24]

Bill Donohue, no doubt exhausted from the seemingly endless discussions over the fate of the island, gave a "thumbs-up" sign. With Donohue having signaled his approval, Chapman gave his support to the compromise. It included much of what he, island residents, and environmentalists had demanded. It opposed further development on the island's south end, eliminated language that would have allowed the authority to sell portions of the island, and reinforced the state's intent that no more than 35 percent of the island could be developed. Borrowing language from the House version of the bill, the revised measure allowed a legislative oversight committee to temporarily block any changes to the island's master plan until the General Assembly had a chance to overturn the amendments permanently at the next legislative session.

A few hours later, the Senate passed the measure unanimously, and then the House did the same. Everyone seemed pleased. Rep. Terry Barnard commented, "We've basically set up the opportunity for Jekyll Island Authority to move forward with the right revitalization plan."[25]

Seven weeks passed before Governor Perdue, on the final day he could do so, at last signed HB 214, relieving environmentalists and Jekyll Island residents who had been worried that he would veto the measure. "Jekyll Island is a fantastic resource with so much unrealized potential for being one of the most popular destination vacation spots on the Atlantic coast," Perdue said in a news release. "I have taken what is a giant step towards ensuring that the very qualities we admire most about Jekyll Island are protected while we set the stage for some much-needed revitalization to occur."[26]

Meanwhile, developers continued to target Jekyll Island revitalization possibilities. It appears that sometime in 2006, Trammell Crow representatives had visited Jekyll in search of new commercial real estate. They reached out to JIA board members to let them know of their interest in certain properties on Jekyll. J. D. Dell of Trammell Crow sent a letter to Ben Porter on February 7, 2007, in which he asked to be put on the board's agenda concerning the Buccaneer site. On February 12, Dell and associated partners introduced their proposals for the Buccaneer site. On June 18, 2007, after HB 214 had been passed, Dell addressed the board and stated that the most important new development was the legislature's extension of the lease to 2089. He also announced that negotiations regarding the project development agreement for the Buccaneer replacement had just been finalized. As reported in the minutes from the June 18 board meeting, "Dell revealed that Trammell Crow was willing to invest $90 million in the new hotel complex, which would offer 300 new rooms, 120 condominiums, a conference center, a spa/fitness center, and a high-quality restaurant, giving a potential maximum of 540 rooms." Board member Bob Krueger announced that there would be some cost abatement during the early years of the lease "to ensure the business will get off on the right foot." These announcements led to a major upheaval within the JIA, and the squabbles were far from over.[27]

The latest uproar stemmed from the authority's decision to grant $10 million in rent breaks to Trammell Crow, one of the nation's largest developers. Some state officials, government watchdogs, and island residents demanded that the incentives be rescinded, and they called for the JIA chair Ben Porter to resign. A Jekyll resident filed a complaint of "serious malfeasance" against Porter for the incentives promised to Trammell Crow. Ed Boshears, a member of the JIA board, called the JIA chair "a liar" and asked him to resign immediately. Porter responded, "We didn't treat it as rent abatement, but as an incentive to get a major developer to get going as quickly as possible."

Over the next few days, board members started condemning one another in emails and in guest editorials in *The Atlanta Journal-Constitution*. Boshears, a Brunswick attorney and former Republican state senator, criticized Porter and fellow board member Steve Croy, both of whom were themselves coastal developers. Boshears argued that the rent deal should be rescinded and made accusations in strong terms: "These people are the most shameless liars I have ever seen in my entire life. They don't want Jekyll Island to [remain] as it has for the last 50 years—a place for average people of this state to come and stay, go to conventions or bring children to the beach. They want to rebuild Jekyll as an upscale resort."[28]

He was not alone in questioning the matter. Senator Jeff Chapman was troubled that the deal with Trammell Crow didn't include any language guaranteeing moderately priced rooms, remarking, "The question remains, why did they have to give the $10 million incentive?" He wanted the island's legislative oversight committee to review the deal. Even some Jekyll citizens entered the fray. Joe Iannicelli, an island resident, charged that Porter "rammed through a proposal to grant an undisclosed number of concessions" to Trammell Crow. "This extraordinary giveaway of Jekyll Island revenues . . . suggests serious malfeasance on the part of Mr. Ben Porter." According to Chapman, most of the board members had known nothing of the Trammell Crow deal before June 18, when they were asked to vote on it. Apparently, the board members unanimously approved the deal before they could review it. Later that day, after Boshears and another board member had finally read the project development agreement, they complained about the incentives and the lack of time to review the deal before the vote. Neill Herring, a Sierra Club lobbyist, went

The JIA selected Linger Longer as its revitalization partner on September 24, 2007. (Scrawls cartoon, courtesy of Janet Rawls)

so far as to argue that Porter "should resign. . . . He's obviously unqualified to run that authority."[29]

Most members of the JIA, however, seemed to support Porter and viewed Boshears as a disgruntled publicity seeker. Nevertheless, Boshears continued to be a voice for affordability and opposed what appeared to be a plan to eliminate such accommodations: "When I raised the issue of keeping affordable hotels like the Days Inn, a developer said, 'We're not building any Section 8 housing over here. . . . [L]et them stay in the campground.'" Boshears complained, "This is the kind of mentality I have to contend with on the Jekyll board." He contended that Porter was "unhappy that I will not conspire with him to conceal the true facts from the people of Georgia."[30]

When the legislature's Jekyll Island Oversight Committee met with the authority a month later to further discuss the revitalization of Jekyll Island, committee members Senator Chapman and Rep. Terry Barnard asked several questions that mirrored recent criticisms of the board's actions, which included the board's selection of a private developer and the $10 million rent abatement. When Barnard raised the issue of affordability, Porter replied, "We do not intend to create a playground for the rich. The master plan will include a full range of bedroom accommodations and prices." Boshears chimed in, saying, "All we have been given is vague generalities. Let's be specific about this."[31]

On September 22, 2007, Boshears received a call from the office of Governor Perdue informing him that he would not be reappointed to the Jekyll Island Authority board. Perdue had decided to replace him with retiring Rep. Richard Royal (R-Camilla). In response, Boshears typed out a long and vitriolic letter accusing the Perdue administration of engineering a "sweetheart deal" with a big Republican donor. He called for a jury investigation and demanded that Perdue cease any involvement in the management and control of Jekyll Island. He also wanted two of his colleagues, Ben Porter and Steve Croy, removed from the authority for "unethical activity." Boshears was unhappy not only about the Trammell Crow deal but also about the JIA board's unanimous decision to select Linger Longer, a subsidiary of Mercer Reynolds, as its private partner in the revitalization of Jekyll Island. An article published in *The Atlanta Journal-Constitution* on September 24, 2007, quotes Boshears as saying, "This was intended to be a massive giveaway of state property to Mercer Reynolds, finance chair for John McCain's presidential campaign, and would have amounted to the greatest theft of state property since the Yazoo land frauds 200 years ago." He accused the governor of removing him from the Jekyll board for "reasons that are obvious. . . . This sweetheart deal [with Trammell Crowe] will cost the authority $10 million that we desperately need."[32]

Over the next few days, there was blowback on both sides. Bert Brantley, the spokesperson for Governor Perdue, responded that "Boshears's allegations are untrue. None of these things are based in reality."[33] However, there was an outpouring of online support for Boshears. The *Constitution* article's comments were overwhelmingly in favor of Boshears, with almost thirty pages of posts condemning Perdue and lauding Boshears for his integrity.

The board's decision to name Linger Longer as the authority's revitalization partner came after months of reviewing private developers' proposals for the possible redevelopment of a new convention center site and adjacent oceanfront property owned by the authority as a mixed-use town center. "Linger Longer's plan is a desirable sustainable proposal that includes convention, hospitality, retail, and entertainment venues," said Bill Donohue, JIA executive director, "as well as other elements that create a signature eco- and family-friendly environment for Jekyll Island."[34]

Linger Longer's plan for Jekyll Island included a new convention center, upgrades of roads and park infrastructure ($25.7 million), the construction of 160 condominiums and 227 vacation homes ($122 million) and a parking garage ($6.4 million), replacement of the Buccaneer Motel ($90 million), and an environmental center. Jim Langford, the project executive with Southeast LandCo, an affiliate of Linger Longer, said there was no plan for a Ritz-Carlton for Jekyll, but he suggested that some upscale properties could be expected. "We're planning an economy hotel, a mid-scale beachfront hotel, and a convention hotel," said Langford, a former state director at Georgia's Trust for Public Land. David Egan of the Initiative to Protect Jekyll Island, a residents' group that had challenged proposals for change, still had questions.[35]

Three weeks later, Wade Shealy, manager of the Jekyll Island Revitalization Group, which had lost its bid to become Jekyll's revitalization partner, accused a consultant from the Bleakly Advisory Group, which had been hired to evaluate various aspects of the revitalization plan, of allegedly manipulating the facts and numbers to make the proposal from Linger Longer appear stronger. Said Shealy, "We had a better land plan and better team and paid the public a better financial return. We also were asking for no money from the state. . . . If Bleakly had not manipulated the numbers, we should have won." For some reason, Linger Longer was allowed to extend development to sixty-four acres rather than limiting its plan to the forty-five acres originally allotted. Shealy argued that if Linger Longer had been forced to confine the new buildings to forty-five acres as the other developers did, Linger Longer's green space and density numbers would have been the worst of the three finalists. According to Shealy, JIA board member Sam Kellett told him, "If you stay cool and don't go to the press, there will be something for you down the road at Jekyll."[36]

As Linger Longer was starting the process of gathering input from stakeholders regarding the revitalization plans, Shealy filed a lawsuit in Fulton County Superior Court claiming that the JIA had unfairly awarded the contract to Linger Longer and seeking an injunction to stop Linger Longer from proceeding with the project. "The whole process was flawed; a lot of the procedures were violated," Shealy said. "Our goal is to get a judge to stop [Linger Longer] from going forward with any contracts signed and to have the bid redone." The lawsuit was an added blow for the revitalization project, as the JIA was struggling with environmental matters, legal issues, and political disputes. The suit alleged that Linger Longer was not responsive to the authority's request for proposals, citing twenty-five allegations and listing twenty legal objections. Senator Chapman proclaimed that any revitalization plans should be halted so that questions around financing, public access, and the affordability of planned hotel rooms and condos could be resolved.[37]

In November 2007, *The Brunswick News* announced that Bill Donohue would likely leave Jekyll Island. Governor Sonny Perdue had recommended Donohue for the role of executive director of the Lake Lanier Islands Development Authority (LLIDA). Perdue's announcement came just as Jekyll was on the brink of a major revitalization. In the years since Donohue had taken control, the island had undergone some important changes. The Georgia Sea Turtle Center, the Jekyll Island Foundation, and events such as the festive lighting and celebrations on the island during the Christmas season had all been added during his tenure. Ben Porter also pointed out that "Bill managed the update of the Jekyll master plan and was instrumental in the development of the revitalization plan for the island."[38] When asked what his greatest challenge at Jekyll Island had been, Donohoe replied, "Building consensus within a very diverse group of people."[39] On November 30, 2007, the LLIDA voted to accept the recommendation of the governor and name Donohue its executive director. At this crucial point, the fight over Jekyll Island's fate had just begun.

The undeveloped south end beach was a major attraction for sea birds and nesting turtles. Environmentalists have fought to preserve it throughout the state era. (Photo by the author)

12

BUILDING TO CAPACITY

In the last quarter of 2007 and on into 2008, the U.S. economy was reeling from the most serious financial crisis since the Great Depression. Years of predatory lending, low-income home buying, and excessive risk-taking by global financial institutions led to a housing bubble whose collapse culminated in a "perfect storm" of foreclosures and declining home values, which in turn precipitated massive bailouts of financial institutions. On October 1, 2008, Congress passed the $800 billion bipartisan Emergency Economic Stabilization Act, which was signed into law by President George W. Bush two days later. However, the measure did not stop the economy's free fall. It was the beginning of the "Great Recession."

On December 10, 2007, Jim Langford, the project executive for Linger Longer, wrote an editorial in *The Atlanta Journal-Constitution* about the problems and possibilities of Jekyll Island. He indicated that while "Georgians are blessed with a beautiful state-owned 5,900-acre island[,] . . . more than 75 percent of it protected from development," in recent decades "visitation has dropped 47 percent . . . [h]otels are just half-full, and the causeway is used at 20 percent of capacity." He believed that vacationers and conventioneers were no longer going to the island because "[a]cres of asphalt give Jekyll a blighted look." The drop in visitation, he pointed out, was a significant detriment to the island in many ways, noting that "Georgia law requires Jekyll Island to be economically self-sustaining. As visitation declines, so does revenue that pays for things like environmental and cultural preservation."[1]

Getting to his primary point—Linger Longer's plan for transforming the island—Langford asserted that "[on] land that is mostly parking lots and outdated buildings, Linger Longer proposes a small 63-acre beach village with three hotels, 79 cottages that include units for rent, a vacation club, a town center and 23 acres of green space." Not only would this development beautify the island and once again make it "a favored destination" of Georgians, he claimed, but "[o]ver the first 15 years, the village will return to the Jekyll Island Authority an estimated $115 million revenues. . . . Linger Longer proposes paying the Jekyll Island Authority $8 million over the first four years to assist with the transition and investing another $350 million in private funds in the project."[2]

Despite Langford's optimistic predictions, many citizens were disappointed with the Linger Longer presentations. Senator Jeff Chapman was openly critical of the company's plans. The concerns of citizens and legislators, Wade Shealy's lawsuit, and the departure of Bill Donohue were all issues that delayed the revitalization process. However, the Shealy lawsuit did not seem to worry Langford, who commented, "I think the judge will agree the lawsuit has no merit and I don't think it will slow us down."[3]

While authority members prepared for the lawsuit, Jim Langford continued to be the largest voice on the island. He had finished a series of public meetings and sought citizen feedback through phone calls, emails, and a website calling for Georgians to vote "yes" for the following proposed resolution: "Be it resolved, in view of the aging infrastructure of and the declining visitation to Jekyll Island, that just 1 percent of the island's acreage including land adjacent to less than 8 percent of the island's total beachfront shall be revitalized to the quality standards that Georgians deserve without reducing public parking or beach access points and with adherence to extensive and rigorous environmental guidelines to create one of the most accessible and eco-friendly communities on the East Coast." The website did not provide an option for "no" votes. In the meantime, Senator Chapman was asking the state attorney general to investigate several components of the Jekyll plan, including whether the proposed development would be in violation of the legislature's directive that Jekyll Island remain affordable to average Georgians.

In several filings in Fulton County Superior Court, the authority was seeking a complete dismissal of the litigation filed in October by Wade Shealy on behalf of the Jekyll Island Revitalization Group. The JIA disputed claims made by Shealy in the lawsuit and asserted that the Jekyll Island Revitalization Group was not, in fact, a legal entity and had no standing to sue the Jekyll Island Authority or the State of Georgia. Wood Partners, which had been a partner in Wade Shealy's effort, had withdrawn from the Jekyll Island Revitalization Group in September. Thus if its request for proposals (RFP) was in fact renewed, restored, or reopened, as requested by the litigation, the Jekyll Island Revitalization Group was no longer in a position to complete the project.

In November, Linger Longer was in the process of finalizing its proposal and completing negotiations to contract with the Jekyll Island Authority to serve as the JIA's private partner in revitalization efforts. Linger Longer also joined the state in seeking dismissal of the complaint filed by the Jekyll Island Revitalization Group. Langford offered that the authority "is hopeful for a ruling on [its] requests for dismissal quickly so that the revitalization of Jekyll can continue to move forward."[4]

In the second week of January 2008, Fulton County Superior Court Judge Jerry Baxter denied the injunction sought by the Jekyll Island Revitalization Group, ruling that the group had no standing to sue. Bob Krueger, who had chaired the private partner selection committee, said, "The ruling vindicates the process used. . . . That means that Linger Longer Communities can proceed with a final design of its proposed multi-million-dollar revitalization of the state park's commercial district."[5]

A grass-roots movement of citizens rallied around Senator Jeff Chapman to defend Jekyll Island. (Photo by the author)

Early in 2008, Senator Chapman was soliciting support for another resolution to protect parking on Jekyll Island's main beach and advocating for the protection of direct beach access on his campaign website. Linger Longer's plan, he contended, would take eighty-eight of the current parking places for the oceanfront center; he believed that Linger Longer would cover that area with hotels, condos, and shops, and that they would have to move the main beach parking area a quarter mile inland. Chapman said, "That's just not right. Building high-priced beachfront condos and shops will displace day visitors from the only beach on the island that is visible at high tide. It goes against everything that is fair and reasonable for the rest of Georgians." He contended that oceanfront parking areas and beach access should remain convenient for day visitors, especially children, the elderly, and people with disabilities. "This isn't about Jekyll Island," said Chapman. "It's about protecting any state park from commercial exploitation." He was the only legislator who was speaking publicly against the Linger Longer plans. Chapman hoped that widespread endorsement of the resolution would show other legislators where the public stood on the issue and bring the matter to the floor of the General Assembly for a vote. Shortly after Chapman posted his critique of the projected $441 million development, Jim Langford offered a rebuttal, claiming that "[u]nder the proposed plan, every current public access point will continue to exist, and the beach will be as open as ever to all visitors."[6]

Most of the island's citizens agreed with Chapman. Jean Poleszak, a long-time resident, had previously been quoted as saying, "The developers are thinking, 'Wahoo! Off we go.'"[7] Her words expressed the concerns of many about the future of Jekyll Island. Art Hurt, a small business owner in Atlanta, was more critical of the JIA. In early February 2008, *The Atlanta Journal-Constitution* published a guest column by Hurt in which he stated that the "JIA has willfully and systematically excluded the public from any participation in the planning process. They have neither sought, nor allowed, any input from the public, and they have ignored pleas from the public for information and for opportunities to submit ideas for consideration for Jekyll's future." Hurt asserted that, consequently, "[t]he public has reacted to being ignored and dismissed. Thus, [the] JIA has created this ugly squabble."[8]

On February 28, to prove his points, Chapman released state audits that demonstrated that the authority had low-balled its earnings by $11 million over the previous eleven years and had overstated the drop in visitation, making Jekyll's financial situation seem more urgent than it was. In response, Ben Porter attacked Chapman for making misleading statements about the JIA's bookkeeping. Porter said that "statements contained in a news release issued yesterday by State Senator Jeff Chapman are false and are intentionally misleading." Porter argued that the comments grossly and deliberatively misrepresented facts and implied impropriety regarding the financial reporting practices of the Jekyll Island Authority. While rejecting most of Chapman's claims, Porter didn't share specific information to refute the senator's numbers.[9]

By the end of that week, the Senate Economic Development Committee had killed three bills sponsored by Senator Chapman that had been intended to overturn current development plans for Jekyll Island. Ben Porter and Steve Croy accused Chapman of lying. Ed Boshears said, "There is a difference of opinion about the interpretation of certain figures concerning Jekyll. Chapman may or may not be right in what he is saying. If Porter and Croy want to make shrill, hysterical accusations that Chapman is lying, then they need to provide proof he is lying and the only way to do that is to have an outside independent agency do an evaluation of the figures."[10]

The JIA and Linger Longer continued to claim that Jekyll Island State Park had suffered a precipitous decline in both visitors and revenues over the previous fifteen years, and that the park was in terrible condition and needed, according to Jim Langford, a "significant revitalization" to make it a "compelling destination." But according to the state auditor, Senator Chapman, and a citizens' group, Jekyll Island's condition wasn't that critical. The park still made money, visitation had dropped on average only 1.9 percent each year, and with a few more hotels and shops, Jekyll would be good as new. "The Authority and Linger Longer are crying wolf and painting this picture of a run-down Jekyll so they can maximize their commercial activity," Chapman said. According to the JIA annual report, the island was $210,575 in the red in 2006, but according to State Auditor John Thornton, the authority turned a profit of $1,950,081 that year.[11] If the auditor was correct, the authority's annual statements had significantly underreported the island's revenues.

The discrepancy resulted in a February 14, 2008, letter from the state auditor to Senator Chapman informing him that "[t]he JIA Annual Reports are not prepared in conformity with generally accepted accounting principles." Consequently, Thornton stated, "we do not believe the JIA Annual Reports from 1997 through 2007 provide an accurate picture of JIA's annual revenues or expenditures." Eric Garvey, the authority's marketing and business development director, denied that figures and facts were misused to give a negative impression of Jekyll. He suggested that the annual reports were more akin to "marketing" documents and "snapshots of our annual performance." In a February 26 statement, Chapman accused the JIA of giving "the distorted impression that it was on the brink of financial insolvency." Looking back at 1997, the first year the JIA had reported losses, state auditors noted that parking fee revenues had barely changed from 1996 to 1997. Authority occupancy records showed that hotel occupancy rates on the island dipped only 1.9 percent during that time, and the number of visitors taking historic district tours actually rose 10 percent. However, the authority and Linger Longer claimed that the estimated number of annual visits to Jekyll during that period had plummeted from 3.5 million to 1.9 million, a 44 percent drop. But the figures didn't add up. According to Ken Cordell, a U.S. Forest Service expert on park visitation, "It is a relatively safe assumption that something about the JIA method of counting and estimating visitation changed between 1996 and 1997."[12]

To make matters worse for the JIA, state lawmakers, island residents, and visitors were once again waging a legislative battle to protect a stretch of open public beach. After considerable public pressure, the authority reconsidered the issue. In a letter to Rep. Jerry Keen (R-St. Simons), Ben Porter indicated that, "[a]fter conferring with our revitalization partner, Linger Longer Communities, we have made the decision to limit use of this area to . . . public purposes [parking] and not development of accommodations, such as hotels or condominiums." Dory Ingram, a volunteer lobbyist for the Initiative to Protect Jekyll Island, expressed her delight: "It looks good, and we congratulate the people of Georgia for holding onto their beach."[13] Nine days later, a state Department of Natural Resources survey showed that nearly half of Jekyll's proposed beachfront village would fall within Georgia Shore Protection Act jurisdiction. The Jekyll Island Authority had anticipated that portions of the proposal would affect development, and they had requested the survey in January. David Kyler, executive director for the Center for a Sustainable Coast, pointed out that "the requirement to protect shoreline areas within the act's jurisdiction is more complex than a simple one-third no-build requirement." Langford suggested that Linger Longer could be flexible: "It might mean moving things around a little bit. It might mean setting things back from the beach."[14]

After months without an executive director, the Jekyll Island Authority board finally selected C. Jones Hooks, president and CEO of the Hampton Roads Economic Development Alliance in Norfolk, Virginia, to fill the position. A native of Metter in southeast Georgia, Hooks had a long history of leadership in Georgia's business community and state government. Earlier in his career, he had served as director of the Kings Bay Impact Coordinating Committee in Camden County, and later as the president and CEO of the Albany-Dougherty Economic Development Commission and the Albany Chamber of Commerce. "Jones Hooks has an impressive background and successful work history, especially in economic development and tourism,"

Jones Hooks was appointed executive director of the JIA in April 2008. (Photo by the author)

Governor Sonny Perdue announced. "His experience will be an asset to the Authority as the revitalization of Jekyll Island proceeds." Hooks seemed equally pleased: "I'm honored by the opportunity to help manage and preserve one of Georgia's most precious natural resources. . . . I look forward to welcoming more Georgians to enjoy all the wonderful things Jekyll Island has to offer."[15]

But almost as soon as Hooks took the job, he realized that he was under siege. He had walked straight into a red-hot mess concerning the ongoing Linger Longer controversy. Hooks said, "I stepped into something that I knew wasn't going to be a cup of tea, but at the same time I had no idea how totally off the wall it was!"[16] Linger Longer's plans were robust and all encompassing, but they led many to believe that the developer was not especially concerned about environmental issues. Jekyll citizens were fearful of potential change, and many were asking, "What's going to happen on Jekyll Island?"

Linger Longer subsequently revised its plan to be more environmentally sensitive, and this new plan was better received by citizens. When Jekyll Island residents and others met to review the revised proposal for the revitalization project, the feedback at the meeting was more positive, though there were still some minor concerns. "I'm very impressed with this new plan," said Bonnie Newell, a Jekyll resident. "Especially if you look where we stood with the original plan, this new one is much more in step with the feeling of Jekyll Island." The JIA hired an Orlando architecture firm, Helman Hurley Charvat Peacock (HHCP), to develop a more detailed design for a new beachfront village area that would evoke a quaint small-town beach center, with such features as a prominent main street, green space, low-rise storefronts topped with swooping awnings, and a spacious public park of oak trees, palms, and sand dunes, in keeping with the natural environment. Michael Chatham, vice president of HHCP, said, "We wanted to keep that feel that is Jekyll Island, that small-town natural beach atmosphere that brings people here." Sandy Cerrato, a Jekyll Island resident, was pleased: "We did not want to lose our state park feel, and it appears that we won't." Residents also praised the authority for listening to their comments and feedback since the original master plan was released in October. Nonetheless, there were concerns about potential vacation ownership units. Mindy Egan, speaking on behalf of the Initiative to Protect Jekyll Island, commented, "We can do better on this island without the 160 time-share units that are being planned. We just don't need them."[17]

At a public meeting on September 29, when a planning consultant from

A series of editorial cartoons by Scrawls depicted the Linger Longer plan in a negative light. (Courtesy of Janet Rawls)

the Bleakly Advisory Group, which the board hired to analyze various financial issues around the revitalization, announced the firm's recommendation that the Jekyll Island Authority build 1,400 new hotel rooms and condos, he was met with "public mistrust." Brunswick resident Lauren Renke commented, "We've heard it said that we are upset about this because we don't want anything to change. . . . We do want a change. We just want a change with moderation."[18]

Meanwhile, negotiations continued between the JIA and Linger Longer as they sought to find a solution to the various problems and concerns. Hooks later noted that "it seemed that the Authority was losing ground. To me that was bothersome." To make matters worse, with so many stakeholders, including people from all over the state of Georgia and out-of-state people as well, the pressure on the JIA board was overwhelming, and the atmosphere was growing increasingly contentious. At one point, a man showed up at a JIA meeting dressed all in black and was angry and hostile at the podium. "After that we would not have board meetings without state police presence," Hooks remembered. "It was that heated, and people were in your face. I was trying to be calm, but underneath I was paddling like crazy."[19]

Almost every week, there was turmoil with residents, Senator Chapman, and the Georgia attorney general, who assigned a representative to keep an eye on the JIA. Hooks said, "I think I got cussed out by everybody on the island. It was extremely stressful." He spent hours upon hours on the phone trying to get the deals done. However, the unraveling of the economy put even more pressure on the situation. "One by one," Hooks remembered,

The discussion between Governor Perdue and JIA board members following the groundbreaking ceremony for the new beach village would prove to be an important turning point in Jekyll Island's redevelopment. (Photo by the author)

"the deals went south because of the economy. But it wasn't just the economy. There were board members who felt that Linger Longer negotiations needed to be redirected." Bob Krueger, who had moved into the role of chair of the JIA, was finally seeing what Hooks was seeing, and they were in sync about the problems with their potential partner. "They talked about a partnership," said Hooks, "but in a meeting, Linger Longer people basically came in telling us, 'Here's what we're going to do, and here's how we're going to do it.'"[20] After that meeting, the JIA concluded that Linger Longer wanted complete control of the entire island. This was the final straw.

When Governor Perdue arrived at Jekyll on December 7, 2009, to preside over the groundbreaking ceremony for the island's new beach village, JIA members were meeting to try to decide how they would express their concerns to the governor. "We had decided that Krueger would ask the governor if they could end their negotiations with Linger Longer," said Hooks. After the groundbreaking and a speech in the convention center, the board had arranged for an island vehicle known as a Red Bug to return them all to the historic district, but Hooks suggested that they walk so that they could have some time to discuss the situation. They explained to the governor that they felt they had reached an endpoint with Linger Longer. Perdue replied, "That's why you guys are on the board. You make the decision."[21]

Shortly after the groundbreaking, Jones Hooks called Jim Langford to let him know that the JIA was going to go another way. The JIA and Mercer Reynolds planned to make a joint media statement the next day, when they would characterize the split as a suspension of the partnership by mutual consent. Instead, Mercer Reynolds made a prior announcement that they were the ones who pulled out and released the JIA from its obligation. Hooks had the impression that the Mercer Reynolds people felt bitter. Bob Krueger made a conciliatory gesture in an opinion piece published on December 22 in *The Atlanta Journal-Constitution* in which he stated, "I wish to thank the members of the JIA board, the professionals at the Reynolds Cos. and all involved for their efforts. I regret that the partnering agreement could not be completed, but we will press on."[22] Senator Chapman was relieved: "I'm grateful they have decided to go about it in this manner. I think there are a lot of companies out there that would appreciate the opportunity to bid on this."[23]

This was the turning point. Hooks's background in economic development, tourism planning, and community development seemed to be a perfect fit to create a better revitalization plan. "Everything that I did, it all came back full circle here on Jekyll Island," he said. Within a month, the Jekyll Island Authority had invited developers from all over the nation, along with hoteliers and building contractors, to consider jump-starting the state park's stalled redevelopment plans. The focus was to find a developer that could deliver one building—a minimum three-hundred-room full-service hotel—by early 2012, when a new convention center was scheduled to open. The response was strong. "We're very pleased," said Eric Garvey. "Hopefully, we can move fairly quickly."[24]

After more than a year of debate about hotels and condos, the Jekyll Island Authority board had reduced the $441 million cost projected by Linger Longer for the revitalization of the island to the earlier suggested target of $99 million. Not only was the new plan more economical, but it also better fit the desires of the citizens. With this lower amount in mind, the JIA planned to rebuild roads and provide funding for the historic district, a new retail district, new hotels, and new visitor attractions. The authority also decided to conduct a capacity study to forecast the effect that new development would have on the island's infrastructure, environment, and visitor experience, as well as its impact on Jekyll's bottom line. Gary Mongeon of the Bleakly Advisory Group reported that, "[t]o raise the needed $99 million, six percent of the island

This facility served as the temporary convention center while the new one was under construction. (Photo by the author)

Construction of the new convention center, beach village, and hotels began soon after the decision had been made not to follow the Linger Longer plan. (Photo by the author)

Jones Hooks kicks off the revitalization, speaking at the new Great Dunes Park on September 20, 2010. (Courtesy of the McCash Collection)

should be redeveloped." The firm's study necessitated that current lodging be more than doubled, from 1,800 rooms to 4,100 rooms or units; a thousand of the new units would be hotel rooms, 500 would be hotel-condos, and the rest would be duplexes, time-shares, cottages, and other vacation rentals. David Egan was cautiously skeptical of the Bleakly study. "The ultimate goal of public land planning is to enhance the quality of the visitor experience," he said. "I didn't hear anything so far about how this development would do that. People come to this place now because it doesn't have the kind of development they say we need to have."[25]

In late September 2008, Ed Boshears, who had been replaced on the JIA board a year earlier, asked for an investigation concerning the dealings between JIA chair Bob Krueger and Ben Porter, Mercer Reynolds, and the current governor, Sonny Perdue, accusing them of conspiring in the earlier revitalization plan. He argued that "[s]everal key aspects of deals to revitalize Jekyll were illegally discussed in secret meetings, and Perdue was intimately involved in the details of the island overhaul." Perdue's office strenuously denied that the governor was micromanaging the board's actions.[26] Boshears called for an outside independent agency, such as a grand jury, to investigate, but no investigation ever took place.[27]

On September 19, 2010, the JIA awarded a $30.6 million project to Georgia-based Brasfield & Gorrie as the general contractor for the new beach village revitalization. The project included public infrastructure and assets, in addition to site preparation for private hotels and retail development. Brasfield & Gorrie would work with HHCP and the JIA design team to complete the project. Authority chair Bob Krueger commented, "This bid is another important milestone that has been successfully completed and keeps revitalization on track." Construction of the new convention center along with two new hotels integrated with a village green and park space was scheduled for completion in 2012. That same day, the revitalization effort was kicked off at the eight-acre Great Dunes Park along Jekyll's beachfront, marking another important step in the island's ongoing redevelopment.[28]

The tension between Jekyll citizens' desires and demands for involvement on the one hand and the JIA's need for increased revenue on the other may never end. Developers will likely continue to salivate over the cherished undeveloped land that characterizes Jekyll Island and for which it is well known, but they will always be met by resistance from those who care about the environment and the unspoiled aspects of the island. Even with the uneasy truce that would be achieved among developers, politicians, authority members, and the public at the end of the first decade of this century, the controversies would go on, and the authority's need to bring in more revenue would not go away.

The houses on Jekyll Island were mostly modest midcentury ranch-style homes built in the late 1950s and 1960s, like this one. (Photo by the author)

LEASES & LOSSES

13

Even as the Linger Longer controversy was still raging, another heated debate between Jekyll residents and the Jekyll Island Authority was also in full swing. HB 214 had extended the authority's lease on Jekyll Island to 2089, but a decision had yet to be made about the possible extension of residential leases beyond 2049. It was a critical issue, for lending agencies would not grant a thirty-year mortgage beyond the life of the lease, and they preferred that the lease extend at least ten years beyond the end of the mortgage. Ben Porter expressed the urgency of the situation: "A decision must be made, so thirty-year mortgages on homes may be written after 2010."[1]

On December 16, 2007, during a meeting between the authority board and the legislative Jekyll Island Oversight Committee, both board members and legislators expressed concern that the cost of Jekyll's residential leases was out of step with lease contracts elsewhere. State Senator Chip Pearson, chair of the oversight committee, noted that the island's residential leases did not align with the price of similar resort properties. He suggested, based on witness observation, that the current value of each of the 628 residential annual leases was $30,000 to $60,000. Pearson was frustrated that the state was projecting budget deficits for the foreseeable future even as Jekyll residents were paying only $250 to $400 a year on leases they had signed in the 1950s and 1960s.[2] It was clearly an issue that the JIA needed to consider carefully.

Inevitably, the question of whether private residences should even be allowed on Jekyll Island arose once again. Bob Krueger pointed out that there had been "recent calls to curb development of private residences on Jekyll Island," which, he suggested, meant that "the public doesn't want to see these existing leases extended."[3] When JIA chair Ben Porter charged the board's Finance Committee with investigating the issue of whether residential leases ought to be continued at all, he claimed that the question had been raised earlier by Senator Jeff Chapman. Chapman disputed that claim, saying that the question he had raised was whether any *additional* residential development should be allowed on the island.

In fact, Chapman, whose district included Jekyll Island, had sponsored a failed bill that would have banned construction of any new permanent resi-

Mindy and David Egan founded the Initiative to Protect Jekyll Island, a citizens' group that fought overdevelopment and sought to protect the island's fragile environment. (Courtesy of Mindy Egan)

dences. The bill was in response to a survey of more than five thousand visitors, many of whom opposed the 277 proposed new condominiums. Because the condos would be privately owned, Chapman and others feared they would not be used for vacation rentals as intended.[4]

During a telephone interview, Chapman contended that statements about not renewing the leases were combative and threatening toward citizens. He clarified his own position concerning existing leases, which he believed should be honored. While he recognized that it was within the authority's power not to renew the leases, he made it clear that he did not support such an outcome. Speaking at an authority meeting, island resident Mindy Egan called the threatened lease action "payback" for residents' opposition to the authority's development plans and added, "I'm so proud there were so many who spoke out against the authority in spite of the intimidating statements that their leases might not be renewed."[5]

In an April 24, 2008, conference call, the authority's Finance Committee discussed the issue of hiring the Bleakly Advisory Group to conduct a financial analysis to exam the issue further. By December the decision had been made, and the Bleakly study was underway. The firm's preliminary results suggested that, compared to similar properties elsewhere, residents should be paying $120,000 to $280,000 per year to lease the land on which their houses were located, considerably more than Pearson had suggested. The same study indicated that Jekyll's hotel properties should be paying the authority

Bob Krueger (fourth from right) replaced Ben Porter (at far right) as chair of the Jekyll Island Authority before a decision on the residential leases was made. Porter chaired the authority during one of its most tumultuous periods. (Courtesy of Mosaic, Jekyll Island Museum)

$48,000 to $72,000 annually to achieve fair rates. Explaining the curious discrepancy in the numbers, Gary Mongeon, vice president and project director for Bleakly, contended that "home lots, which are usually a quarter acre, can sometimes be worth more on a per-acre basis than commercial property, because they can be sold in smaller units." Skip Adamson, a real estate agent on Jekyll, argued that "[t]here's no way a homeowner can afford that kind of rent on top of their house mortgage." While some owners used their homes as vacation rentals, earning as much as $20,000 per year, the authority did not collect a percentage of those rental fees. Residents were open to the idea of restructuring their leases, but they seriously questioned whether Bleakly's calculations were sound.[6]

On February 9, 2009, Mongeon told the authority that the study was still in its very early stages and that he needed more time to investigate the issue before making recommendations. "Finding out the leases were far below value isn't news," Jones Hooks commented. "Leases need to be modified and this is a healthy process that we are undertaking. We are looking at all ideas right now." Bob Krueger, now the JIA chair, noted that "[t]his is an issue that concerns our residents. It's only fair that we hear what they have to say."[7]

Nevertheless, something needed to be done. This became even clearer when, nine days later, the Jekyll Island Oversight Committee, led by Senator Tommie Williams (R-Lyons), sponsored Senate Bill 161, which would ensure that Jekyll leases be brought in line with fair market values. Krueger, still concerned about residents' reactions, indicated that the authority would continue to examine the issue and would seek to "bring the agreements to fair market value without penalizing residents of the island."[8]

Two important time concerns complicated the lease matter: the looming deadline beyond which thirty-year mortgages could no longer be financed, and the scheduled expiration of the leases in 2049. Mindy Egan tried to be optimistic and indicated that she was holding out hope that the authority

A Scrawls cartoon urging the JIA to "do the right thing." (Courtesy of Janet Rawls)

would do the right thing. Joe Iannicelli, a homeowner on the south end of the island, was more pessimistic, commenting that "[t]his whole project of redevelopment and revitalization is a plot, a way for the governor to sell Jekyll Island to private developers." Eric Garvey, Jekyll's marketing director, rebutted that, saying, "If we didn't want citizens on Jekyll, we wouldn't even look at this issue."[9]

When the Bleakly Advisory Group set out to conduct its yearlong study, the lease policy had not been updated since the 1960s. Bleakly's recommendations called not only for new residential lease policies on Jekyll but also for not renewing leases at all for some houses. Some homeowners worried that the lease issue was retribution for their opposition to authority plans for a $352 million hotel and a new condominium project. Frank Mirasola, president of the Jekyll Island Citizens Association, said, "Not renewing leases was an inappropriate option meant to terrorize residents. You have [more than] 600 houses here on the island. What's the state going to do with all these houses? Bulldoze them? Buy people out?"[10]

Residences in one particular part of the island were under scrutiny—the homes in the St. Andrews subdivision on the ecologically sensitive south end. Mirasola contended that the HB 214 bill that ensured Jekyll leases with fair market values had been twisted by some to say that nobody should live on the south end, but he argued against that interpretation: "What it really does in essence is to grandfather in everything on the south end and say it can be replaced, but only in kind." For many citizens, a home on Jekyll was the largest part of their estate, and cancelling a lease would have a life-changing effect. Authority project manager Jim Broadwell tried to calm the waters, pointing out that "reexamining leases is just one part of the island's revitalization plans and residents shouldn't read too much into the questions being asked."[11]

After a full year of studying the complex lease issues and analyzing property payment values on the island compared to similar residences in Glynn County, Gary Mongeon reached the conclusion that residents who leased property on the interior of the island paid about the same home value as residents of St. Simons Island. Residents living on beach or waterfront property, however, paid significantly less. Eric Garvey took note: "This is something that needs to be changed . . . as we progress with the structure of residential lease renewals."[12]

It was critical that the authority decide on the controversial issue in the very near future, and it was apparent to everyone that if the leases were renewed, they would have to be adjusted. The authority decided to delay action until the Bleakly Group had made its final recommendations. At that point, the board planned to convene with legal counsel to determine whether such actions were feasible and sensible.

By this time, the Bleakly Group had concluded that its preliminary recommendations for lease increases were too high. Instead, the firm examined strategies to lure homeowners to renew leases under terms that would increase payments gradually from the current average of $350 per year. "We're looking for a formula that provides some equity," said Mongeon, "one that brings us closer to market value, but doesn't destroy property values and isn't so regressive that people opt not to renew their leases." These new ideas changed the tone of the discussions between residents and the authority. Frank Mirasola expressed his reaction: "My personal feeling is the presentation did a good job of pulling the facts together. The bottom line is it will be up to the authority to decide what to do."[13]

Some residents were not happy about there being any tinkering at all. Gil McLemore, a Jekyll Island leaseholder since 1972, opposed any change in the leases, arguing that "[r]esidents already pay too much in government fees." He added, "It was the state's deal, and the state's price, under the state's terms," referring to the lease agreement established in the 1950s.[14]

Under Bleakly's proposal, leaseholders could continue their present ninety-nine-year lease until 2049 without an increase in what they were paying. However, any new leases would fall under new rules that would include a lease value of .5 percent of the fair market value of the property adjusted against a consumer price index of 3.85 percent every five years, which was the cumulative average over the last fifty years. Mongeon said, "It's necessary to have a mechanism in place to adjust leases. We're tying the lease pattern to the market." The problem was not with the original leases established, he contended, but with "the lack of any periodic adjustment," which had been costly to the authority.[15]

In the end, the JIA and the Bleakly Group tested the waters with several lease options. One option allowed leaseholders to continue their present leases until 2049 with no increase. However, what would happen after 2049 was uncertain. Residents worried that the authority was trying to coerce them into signing into a new, costlier deal by suggesting they could be in jeopardy of losing their property rights if they waited until 2049, the end of the current lease period. "What will happen to my lease option in 2049?" asked Mark Lichtenstein. The JIA board said the state could even elect to eliminate all private residents—if it wanted to.[16]

After months of meeting with Jekyll Island residents, conducting peer reviews, and meeting with Ken Bleakly, president of the Bleakly Advisory Group, the authority was finally ready to decide the issue and planned to vote on it at the next board meeting. "We need to make sure residential leases are kept simple, equitable, and affordable," said board member Mike Hodges. "We will base whatever fees we charge on land evaluations only, and those will be made by the county."[17]

On November 9, 2009, Jones Hooks revealed the proposed new lease options. Despite all the months of distrust of the authority, residents were pleasantly surprised. Hooks stated the four main points: keep it simple; make it equitable; assure affordability; and base fees on land valuations. Starting from there, he discussed the new lease options, which would be offered for a twelve-month period and would begin in 2011. All leases would extend to 2089. For leaseholders who converted their existing leases within the twelve-month period, the lease rate of four-tenths of 1 percent (0.4 percent) of land, as determined by the Glynn County tax assessor, would apply.[18]

On January 26, 2010, the authority unanimously adopted the new lease agreement. At an open meeting on April 19, the terms were disclosed to the public. Jekyll citizens finally had some clarity about how much they would pay annually for their residential leases. "If a person chooses to do nothing, they will [after 2049] no longer have a leasehold interest or the right to occupy that property of land," said Eric Garvey, marketing director and spokesperson for the authority.[19]

On April 20, 2010, the authority delivered lease agreements both by mail and by email to all single-family homeowners as well as to multifamily building owners on Jekyll Island. Whereas in 2010, under the old system, the authority's income from leases was only about $209,000, if all homeowners were to convert to the new lease agreement by the end of the year, the authority would receive approximately $328,000 in 2011, followed by annual assessments based on the new formula.

The deadline for signing the new leases was set for September 1, 2010, to give the authority enough time to process the leases and have them in place by January 1, 2011. Homeowner Frank Mirasola said, "The good news is that they finally got the lease corrected. . . . It's as good an offer as we're going to get. The bad news is I hope I can get it done in time." Board members acknowledged the time crunch and said the staff was moving as fast as possible to finish the leases.[20]

As it turned out, the new agreement was, by and large, a huge success, with approximately 98 percent of leaseholders signing the new lease. Only thirteen homeowners refused to sign and clung to the leases that expire in 2049. "It has been, in some cases, a rocky road, but we have gotten there," said Gary Mongeon.[21] At long last, one of the island's most serious problems and major controversies had been settled to almost everyone's satisfaction.

This aerial view of the north end of Jekyll suggests how small the island really is. (Shutterstock)

MARSH, LAND, ENVIRONMENTALISM & OTHER CONTROVERSIES 14

Great strides have been made on Jekyll Island in the last quarter century—some examples being the revitalization of the island, the establishment in 1999 of a new Jekyll Island Foundation to raise funds for various projects, and the building of the popular Georgia Sea Turtle Center. However, a series of disputes characterized the first two decades of this century. As the Jekyll Island Authority began its plans in 2009 for both revitalization and a new master plan, it consulted the engineering firm of Thomas & Hutton to determine how much land, if any, could still be used for development, to ensure that it did not exceed the 35 percent limit established by law. In January 2009, Bill Foster, project manager for Thomas & Hutton, informed the JIA that it had about fifty-five acres left to work with before it exceeded the legal limit. Foster, who utilized LIDAR (light detection and ranging) technology, announced that, by his calculations, the total area of Jekyll Island was 4,125 acres, and that 1,397 acres, or 33.66 percent of the island's land area, had been developed. A month earlier, however, a University of Georgia student's doctoral thesis had suggested that the 35 percent development limit on Jekyll had already been breached. Unlike Thomas & Hutton, however, the student had used a mean high tide figure of seven feet. Such discrepancies in methods of determining the landmass of the island would set off another lengthy brouhaha.[1]

Jekyll's 1996 master plan had defined developed land to include paved roads and rights-of-way, bike paths, and golf courses, as well as lakes and ponds for recreation. Even so, and given the recent contradictory conclusions about the percentage of land that had been developed, the JIA wanted an additional study of the matter. As it prepared in 2010 to update the Jekyll master plan in accordance with state law, the authority appointed seven task forces to take up a variety of issues. The most controversial of these would prove to be the 65/35 Task Force, named for the state law requiring that 65 percent of land on the island remain undeveloped. That task force was charged with determining how much land, if any, might still be open for development on Jekyll.

Definitions of what constituted developed and undeveloped land were debatable, and task force members did not always agree. They were unsure how to help create a new master plan with so much uncertainty. Should golf courses, which are man-made and artificial, be considered developed land, as the

The 65/35 Task Force struggled with the question of whether golf courses should be considered "developed" land or wildlife habitat. (Courtesy of the Jekyll Island Authority)

earlier master plan had indicated? "Frankly, these are constructed wetlands," said Keren Giovengo, a program planner for the University of Georgia Extension Service. JIA members contended that the golf courses, while artificial, also provided an important area for wildlife, such as alligators and freshwater turtles. "From the standpoint of the Jekyll Island conservation plan, the golf course is a very important area," said Ben Carswell, the JIA conservation manager and the main author of the JIA conservation plan. Task force members also had questions about dirt roads, man-made ponds, and parcels of land that had been cleared but not used for construction. Above all, what about marshes? Pierre Howard, president of the Georgia Conservancy, stated his opinion quite simply: "Marsh is not land. I think it's regrettable that someone now would seek to change the deal and make it appear that marsh is land."[2]

Over several months, members of the 65/35 Task Force continued to discuss how to keep the island in compliance with the state law mandating limited development, but without making their final conclusions. At a meeting in July 2012, they agreed to use a National Oceanic and Atmospheric Administration standard on the eastern shore between Clam Creek and Beach Creek. The task force also chose to use LIDAR data to measure the marsh side of the island, but the group remained indecisive about whether to include inland marshes, the swampy areas between the east and west shores of the island, in Jekyll's landmass.[3] The task force spent more than a year debating the issue before concluding that if an area cannot be leased, subdivided, or sold, it cannot be land, thus discounting marsh when measuring the island's landmass.

This last decision essentially decreased the island's total land area from the measurement used in the master plan of 1996, putting the authority over its developable limit by three percentage points. The authority, however, disputed the task force's conclusion and claimed that the recommendations of the task force were not in compliance with Georgia law. According to John Hunter, the director of historic resources at Jekyll Island, the members of the task force "established their own interpretation." The authority argued that they were wrong and that the amount of land that had already been developed was only 32 percent. Task force members had counted total island land as 3,817 acres, while the authority now claimed it was 5,543 acres.[4]

In late April 2013, the controversy escalated when the authority reached out to the state attorney general and asked him to review the task force's findings. It was not until late June that Attorney General Sam Olens announced his nonbinding opinion that the Jekyll Island Authority must continue to include marsh above mean high tide in calculating the land that could be developed. In short, he indicated that to eliminate all marsh calculations from land definitions would not be "in compliance" with state law. Olens's opinion was contrary to the hopes of both environmentalists and the task force working on the new master plan. Given the attorney general's ruling, the Jekyll Island Authority

For several years the JIA debated the question "What is land?" and whether it included marsh areas. (Scrawls cartoon, courtesy of Janet Rawls)

was about 100 acres under the development limit, rather than 136 acres *over* the limit as the task force had concluded. "If marsh can be counted as land, then that has major implications in terms of how far development can go," asserted David Egan, cofounder of the Initiative to Protect Jekyll Island.[5]

Pierre Howard, president of the Georgia Conservancy, did not consider Olens's opinion to be the final word, contending that "[u]ltimately only the courts can interpret the law with full force and effect." Olens did not disagree with Howard, writing to Jones Hooks that "[i]f the authority has any plans to substantially increase the island's measured land area above mean high tide, such a proposal should be thoroughly evaluated in a public process, and no final action should be taken until the General Assembly has the opportunity to act on it."[6]

Those involved in the master planning process as well as state environmental groups alleged a lack of transparency on the part of the authority, especially after it had so quietly sent the task force's recommendations to the attorney general's office seeking legal advice. In an open letter, Brenda Costain, a member of a separate recreational planning task force, called the authority "reprehensible" for ignoring the recommendations of the 65/35 Task Force. The Georgia Conservancy said, "It is patently obvious that because the island is actually beyond the 35 percent statutory limit and because the Jekyll Island Authority wants to develop beyond, they are continuing to count marsh as land in order to achieve their development goals." While the JIA maintained that marsh should be counted as land by precedent, task force members argued that prior master plans were inaccurate and that counting marsh as land "could create a dangerous precedent for development along the Georgia coast."[7] What seemed to cause the most outcry was the authority's response to and rejection of the finding of a task force it had appointed. The matter was far from settled.

David Egan of the Initiative to Protect Jekyll Island said, "I think what we need to do is go back to the original legislation . . . and find out what the law intended at that time." In 1971, Rep. Michael Egan (R-Sandy Springs), who had worked with Rep. Reid Harris (D-St. Simons), the principal author of the Coastal Marshland Protection Act, sent a letter to the JIA executive director in which he wrote that "two-thirds of the land and all of the marshes will be left in their natural states," implying that marshes and land are two separate entities.[8] Rep. Egan thought that legislators had "made it clear in the act, but I guess we did not. . . . I just think that land is dry land, not marsh."[9]

In a late morning workshop on the Jekyll Island master plan in mid-July 2013, JIA board member Buddy DeLoach suggested an alternative: If acreage were used as part of the determining factor, it could end the need for basing development on the legally mandated 35 percent of the island. Acreage would fall within the 35 percent limit. It was a breakthrough that solved some of the problems, because it was the percentage standard for measuring the island that had caused turmoil among the people who were trying to complete the Jekyll master plan. Steve Caley, a senior lawyer at the Atlanta environmental firm GreenLaw, agreed that setting acreage as the measure could be a solution. David Egan seemed to concur, saying that "this fixed acreage idea does have appeal." When JIA board member Bob Krueger remarked that the board did not have any plan to develop any land outside its existing footprint (with the qualifier that the authority might need "100 acres in our pocket in case something happens"), his statement drew a favorable reaction.[10]

John Hunter worked at Jekyll Island for fifteen years, from February 2000 to July 2015, serving as chief curator and assistant director of historic resources for four years before being promoted to director of historic resources. (Courtesy of John Hunter)

In mid-September, the authority agreed to set aside sixty-five or more additional acres for future development, with forty-six of those to be restricted to uses of health, public safety, and recreation. Krueger indicated that he would prefer to set aside a minimum of seventy acres for future development, out of caution: "Who knows down the road? We're locked in and something could happen." JIA secretary Mike Hodges reminded Jones Hooks that such action would bind future authorities for a "very long time." Hooks conceded that Hodges might be right, but he contended that "[t]he greatest asset of the island is the natural beauty" and that the authority had the responsibility to protect and preserve Jekyll's natural areas. The board agreed that the additional undeveloped acreage would become part of the master plan. John Hunter, the island's director of historic resources, recommended setting aside only forty-two acres for development and twelve acres for expanding the island's popular campground, with the remaining acreage to be used for the expansion of the water and sewer system and for clearing approaches to the airport.[11]

The new numbers, which would be incorporated into a draft of the island's revised master plan, would be the first step toward establishing the firm acreage that could be developed on the state-owned barrier island. Because it believed that the percentage of already developed land fell below 35 percent, the Jekyll Island Authority sought legislation, as Attorney General Olens had recommended, to drop the percentage requirement and establish a substitute set of numbers of acres.

But until a legislative bill could be passed, the squabble would continue. Steve Caley of Greenlaw saw the acreage limitation as "a step in the right direction," though he agreed with conservationists' contention that the authority had already developed more land than was allowed under the limiting law. "Any increase further violates the statute," he asserted. David Kyler, executive

Image of the 2014 master plan. (Courtesy of Mosaic, Jekyll Island Museum)

director of the Center for a Sustainable Coast, echoed Caley, saying "That's bogus" of the authority's assertion that only 29 percent of the 5,543 acres had been developed: "They're already at thirty-eight percent."[12]

In the meantime, the Jekyll Island Authority initiated the next steps with the University of Georgia's Carl Vinson Institute of Government to begin a draft of the new master plan. The master plan would define what was meant by undeveloped and developed land, as well as provide classifications and land use definitions. Lanford Holbrook of the Carl Vinson Institute led the session on planning on September 16, 2013, and it was clear that the master plan was nearly finished. At a meeting with the Jekyll Island Legislative Oversight Committee, the JIA scheduled a session for October 22 for the master plan public hearing.[13]

On April 14, 2014, Governor Nathan Deal finally signed into law two legislative bills that would end four decades of bickering over development on Jekyll Island. Together, House Bill 715 and Senate Bill 296 capped the number of acres that could be developed at 1,675, replacing the older state law that had limited development to 35 percent of the island. Governor Deal called the bills historic and noted that, of the approximately 70 acres that could still be developed, only 20 of them could be used for new residential projects; 12 acres would be used to expand the island's campground, with the rest of the acreage allotted to public projects such as trails, roads, and infrastructure projects.[14] Pierre Howard of the Georgia Conservancy praised the compromise: "This shows me people can still work together and get things done."[15]

Up to that point, only one new motel or hotel had been built on Jekyll since 1974—the Hampton Inn and Suites, which opened in 2010. It was constructed as a "green" building, sensitive to concerns like sustainability and resource efficiency and in harmony with the environment. The new hotel,

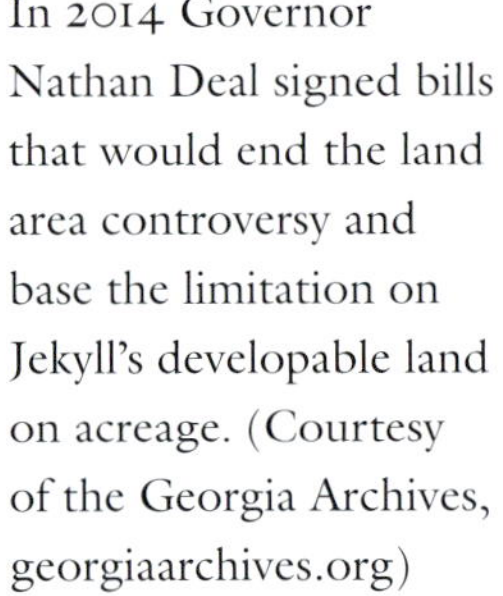

In 2014 Governor Nathan Deal signed bills that would end the land area controversy and base the limitation on Jekyll's developable land on acreage. (Courtesy of the Georgia Archives, georgiaarchives.org)

When the Hampton Inn and Suites opened in 2010, it was Jekyll Island's first new hotel in almost four decades. (Courtesy of David Curtis)

unlike all previous ones on the island, stood behind the protective dunes, which remained untouched. It would set the standard for the future building of new hotels on Jekyll Island.

With the land issue decided, one of the greatest disputes in island history had finally ended, and at last the JIA could get on with revitalization. Nevertheless, smaller disagreements would arise, such as a brief but heated controversy over Jekyll Island mail delivery. Rumors circulated that the JIA had been discussing with the U.S. Postal Service (USPS) the possibility of ending home mail delivery on the island. Concerned about a bill pending in Congress that would give the Postal Service power to end home delivery at its discretion, JIA attorney, Chris O'Donnell, told members of the Jekyll Island Citizens Association (JICA) that the island might soon lose its post office, which had been relocated to a trailer during revitalization efforts. Such a possibility upset residents, especially retirees who received their medications by mail. Jim LaPean, a JICA member, asked, "Why is the Postal Service even talking to the [authority]? This is not a state issue. This is a federal issue."[16]

Another association member, Bonnie Newell, investigated the matter and found a regulation prohibiting the Postal Service from stopping home delivery without the consent of those who would be affected. According to the rule, she said, "[c]ustomer signatures must be obtained prior to any conversion"; thus, decision-making power over whether to end mail delivery on the island belongs to residents, not the authority. In response to a *Florida Times-Union* inquiry, USPS spokesperson Stephen Seewoester denied that there had been any formal discussions with the authority but said the Postal Service would soon explore possible options for Jekyll mail service.[17] Bonnie Newell claimed that "[t]he deal was with Mr. Rawski, the postmaster of Brunswick, that if we give up our home delivery, they would build a historic post office."[18] According to an article in *The Florida Times-Union*, at some point during the discussions between the USPS and the JIA, the scope of the negotiations expanded beyond the topic of a new post office. It appeared that the Postal Service had suggested—or at least implied—that it would close the Jekyll Island post office altogether unless residents agreed to give up home delivery. But there apparently was some misunderstanding. A few weeks later, the authority sent island residents apologetic letters acknowledging that it had made a mistake. Consequently, the matter ended amicably; home mail delivery continued, and the Jekyll post office was eventually moved into the historic district.[19]

Within a few months, yet another debate about the proliferation of deer on Jekyll Island began to heat up. A 2012 analysis indicated that the island's deer population had increased between 2011 and 2012. According to Ben Carswell, director of conservation at Jekyll Island, evidence indicated that the deer population was near or exceeding biological carrying capacity—that is, the maximum population the environment could support indefinitely. He initiated a series of spotlight survey assessments in early October 2013 to determine the number of deer on the island. Carswell suggested "that a white-tail deer population control program could contribute to enhanced ecological diversity on Jekyll Island" and expressed his confidence that "such a program would not detract from the [island's] conservation goals." He recommended reducing the deer population to address the problem. However, he and the Department of Natural Resources realized that the options for managing the population could be problematic, especially on Jekyll Island, where the issue concerned many residents. The Deer Management Committee considered measures such as deer relocation, contraception and sterilization, native predator reintroduction, controlled public hunting, and sharpshooting. The committee's final recommendation was for sharpshooting, to be conducted by the USDA's Wildlife Services program.[20]

Jekyll resident Bonnie Newell was especially concerned about the post office controversy. Her husband, Steve, was also an important voice on island issues, in particular the beach lighting ordinance concerning sea turtles. (Courtesy of Bonnie Newell)

On July 21, 2014, Carswell presented the draft summary of the white-tailed deer management recommendations to the Jekyll Island Authority. His three-year study conducted with the Department of Natural Resources and the Deer Management Committee agreed that professional sharpshooters should harvest about eighty deer, with the meat

White-tailed deer were overpopulating Jekyll Island. (Courtesy of the McCash Collection)

to be donated to the White Oak Wildlife Conservation. After Carswell had finished his report, the authority allowed citizens to comment. Lisa Norton, president of Citizens for Humane Animal Treatment, along with ten other Jekyll citizens, questioned the methodologies used to count deer numbers and urged the board to reconsider alternative options, such as deer contraception. Bonnie Newell reached out to Laura Simon, a wildlife ecologist at Yale University's School of Forestry and Environmental Studies, who reviewed Carswell's documents and offered a response that cited several studies demonstrating the efficacy of deer contraceptives. To his credit, Carswell followed the science and eventually changed the island's course of action to include deer contraception.

Nearly a year after he had recommended the use of government sharpshooters to kill eighty deer, Carswell decided to delay any hunting to thin the herd. Even though the Jekyll Island Club had been founded primarily as a hunting club back in 1886, shooting deer on the island was not a popular solution. Instead, the authority voted to spend $150,000 on a four-year study to be conducted by the University of Georgia to determine the effect deer have on the island vegetation.[21] Wildlife conservation would continue to be a priority, though balancing the flora and fauna could become a serious problem if the deer continued to proliferate. A second study agreed that there were too many deer on Jekyll Island—as many as 95 to 196 deer per square mile. However, Carswell concluded that it was not an extremely urgent issue: "I don't feel like we're being cruel to the animals by letting nature . . . take its course in this case."[22] And it seemed that nature *had* begun to take its course when bobcat tracks began to be spotted on the island as early as 2014. Bobcats, which are natural predators for white-tailed deer, had apparently wandered onto the island from the mainland.[23]

Lighting ordinances protect the sea turtles who lay their eggs on the island, as well as the vulnerable sea turtle hatchlings. (Photo by the author)

One other long-standing issue needed to be addressed, but it was less a controversy than a concern that gained traction with the opening of the Georgia Sea Turtle Center in 2007, which had in turn increased interest in protecting the turtles and luring them back to Jekyll Island. Authority members shared their worries about the decrease in the populations of sea turtles, especially the loggerhead turtles that commonly laid their eggs on the Georgia coastal islands. For decades, people had walked on the beach at night with flashlights, beachside hotels had bright signage, and beach pavilions were lit up. In the summer of 2009, however, the Jekyll Island Authority passed an improved "sea turtle friendly" lighting ordinance to keep the threatened loggerhead sea turtles and their hatchlings from being disoriented by artificial light and losing their way back to the sea. "Basically, the new ordinance means we're doing it the right way now," said biologist Steve Newell. It was an important step in helping visitors to understand why regulating lighting along the beaches was so important for turtle nesting.[24] On March 30, 2009, hundreds had watched and cheered as the staff of the Georgia Sea Turtle Center released four turtles back into the ocean on the Jekyll Island beach.[25]

By 2015, the artificial light problem had not been fully resolved. At that point, the Department of Natural Resources, Ben Carswell, and Katie Mascovich, a graduate student and research assistant, did a study on the effect of the 2009 lighting ordinance on the island. They found that sea turtles were now nesting in record numbers all along Jekyll's beaches, except for one spot—in front of the new Westin Hotel. Although it was early in the nesting season, there were already 111 turtle nests on the island. However, it appeared that the Westin was not in compliance with the recent lighting ordinance. Another lighting survey in May 2015 by biologist Mark Dodd confirmed that the Westin Hotel was noncompliant with the ordinance on ten issues. But the Westin was not the only problem. The Holiday Inn had eight ordinance violations, the Days Inn had five, and the Beach Club had two. Dodd pointed out that compliance with the lighting ordinance was "particularly crucial at this time of the year when turtles come in from the sea to nest and when eggs laid early in the season are about to hatch." According to the ordinance, violations were to be corrected within ten days of notification. Failure to remedy all issues could potentially result in forfeiture of the violator's lease.[26]

By August 2015 most of the violations had been resolved, though a few problems persisted at various hotels, at the Great Dunes Pavilion, and with streetlamps located along North Beachview Drive. Carswell and Mascovich planned to continue tracking the issue until all violations were resolved. Overall, the ordinance is working well, and turtle nests on Jekyll Island have continued to increase. "Making our beaches safe for both turtles and people is incredibly important to the JIA," said the island's executive director, Jones Hooks. "We take the beach lighting very seriously and have one of the strictest lighting ordinances along the Atlantic coast."[27]

The latest but probably not the last controversy began on September 19, 2023, when the Jekyll Island Authority notified shop owners along Pier Road in the historic district that their leases would not be renewed for 2024. The business owners were given until December 31 to liquidate and vacate the premises, though no other retail space was currently available on the island. Some shop owners had been in operation for almost a quarter of a century and were now at risk of losing their businesses altogether, and they were deeply upset by the situation. Juliana Germano, owner of two of the shops, indicated to the authority that she was "shocked and devastated" by the news.[28] Following a petition and protests, the shops were given a lease extension until after Labor Day 2024. The authority indicated that it had other plans for the small buildings, which in the club era had housed club workers or provided other services. The JIA board discussed these plans at a meeting on January 16, 2024. The vacated shops would become part of a "Lost Trail" connecting them to the old infirmary (now a "merchandise shop" for the *31•81* magazine published by the authority). The shops would be converted to "a beer garden with a stage, an ice cream and candy store, a year-round Christmas store, a coffee shop, and a living history exhibit that will be an extension of the Mosaic museum."[29]

TOP Sea turtle hatchlings that are lucky enough to avoid waiting predators, such as sea birds, make their way as quickly as they can to the ocean. (Shutterstock)

BOTTOM The shops on Pier Road were operated by independent business owners until 2024. (Photo by the author)

While some of the controversies and problems Jekyll has experienced have clearly been more important than others in shaping the island's future, questions about the JIA's plans and actions persist and will most likely continue to do so. Disagreements will no doubt arise from time to time, given the various interests the authority must serve—among them residents and business owners; tourists, with their need for lodging, shopping, and dining; environmentalists; and those who are concerned about the preservation and interpretation of historical sites. The Jekyll Island Authority's stewardship of an island as diverse and complex as Jekyll, where the authority must address so many interests, will no doubt never please everyone. However, in recent years, there seems for the most part to have been greater clarity and harmony among the expectations and efforts of all concerned. Since the island's revitalization and the recent celebration of its seventy-five years under state ownership, the waters seem to have calmed somewhat. Under the stable leadership of Jones Hooks, the most serious issues seem to have been resolved. Whether that will continue to be true in the future remains to be seen.

The new Jekyll village, a remarkable contrast to the old village and far more inviting, is essentially complete. (Photo by the author)

CONCLUSION

Despite all the controversies, especially those over revitalization and the new master plan, it seems that Jekyll Island has finally reached a period of stability, leading to a virtual rebirth of the island. Consequently, Jekyll has in recent years experienced significant growth in facilities and tourism. Currently, it attracts and accommodates more than three million visitors each year.

Revitalization is essentially complete. The former 4-H learning center was not moved but rather was rebuilt and enlarged. It reopened in 2016 as the top-notch $17 million Camp Jekyll. In addition, an expansion of the Jekyll Island Campground to add fifty-six new campsites is underway. The island's infrastructure now includes new hotels in different price ranges to accommodate visitors of various income levels, and the Jekyll village is thriving, as is the restored historic district. The Georgia Sea Turtle Center and the Mosaic museum draw many visitors. And the beloved south end of the island has been preserved and is better interpreted. While many important changes and developments have occurred on Jekyll in recent years, and many new and improved facilities have been added, the island has remained true to its conservation goals, maintaining large expanses of undeveloped areas teeming with wildlife. Along with beachgoers and sightseers, the island also attracts large numbers of environmentalists and bird-watchers.

The revitalized island has won a significant number of awards, as well as recognition in such magazines as *Travel and Leisure* and *Southern Living* as one of the best places to visit in the United States. The successful revitalization came at a cost of $195 million.[1] On November 16, 2015, Governor Nathan Deal was on hand to celebrate the rededication of Jekyll Island. "Look how far we've come," Deal said. "Some 60-plus years after Georgia first proposed opening up Jekyll Island to all its residents, we've come full circle, and it all looks wonderful." JIA Executive Director Jones Hooks commented that the "big, big, big projects have been completed. There's more to be done, but it's time to stop and celebrate with friends."[2] Since then, a great deal more work *has* been done.

In recent years there also have been far fewer controversies, as the JIA has made an increased effort to listen, take into consideration the concerns of others, and better communicate with those it serves. For example, in the

LEFT The 4-H learning center was rebuilt and reopened as Camp Jekyll. (Photo by the author)

RIGHT The campground expansion is underway. (Photo by the author)

OPPOSITE The Jekyll Island Airport, unsuitable for commercial flights, is used by private planes and for scenic tours. Plans to enlarge and update it so that it can accommodate larger aircraft are under consideration. (Photo by the author)

spring of 2023, the authority became aware of unfounded rumors circulating about plans for a new airport terminal, which the JIA had considered "as a result of island revitalization and increased visitation, and the need to serve those traveling via air with a larger, ADA-compliant terminal." Although the updating of the airport has been delayed as a result of insufficient funding for the type and quality of the facility the authority is seeking, the JIA felt it helpful to issue to the island's citizens a full explanation of what had occurred and why, in order to quell "the spread of misinformation . . . and give a clear understanding of how the JIA manages the operations of its airport."[3] The authority seems to have learned that the more information citizens have about the reasons and deliberations behind its decisions, the better they might understand why certain changes are being made. The JIA does not always please everyone and probably never will, for its task is complex. But there is no doubt that today's JIA strives to do what is in the best interest of the island.

Although the airport has not yet been updated, revitalization has brought about many important changes. The JIA has added new structures such as hotels and the village that surrounds them. It has commissioned archaeologists to determine whether historical artifacts are hidden belowground in the historic district and to identify other potential archaeological sites on the island. The authority has taken advantage of a state-issued general obligation bond of $1.6 million to enhance disability access at multiple places on the island. After earlier criticism on the matter, the JIA not only worked to improve beach access for the disabled in compliance with the Americans with Disabilities Act (ADA), but it also claimed that it wanted to "go beyond beach access" with ADA requirements.[4] The authority created an impressive Georgia Sea Turtle Center, which has rescued and rehabilitated turtles along the Georgia coast and from as far away as New England. More recently the JIA has restructured the Jekyll Island Museum, now called Mosaic, a project that received substantial

N421AP

The JIA has completed its efforts to make the beaches ADA compliant. (Photo by the author)

The new Mosaic Museum opened in 2019. (Photo by the author)

funding from the Jekyll Island Foundation, the Woodruff Foundation, and other important donors to surpass its goal of $3.134 million.

There have also been new efforts in recent years to tell the story of Black Americans on the island, such as through improved signage at the south end and the restoration and preservation of the St. Andrews Beach Pavilion within the new Camp Jekyll. Another important recent project at the south end is the revamped *Wanderer* exhibit, which tells the story of the enslaved Africans who were illegally landed on Jekyll Island in 1858. The exhibit, entitled "A Memory Trail: The Story of the Survivors of the Slave Ship *Wanderer* Through a Family Learning Experience," has been recognized by UNESCO as a "Site of Memory."

Additional planned projects have been completed or are now underway on the island. One recent project is the Mercer Medical Clinic, which opened in 2023 in the Jekyll village to provide needed services for residents and visitors.

The exhibit "A Memory Trail: The Story of the Survivors of the Slave Ship *Wanderer* Through a Family Learning Experience" has been recognized by UNESCO as a Site of Memory. (Photo by the author)

Another is the JIA's golf improvement plan, which will reduce the island's total number of holes by nine but will improve the golf facilities overall and add nine holes to the historic Great Dunes course. The first phase of the golf improvement plan was celebrated October 30–November 1, 2024, when the redesigned Pine Lakes course hosted the fifth annual Paulk Cup Classic, named for the course's longtime golf pro Johnny Paulk, who cofounded the Georgia-Florida Golf Classic more than forty years ago. A third project that has come to fruition is the new Public Safety Complex, which held its grand opening on October 28, 2024. It will provide facilities for the Jekyll Island Fire Department, including sleeping quarters for firefighters on duty, as well as for the Georgia State Patrol. At the time of this writing, work is under way to enlarge the campground space and improve facilities for campers. The authority has also broken ground at the site of the former Buccaneer Motel for the construction of another twenty-four cottages, a subdivision to be called Seaside Retreat.

Not surprisingly, Jones Hooks, with his many accomplishments as executive director of the Jekyll Island Authority, was recognized with Leadership Georgia's Frederick B. Kerr Service Award in recognition of his dedicated service to the state and support of the organization. The Georgia House of

The new public safety building under construction. (Photo by the author)

Implementation of the recommendations of the authority's golf improvement plan is well underway. (Photo by the author)

In March 2023 the Georgia House of Representatives passed a resolution commending JIA Executive Director Jones Hooks (second from right) for his success at Jekyll Island. Hooks's wife, Stephanie (fourth from right), joined him for the presentation. (Courtesy of the Jekyll Island Authority)

Representatives has also recognized his work with a resolution applauding his "outstanding public service and outstanding stewardship and commitments to revitalize, retain, and protect" Jekyll Island.[5] There is no denying his success. When Hooks became the island's executive director in 2008, the JIA budget had been $15.5 million. By 2021, it had more than doubled to $30,428,000, thus enabling many of the improvements discussed here. The proposed budget for 2024, determined before Hooks left his position as Jekyll's executive director, was $41 million.[6]

Remarkably, partisan politics and disagreements between state officials over issues at Jekyll Island have subsided in recent years. Most Georgia politicians have apparently realized that, under strong leadership, and with good visitation numbers and an ability to meet its budget, Jekyll Island is finally a self-supporting and successful state entity, and so they have decided to "let them roll."[7] After fifteen years as executive director, the longest term of anyone in that position on Jekyll Island, Jones Hooks announced his retirement effective June 30, 2023.

While there has been much to praise in recent years, questions remain about the future of the island, and new problems and disputes will no doubt arise. The greatest challenge the island will face is that of climate change and the rising sea levels and increasing frequency and strength of storms it brings. Additionally, even though environmentalists won the fight for the south

Mark Williams, formerly Georgia's commissioner of natural resources, has been the executive director of the Jekyll Island Authority since July 2023. (Courtesy of Mosaic, Jekyll Island Museum)

end, pressure from developers and even politicians may well resurface in the future. At this juncture, it seems improbable that privatization will take over whole parts of the island, but over time there may be a push for more high-end development.

Since the 1970s, several successful public-private partnerships and consultants have helped to shape the island in important ways, for better or worse. However, throughout Jekyll Island State Park's history, there have been key people who helped to "save the island," among them political figures from the 1940s like M. E. Thompson and, more recently, State Senator Jeff Chapman, preservationists such as Larry Evans and Vance Hughes, conservationists such as David and Mindy Egan, the Jekyll Island Citizens Association, and past Executive Directors Jones Hooks, Bill Donohue, and George Chambliss and other JIA board members and staffers, as well as many other activists and environmentalists.

The person hired to succeed Jones Hooks, Mark Williams, became executive director on July 1, 2023, and has been carrying on the good work. He came to the job with important experience, having served on the Jekyll Island Authority board of directors for thirteen years by virtue of his role as the state's commissioner of natural resources. The first dispute made public under his administration was that concerning the shops on Pier Road. It will probably not be the last, and he will undoubtedly face future challenges.

Perhaps the most difficult challenge for the future of Jekyll Island is sustainability amid the growing threat of climate change. As early as 1944–1945, while Sea Island was overseeing Jekyll during World War II, Jim Compton was concerned about erosion of the beach and the golf course. On June 20, 1962, *The Brunswick News* headline was "Ocean Chews Up Beach, Seawall Erection Rushed." The seawall referred to in the article only exacerbated the problem. When there was another major erosion event two years later, the situation became even more critical.[8] Only eight months after that, in September 1964, Hurricane Dora, the most damaging hurricane to hit Jekyll Island since the state park opened, brought additional damage, not only to the beaches but to the trees and hotels as well. Peppermint Land, a beachfront amusement park, was virtually destroyed by high winds that toppled its Ferris wheel. After the hurricane, President Lyndon Johnson visited Georgia and offered large revetment rocks to help protect the island. Islanders dubbed them "Johnson rocks," but even rocks did not stop the erosion.

On December 1, 1972, Horace Caldwell notified Governor Jimmy Carter that the unprotected three miles of Driftwood Beach had recently lost more than 1,500 trees. Caldwell wrote, "The Corps of Engineers estimate that it will continue to lose . . . approximately eight feet of land per year." At that time, extremely high tides broke over the beach into the Clam Creek marsh. On January 9, 1974, the ocean sloshed a few feet beyond the high-water mark.[9] Driftwood Beach at the north end of the island continues to suffer from high tides and erosion.

By the 1980s, there was more understanding and awareness about the crisis of beach erosion. Already, Georgia's barrier islands have been designated as having "critical erosion problems." The bad news is that sea levels continue to rise, and coastal erosion is likely to get even worse in the future. The problem on Jekyll's north end is complicated by earlier building so close to the shore. In subsequent years, anyone concerned with coastal issues has recognized that sea walls generally make beaches steeper, which means that visitors have less recreational beach area.[10] Efforts to rebuild the dunes wherever possible are well evident on the island, and more recent building projects have left the dunes undisturbed or are helping to restore them. However, for some parts of the island, notably those near the north end developments, it appears to be too late.

Another perennial problem is the dredging of St. Simons Sound, which contributes significantly to the erosion of Driftwood Beach and the rest of Jekyll's north end. Ever since World War II, the dredging of shipping channels

Erosion at Driftwood Beach on the north end of the island is particularly severe. (Shutterstock)

has been a serious issue. As Brunswick has become a more important port, and because of the increasing weight of large carriers, more dredging has been done to dig deeper channels. The large cargo ships are crucial for jobs in Brunswick, but in September 2019, the *Golden Ray* cargo ship capsized in St. Simons Sound due to incorrect calculations about the vessel's stability. Investigators also found that two watertight doors had been left open, which caused the ship to flood after it capsized. Four of the ship's crew members were trapped inside for over thirty hours. The shipwreck resulted in more than $200 million in damage. The subsequent removal of the wrecked ship was a difficult and complicated operation, taking almost three years and requiring more than three million man-hours, with the cost estimated to be in excess of $840 million, making it the most expensive shipwreck in U.S. history. The 656-foot cargo ship was carrying 4,100 vehicles when it capsized. Despite measures to avoid oil slicks, oil residue washed onto the beaches and into the marsh and Clam Creek. While there may not be another disastrous cargo ship accident so close to the island, pollution of the oceans will continue to be a potential issue.[11]

There is always the possibility, even the probability, of future hurricanes. Over the last several decades, Jekyll Island has not experienced a Category 4 or 5 hurricane. The so-called "Georgia Bight" has prevented devasting storms for many years, but there is always the risk of a direct hit by a major hurricane. Such an occurrence could be devastating—"it would change the landscape forever," according to Jones Hooks. One scenario is that Jekyll Island might break up into three smaller islands. In the JIA 2020 Conservation

The *Golden Ray* cargo ship capsized in St. Simons Sound in September 2019. (Photo by the author)

Despite its history of problems and controversies, Jekyll Island has become one of the most beautiful and best-loved state parks in Georgia. The majority of the island remains undeveloped today. (Courtesy of the Jekyll Island Authority)

Plan, there is a stated recognition that "[s]ea-level rise will radically redefine the coastline of the 21st century" and that coastal regions "will see significant changes to coastal flooding regimes, which poses a major risk to the safety and sustainability of coastal communities worldwide." In recent years, following brushes from Hurricanes Matthew and Irma, the authority has established useful policies and operations to be implemented in the event of another major storm.

One important advantage is that Jekyll Island is now at last self-sufficient. The increased budget for the island includes funds for such things as a conservation department and investment in the reforestation of live oak trees. Additionally, cultural resources staff members have identified archaeological sites ranging from the Middle Archaic period to the Mississippian period that are still to be explored.

When asked about his concerns for the future, Hooks said, "It goes back to preserving the nature of Jekyll Island. That's why we do reforestation. That's why we spend for future conservation."[12] The Jekyll Island Authority's mission statement articulates this succinctly: "As stewards of Jekyll's past, present, and future, we're dedicated to maintaining the delicate balance between nature and humankind." One can only hope the authority will be successful and remain committed to that effort.

Numerous executive directors and JIA board members have continually sought the improvement and success of Jekyll Island, and although their efforts have varied over the years, none of what they attempted or accomplished would have been possible without the vision of M. E. Thompson. Few governors are well remembered more than three-quarters of a century after their departure from office. Yet Thompson, though he served as governor for only a year and a half, is still recognized and applauded for what he considered his greatest accomplishment—the acquisition of Jekyll Island as a state park for the "plain people of Georgia." Up to now, the governing board has remained true to his vision by ensuring that the island has not become an exclusive enclave for the wealthy. Even at the outset, Thompson realized that change would be an inevitable part of the island's future. In 1947, the year he succeeded in purchasing the island, he declared on his weekly radio broadcast that "Jekyll Island, like the rest of Georgia, was left to us as a heritage in trust for our children and their children's children. It is never to be finished, but always to be improved."[13]

ACKNOWLEDGMENTS

To all those whose help I recognized in the preface, I would like once again to say thank you. Without your generosity, this book could not have been written.

There were others, of course, who helped in various capacities along the way and whose contributions I appreciate very much. I especially want to thank the archivists, who have helped to preserve and provide access to so many valuable materials: Andrea Marroquin, Faith Plazarin, Mimi Rogers, Jill Severn, Jena Jones, and so many others too numerous to name, I am profoundly grateful.

I am also grateful to those individuals and families who have shared information and photographs, especially Janet Rawls, for allowing me to use some of her late husband's incisive political cartoons; the family of Andre Steiner; Vance Hughes; David Curtis; and Harold Schaitberger.

A word of appreciation goes to Middle Tennessee State University's Department of History for generously providing funding for the indexing of the book.

Accolades go to my copyeditor, Arthur Johnson, for his thorough and careful editing of my book and his many helpful suggestions, as well as to the various staff members at the University of Georgia Press who helped throughout the publication process.

To my mother, June McCash, who passed on to me her love of Jekyll Island and whose encouragement and editorial suggestions have helped to make this a better book, I offer my deepest gratitude.

Above all, I would like to express my appreciation and devotion to my wonderful wife, Leah, who has stood beside me throughout the process and without whose inspiration, love, patience, and support I would never have made it through this project.

NOTES

PREFACE

1. See the introduction to Starnes, *Southern Journeys*, 6–7.

2. The article originally appeared in Starnes, *Southern Journeys*, 154–76.

3. Fiese, "Jekyll Island," 152.

4. Ga. Law 1953, Jan–Feb Session, 261.

1. WORLD WAR II AT JEKYLL ISLAND

1. McCash and McCash, *Jekyll Island Club*, 1, 191–92.

2. Marian Maurice Diary, March 29, 1942, Maurice Family Papers, Southern Historical Collection, Library of the University of North Carolina at Chapel Hill. For a fuller description of the final days of the Jekyll Island Club and the Maurice sisters, see McCash and McCash, *Jekyll Island Club*, 211–15.

3. Bernon Prentice to Bill Jones, September 6, 1942, Sea Island Company Records, Georgia Historical Society. Henceforth, this source will be referred to as SICR.

4. Marian Maurice Diary, March 29, 1942, Maurice Family Papers.

5. Hendrick, "German U-Boat Commander"; Goldstein, "Reinhard Hardegen, Who Led U-Boats."

6. Ford, *Jekyll Island*, 51.

7. Daraskevich, "Reinhard Hardegen, 1913–2018."

8. Lillian Schaitberger, interview by Tyler Bagwell, June 3, 1998, oral history transcript at Jekyll Island Museum Archives, 19.

9. Faulkenberry, *Project Glynco*, 16.

10. "Hercules Plant Gets 'E.'"

11. Bill Jones to Bernon Prentice, August 27, 1942, SICR.

12. Schaitberger interview, 6–7.

13. Schaitberger interview, 20.

14. Other Jekyll employees included Ralph Henderson's wife, Rose, who also lived on the island; William Smith, assistant foreman of the grounds; Lonnie Stafford, a grounds worker; and Sam Wesley, who maintained the landscaping. Additionally, since the Sea Island Company was overseeing the island during the war, some Sea Island Company employees worked at Jekyll periodically, including T. M. Baumgardner, Karl Keiffer, and R. J. Reddick, who became the watchman in 1944.

15. Schaitberger interview, 19.

16. Schaitberger interview, 6.

17. Bagwell, *Jekyll Island*, 18.

18. Faulkenberry, *Project Glynco*, 23.

19. Bernon Prentice to Bill Jones, January 18, 1943, SICR.

20. Bernon Prentice to Bill Jones, January 25, 1943, SICR.

21. Bernon Prentice to Bill Jones, July 28, 1943, SICR.

22. Bill Jones to Bernon Prentice, November 26, 1943, SICR. Curiously, handwritten across the top of the letter are the words "Not sent." Nevertheless, the letter clearly explains the problems that Prentice would face if he tried to reopen the club after the war.

23. Roy Hawkins to Bill Jones, February 1, 1944, SICR.

24. Jim Stockton to Bill Jones, February 19, 1944, SICR.

25. F. M. Scarlett to Bernon Prentice, February 9, 1944, SICR.

26. Transcript of telephone conversation between Jim Compton and M. L. DeZutter, July 2, 1946, SICR.

27. W. H. Lovett v. State Park Authority, J. D. Compton affidavit, July 1946. SICR.

28. Minutes of the adjourned special meeting of the stockholders of the Sans Souci Association, SICR.

29. Arthur Young and Company to board of governors audit committee, April 30, 1944, SICR.

30. F. M. Scarlett to Bernon Prentice, May 1, 1945, SICR.

31. F. M. Scarlett to Bill Jones, August 22, 1945, SICR.

2. THE END OF SPLENDID ISOLATION

1. Boring, "Jekyll Isle, 2d to Heaven."

2. Jekyll Island survey, March 29, 1946, SICR.

3. Bernon Prentice to Bill Jones, telegram, June 27, 1946, SICR.

4. Transcript of telephone conversation between Jim Compton and M. L. DeZutter, July 2, 1946, SICR.

5. Ibid.

6. Sullivan, "Blackbeard Island."

7. Telephone transcript from Charlie Gowen regarding M. E. Thompson discussion of Jekyll Island, August 20, 1946, SICR.

8. Bernon Prentice to Bill Jones, August 14, 1946, SICR.

9. Transcript of telephone conversation between M. E. Thompson and Jim Compton, September 5, 1946, SICR.

10. Governor Ellis Arnall to Alfred Jones, telegram, September 9, 1946, SICR.

11. Eugene Cook to Bill Jones, September 16, 1946, SICR.

12. Charles Gowen, interview by Brenden Martin and June Hall McCash, May 1, 2000, Jekyll Island Museum Archives.

13. Statement made by John Gilbert, attorney for the Jekyll Island Club, to a representative of *The Brunswick News* respecting the proposed acquisition of Jekyll Island by the State of Georgia, September 25, 1947.

14. Kytle and Mackay, *Who Runs Georgia?*, xiv.

15. Bullock, Buchanan, and Gaddie, *The Three Governors Controversy*. See also https://en.wikipedia.org/wiki/Benjamin_W._Fortson_Jr.

16. Kytle and Mackay, *Who Runs Georgia?*, 6.

17. Gowen interview.

18. Ibid.

19. Thompson v. Talmadge, 201 Ga., 867.

20. Gowen interview.

21. Bernon Prentice to M. E. Thompson, May 26, 1947, SICR.

22. Constitution State News Bureau, "Jekyll Island Action Filed."

23. Unidentified clippings, June 4, 1947, Everett Collection, Coastal Georgia Historical Society.

24. "Jekyll Island Plan Is Wrong!"

25. Lawrence R. Condon to Edward Sunderland, October 27, 1947, SICR.

26. Margaret Maurice to Bill Jones, June 21, 1947, SICR.

27. Final decree and judgment, Superior Court, Glynn County, Georgia, October 4, 1947, SICR.

28. Bill Jones to Bernon Prentice, June 5, 1947. SICR.

29. Marian Maurice Diary, February 14–March 7, 1947, Maurice Family Papers.

30. Minutes of the special meeting of the stockholders of the Jekyll Island Club, November 5, 1947.

31. The club era of Jekyll Island is explored in McCash and McCash, *The Jekyll Island Club: Southern Haven for America's Millionaires*. The book includes a final chapter on the transition of Jekyll Island from private to state ownership.

3. A STATE PARK FOR THE PLAIN PEOPLE OF GEORGIA

1. *Brunswick News*, October 8, 1947, 1.

2. Todd, "Convict Lease System."

3. Transcript of telephone conversation between M. E. Thompson and Jim Compton RE Jekyll Island, September 5, 1946, SICR; *Brunswick News*, October 25, 1947.

4. *Brunswick News*, October 25, 1947, 10.

5. *Brunswick News*, November 6, 1947, 8.

6. *Brunswick News*, November 11, 1947, 5.

7. "Jekyll Island State Park Contracts."

8. Gowen interview.

9. *Savannah Morning News*, March 3, 1948, 14. Tallulah "Tallu" Fish would become curator of the Jekyll Island Museum.

10. *Brunswick News*, October 12, 1947, 8; *Savannah Morning News*, February 5, 1948, 9.

11. *Atlanta Constitution*, June 14, 1947.

12. Cannon Davidson, interview by Tyler Bagwell, July 14, 1998, Jekyll Island Museum.

13. Gowen interview.

14. "Thompson's Folly Revisited."

15. "Willing to Sell Jekyll."

16. Gowen interview.

17. "Bill Calls for Five-Man Board," 10.

18. Ibid.

19. "Jekyll Bill May Die."

20. "House Committee OKs Jekyll Bill."

21. "Talmadge Seeks Jekyll Study"; "Talmadge Group Seeking Decision." See also "Committee to Lease Jekyll."

22. "Coalition Formed."

23. "Talmadge Approves Plan."

24. "Talmadge Appoints Group."

25. *Savannah Morning News*, April 16, 1949, 1.

26. *Savannah Morning News*, July 10, 1949, 29. Whitaker reported a "big drop from the last season."

27. Paul Murphey, interview by Brenden Martin, oral history, August 17, 2011, Jekyll Island Museum.

28. Murphey interview.

29. Bagwell, *Jekyll Island*, 44.

30. "Solons Likely to Carry On."

31. *Savannah Morning News*, February 15, 1950, 7.

32. "Gowen Pleased with Set-Up"; Jekyll Island State Park Authority, Ga, Laws 1950, 152.

33. Gowen interview.

4. A NATURAL BEAUTY PLAN

1. JIA minutes, March 4–5, 1950; "Jekyll Authority Coming Here," 1, 3, 8, 10.

2. *Brunswick News*, March 6, 1950.

3. "Bill Would Give Plot."

4. JIA minutes, June 10, 1950.

5. "Hendry Nearing Completion."

6. "Steel Strike of 1952."

7. JIA minutes, October 5, 1950.

8. Sparks, "Georgia's Padlocked Island."

9. "Jekyll Authority Holds Meeting."

10. JIA minutes, April 21, 1951.

11. JIA minutes, November 17, 1951.

12. "Dedication of Jekyll Island Causeway."

13. "Thompson's Folly Revisited."

14. JIA minutes, March 7, 1953; legislative resolution mentioned in minutes.

15. JIA minutes, January 9, 1951.

16. JIA minutes, April 26, 1952. Steiner signed his name as "Andrew Steiner" on a 1973 update of the master plan.

17. Auchmutey, "Deals with the Devil," 1E.

18. Ibid., 4E.

19. McCash and Martin, "Odyssey of Andre Steiner," 56–57.

20. Ibid.

21. Andre Steiner, interview by Brenden Martin and June McCash, oral history, 2001.

22. Steiner interview.

23. JIA minutes, August 23, 1952.

24. "Jekyll Convicts Apprehended."

25. "Jekyll Convicts Elude Searching Party."

26. "Fugitives from Jekyll Caught."

27. JIA minutes, July 18, 1953.

28. "Convicts Start Fires," 10.

29. JIA minutes, May 11, 1953.

30. "Jekyll Prison Camp," 8.

31. "Thousands Visit Jekyll Opening."

5. THE WHITE ELEPHANT

1. "Applicants Assigned All Jekyll Island."

2. *Brunswick News*, May 25, 1955.

3. Nelson, "Long-Term Politico Jimmy Dykes."

4. JIA minutes, special call meeting, November 3, 1954.

5. Nelson, "Costly 'Little Executive Mansion.'"

6. Ibid.

7. Pou, "Dykes Record Bared," 1–11. The hotel lease was approved in the name of L. L. Phillips of Cochran, Georgia, for Jekyll Island Hotels, Inc., at the JIA meeting on May 14, 1955.

8. Jim Compton, private letter to D. B. Blalock, June 17, 1955, Sea Island Company Records, Georgia Historical Society.

9. "Compton Leaves Jekyll Authority," 12; "Dykes Moves to Spread."

10. Compton to Blalock, June 17, 1955.

11. "Jekyll Paint 'Evaporates.'"

12. "Jekyll to Need Another $500,000."

13. "Solons Demand Jekyll Authority," *Brunswick News*.

14. "Governor to Ask Sale."

15. St. John, "Griffin Asks Sale of Jekyll."

16. "Governor Shifts Stand on Jekyll."

17. "Thompson Gets into Discussion."

18. "Governor Tells Jekyll Board."

19. "Governor Says He'll Ask Sale."

20. "Thompson Gets Into Discussion."

21. Nelson, "Sen. Dykes Moves to Spread."

22. Nelson, "Longtime Politico Jimmy Dykes."

23. Nelson, "Jekyll Authority Employee Bought Supplies."

24. Nelson, "Costly 'Little Executive Mansion'"; Nelson, "Jekyll Architect Gains 4 Pct. Fee."

25. "Warehouse Run by Dykes," 1–14.

26. "Dykes Offers to Give Up Leases."

27. Nelson, "Jekyll Island Sale Favored, Opposed."

28. "Jekyll Boom Attributed to 'Curiosity.'"

29. LeCraw, letter to the editor.

30. Drozeski, letter to the editor.

31. Nelson, "Chairman Blalock, Tarbutton Quit Jekyll Board."

32. "Governor Gives Jekyll and Port."

33. "Governor Names Panel to Study."

34. "Governor Gives Jekyll and Port."

35. Nelson, "Joint Panel Will Study"; "Governor Names Panel."

36. "Average Person Said 'Latching Onto.'"

37. Gauphin, "Thrasher Raps Jekyll Compromise."

38. "Thrasher Assails Selling of Lots"; "Sale of Lots on Jekyll."

39. "Amendment Seen Requirement"; "Solons Demand Probe."

40. "Senate Votes New Jekyll Island Authority."

41. "Thrasher, Cook Disagree."

42. "Tightening of Jekyll Fund."

43. "Thrasher Cracks Down."

44. "Governor Signs Bill."

45. Neal, "Fabulous Jekyll Island."

46. "Governor Pours Another Quarter Million."

47. JIA minutes, September 9, 1957.

48. Nelson, "Jekyll—A Golden Elephant."

49. "Attractive New Facilities."

50. Nelson, "Jekyll—A Golden Elephant."

51. "Cochran's James Dykes Found Dead."

6. Separate and Unequal

1. JIA minutes, August 23, 1952.

2. Jim Bacote, interview by Gretchen Greminger and Andrea Marroquin, July 24, 2013, 622 Ways Temple Road, Riceboro, Ga.

3. White, "60 Years Ago, Springhill Mining Disaster."

4. Greene, *Last Man Out*. See also Block, "Maurice Ruddick."

5. "Jekyll Trip as Griffin's Guests."

6. Ibid.

7. Ibid., 249–56.

8. Bacote interview.

9. Ibid.

10. "Miners Enjoy Sun on Jekyll."

11. Block, "Maurice Ruddick."

12. Dubay, "Marvin Griffin," 108.

13. "Ex-Miner Ruddick Sets Return."

14. "Negro Farmer Leases Jekyll Beach Motel."

15. Bacote interview.

16. Wikipedia, "Chitlin' Circuit."

17. Dr. W. Ray Hill, interview by Janine Hunter, August 26, 2008, Jekyll Island Museum.

18. Henry Armstrong, interview by Brenden Martin, May 16, 2001.

19. "Apartments and Negro Project Start."

20. Bagwell, *Jekyll Island*, 104–5.

21. "Thrasher Hits Move to Close."

22. "State to Build $75,000 Jekyll."

23. Bacote interview.

24. "Jekyll Unit Is Cautious."

25. Law v. Jekyll Island State Park Authority; Ben Fortson to Julius C. Hope.

26. "Desegregation at Jekyll Asked."

27. "Group Plans Court Action."

28. Henderson, *Georgia Governors*, 179.

29. "Judge Signs Jekyll Isle Racial Edict."

30. Hill interview.

31. Ibid.

32. Ibid.

33. Montoya, "50 Years Later"; "At Issue; 51; Quiet Conflict."

34. Hill interview.

35. Sandra Mungin, interview by Gretchen Greminger and Andrea Marroquin, July 18, 2014.

36. Bacote interview.

7. EXPANDING TOURISM AND DEVELOPMENT

1. "They Nabbed This New York Tourist." Brief portions of this chapter appeared as an article by Martin and McCash, "From Millionaires to the Masses," in Starnes, *Southern Journeys*, 154–76. Used with the permission of the University of Alabama Press.

2. Henderson, *Ernest Vandiver*, 179–80.

3. "Vandiver Asks for $1,218,000."

4. "Hartley Quits State."

5. "Husband Hunted; Wife Fights for Life."

6. "Jekyll Woman Slain, Husband Takes Life."

7. "Two-Week Theft Spree."

8. "Jekyll Motel Embezzler."

9. "Escaped Convict Is Object of Hunt."

10. "Convict Emerges from Hiding Spot."

11. "Two Convicts Shot."

12. "Convict Pair Flushed from Jekyll Woods."

13. "Jekyll Owes $2.5 Million for Prisoners."

14. "Jekyll Fugitives Captured at Waynesville."

15. "Wayne Prisoner Escapes Detail."

16. "Jekyll Bridge Span Fails."

17. "Jekyll Bridge Again Blocked."

18. "Jekyll Bridge Still Closed."

19. "Heavy Jekyll Lift Traffic."

20. "Jekyll Span Fixed."

21. "Jekyll Bridge Failure Brings 10-Hour Delay."

22. "Jekyll Sparkles for Lawmakers."

23. "Jekyll Sewage System to Serve."

24. "Dora: Jekyll Island Light."

25. "Hartley Is Harassing Him."

26. "Jekyll Officials Deny Knowledge."

27. "Commission OK's Jekyll Liquor."

28. "Methodists Ask Halt to Jekyll Liquor."

29. "Court Refuses to Halt Drink Sales."

30. "Ex-Jekyll Cleaner Asks Board."

31. "Hearing Sought on Jekyll Firing."

32. Nelson, "Liquor and Segregation Fading."

33. "Jekyll Co-ops Apartment."

34. Shannon, "Jekyll at the Crossroads."

35. Coastal Marshlands Protections Act (CMPA) of 1970, Ga. L., p. 939, or OCGA. The legislation defined the estuarine area of the state as "all tidally influenced waters, marshes, and marshlands lying within a tide-elevation range from 5.6 feet above mean tide level and below."

36. Nesmith, "State Forgets Its Marsh Act."

37. "Fishing Pier Construction Starts"; "Jekyll Island's New Fish Pier."

38. "Ben Fortson to Resign."

8. "WHAT'S WRONG AT JEKYLL ISLAND?"

1. RGB-27435 001-01-005. Governor-Executive Dept. Governor's Subject Files-1971–1974-Gov. Jimmy Carter County Files, Glynn through Grady. Consignment #1975-0032A.

2. Harrell, "Dispossessed of 'My' Jekyll Island."

3. "Downhill for Jekyll Island."

4. "Development of Jekyll Should Halt."

5. Riner, "Jekyll Land Fight Heats."

6. Shannon, "Jekyll at the Crossroads."

7. On February 22, 1971, Caldwell received a letter from DuPree Jordan, one of the partners in the Super Slide, a subsidiary of Fun Products, Inc. Jordan sent the letter to clear up "several misconceptions" around the contract.

8. "'Sea Circus' Must Treat Own Waste."

9. Shannon, "Jekyll at the Crossroads."

10. Ibid.

11. Wells, "Park's Wiggins Clamps Lid."

12. Georgia State Archive, RCB 31386 001–01–005, Governor Executive Dept.-Governor's Subject-Files, 1972–1974-Gov. Jimmy Carter-Agency-Memos-Department of Natural Resources-Consignment #1975-0032A.

13. "Trouble Has Struck Lanier Before."

14. Carter to Horace Caldwell, November 28, 1972.

15. Constitution State News Service, "Carter Hit for Vetoing Funds," 2A.

16. Allen, "Closing of Jekyll Island Threatened," 6A.

17. "Jekyll's Water OK, PSC Says."

18. Allen, "EPA Chief Hits Jekyll Inaction."

19. McCash, *Jekyll Island Cottage Colony*, 101–2.

20. Christensen, "Jekyll's Water Makes Waves," 2-A.

21. Townsend, "Jekyll Authority Seeking Power," 2A.

22. Hopkins, "Jekyll Board Terminates," 3A.

23. "Busbee Vetoes Bill," 2.

24. Salter, "Jekyll Motels Delay Opening," 6C.

25. "Jekyll Island Decline Set," 8A.

26. Salter, "Jekyll Rejects Condo Switch," 5C. As a result of his financial problems between 1971 and 1977, Larry Morris would default on the loans. In later years, as a consequence of his football career, he developed

chronic traumatic encephalopathy (CTE); he was one of the first former players to be diagnosed with the disease. See Holcomb, "Best Player in School History."

27. Eason, "Useless Marina Tops Jekyll Agency's," 12A.

28. Hopkins, "50-Cent Entrance Fee Proposed."

29. "Jekyll Status Preservation Urged," 2C.

30. Davis, "What's Wrong at Jekyll Island?"

31. Shipp, "Jekyll Island: Painful Move," 2B.

32. Shipp, "A New Chapter in Jekyll's Sad Story?," 4A.

9. SAVING THE HISTORIC DISTRICT

1. JIA minutes, February 31, 1951. JIA members reviewed a Memorandum of Insurance Valuations and Fire Coverage that Jim Compton prepared. Among the listed vacant structures of Red Row were two abandoned "Negro Servants Quarters," a single-family house, "Negro Camp Buildings" with eleven connected two-room units, and a guardhouse. The valuations added up to $6,600.

2. JIA minutes, June 23, 1951. Mike Benton suggested razing the Albright House (formerly the Pulitzer Cottage) using convict labor, and Jim Compton estimated that it would cost $2,000.

3. *Brunswick News*, March 1, 1960; JIA minutes, July 8, 1963; Galphin, "Aldred Says 'Hecklers' Hurt Jekyll"; Daniel, "Jekyll to Show 'Rich' Cottages"; *Brunswick News*, December 1, 1965.

4. "Archaeologist Studying Ruins."

5. "Virginia Architect Named to Restore."

6. Fauber to E. B. Davis, secretary-treasurer, Jekyll Island State Park Authority, re: Faith Chapel and Rockefeller Cottage, JIA.

7. Beedle diary, July 28, 1969, Jekyll Island Museum.

8. Beedle diary, August 12, 1969, Jekyll Island Museum.

9. Beedle diary, July 22, 1971, Jekyll Island Museum.

10. Beedle diary, September 5, 1973, Jekyll Island Museum.

11. Beedle diary, September 10, 1973, Jekyll Island Museum.

12. Harris, Kerr, Forster and Company to Ernest Davis, state auditor, September 21, 1972, Jekyll Island Museum.

13. Larry Evans, interview by Brenden Martin and June McCash, June 25, 2000, Jekyll Island Club Hotel. Transcript and recording at JIM archives. Vance Hughes, interview by Brenden Martin and June McCash, February 3, 2011, Jekyll Island Club Hotel. Transcript and recording at JIM archives.

14. David Curtis, interview by Brenden Martin and June McCash, February 7, 2011, Jekyll Island Clubhouse. Curtis was an associate partner with Leon N. Weiner; his role on the project was to raise $20 million in capital.

15. Curtis interview.

16. Davis, "Century-Old Millionaires' Club Revived."

17. Evans interview.

18. Curtis interview.

19. Patton, "Refurbished Club Reopens at Jekyll," D-1.

20. Curtis interview.

21. Warren Murphey, interview by Brenden Martin and June McCash, May 13, 2000, Villa Ospo, Jekyll Island.

10. CONTROVERSY AND PROTEST

1. John McTier, interview by Brenden Martin, telephone interview, August 7, 2001. Transcript and audio at Jekyll Island Museum Archives.

2. McTier interview.

3. Williams, letter to the editor.

4. Rhodes, "Long-Range Plans."

5. Hussy, Fry, and Bell report, September 28, 1993, JIM archives; "Improving Jekyll."

6. Thomas, "Jekyll Put on Solid Footing."

7. Davis, "Develop 'Dull' Jekyll, Planners Urge."

8. Davis, "Jekyll Fighting 'Asphalt Image,'" 10-A.

9. Jim Morrison, "Bridge Malfunction."

10. McTier interview.

11. "Golf Course Construction Halted," 10-A.

12. McTier interview.

13. Ibid.

14. Layman, "Jekyll Chief Resigns."

15. Dickson and LoMonte, "Jekyll Authority Chief Quits," B-1, 8.

16. Shaw, letter to the editor.

17. "Jekyll Bill Deserves Support."

18. *Jekyll's Golden Islander*, May 23, 1996.

19. "Frequent Visitor Dislikes the Fence."

20. "JIA Shuffle."

21. Bill Donohue, interview by Brenden Martin and June McCash, May 31, 2000. At the time of the interview, Donohue was in his third year as executive director.

22. Jim Morrison, "Supreme Court Rule for JIA."

23. Dickson, "Island Eyes Portion of Glynn's."

24. "Jekyll Leaders Urge Residents."

25. Dickson, "Jekyll Island Tax Fight."

26. Dickson, "Glynn Lawsuit Attacks Sales Tax."

27. Ibid.

28. Grass, "State-Owned Jekyll Island's Money."

29. "Director of JIA Awaits Reply."

30. Stepzinski, "Jekyll Project Aims to Help."

31. Bynum, "Ga's Jekyll Falling into Disrepair."

11. THE PERILS OF REVITALIZATION

1. JIA minutes, October 16, 2006.

2. Jim Morrison, "Controversy over Development."

3. JIA minutes, January 8, 2007.

4. Stepzinski, "Jekyll Bills Land in Chapman."

5. Jim Morrison, "Controversy over Development"; Jim Morrison, "Jekyll Bill Lands in Chapman," 4. The first Morrison article is accompanied by a photograph showing thirty-three residents traveling by bus to Atlanta, but all other accounts indicate that there were fifty or more people in their contingent.

6. JIA minutes, June 18, 2007, and October 23, 2007.

7. Jim Morrison, "Controversy over Development."

8. Jim Morrison, "Jekyll Bill Lands," 4–5.

9. Chapman, "Future Is Foggy on Jekyll," E-1.

10. Ibid.

11. Larrabee, "Future of Jekyll Starts Today," B-1.

12. Chapman, "Legislature 2007: Fight over Jekyll's Future."

13. Larrabee, "Jekyll Residents Hope Better Luck," B-3.

14. Ibid.

15. Jarvie, "Jekyll Island Personality May Be Split."

16. Associated Press, "Faded Island, Still Adored."

17. Chapman, "Legislature 2007: State Senators Cast," D5.

18. Ibid.

19. Chapman, "Legislature 2007: Options Stay Open," D6.

20. Larrabee, "Cry Goes Out to Save South," A-1.

21. Larrabee, "Future of Jekyll Island Starts," B1.

22. Shipp, "Joke About Jekyll Island."

23. Larrabee, "Thumbs-Up Seals Jekyll Deal," B-1.

24. Ibid.

25. Ibid.

26. Larrabee, "Jekyll's Residents Relieved," A-1.

27. JIA minutes, June 18, 2007. At this JIA meeting, Ben Porter made his first public comment about rent abatement.

28. Chapman, "Jekyll Developer Incentive Stirs Mud," C-1.

29. Ibid.

30. Starr, "Jekyll Board Hurling Insults."

31. Hawkins, "Jekyll Authority Defends Its Plans," A-1.

32. "Ousted Jekyll Board Member Alleges," A-1.

33. Ferguson, "Jekyll Critics' Claims Dismissed."

34. "Jekyll Island Authority Selects Private."

35. Starr, "Jekyll's Vision for the Future."

36. Hawkins, "Losing Bidder Protests Jekyll's Choice."

37. Chapman, "Jekyll Island: Suit Filed," B-1.

38. Rowland, "Donohue May Run Lanier Authority."

39. Starr, "Former Director Put Jekyll."

12. BUILDING TO CAPACITY

1. Langford, "Jekyll Island Development," A13.

2. Ibid.

3. Robinson, "Developer—Jekyll Plans."

4. "Jekyll Island State Park Authority Seeks."

5. "Jekyll Says Judge Clears Plan."

6. Rowland, "Jekyll Developer Says Chapman Wrong"; Egan, "Jekyll Island: Revitalize, but Sensitively," A17. Egan challenged the statistics in Langford's assertions.

7. Jarvie, "Jekyll Island Personality May Be Split."

8. Hurt, "A More Constructive Approach," A-11.

9. Larrabee, "Senator's Claims 'False,'" B-1.

10. Galloway and Kemper, "Political Insider."

11. Chapman, "Jekyll Island Figures Just Don't Add Up."

12. Ibid.

13. Larrabee, "Jekyll Developer, Agency Drop Beach."

14. Hawkins, "Jekyll Defense Now Up to Plan B."

15. "Jekyll Island Selects New Executive."

16. Jones Hooks, interview by Brenden Martin, August 2, 2010, Jekyll Island, Ga.

17. Ferguson, "Jekyll Plan Well Received."

18. Hawkins, "Jekyll Residents Question Consultant," B-1.

19. Hooks interview.

20. Ibid.

21. Ibid.

22. Krueger, "Revitalization of Jekyll Island."

23. Hawkins, "Expansion Is Linger No Longer," A-1.

24. Chapman, "Developers to Discuss."

25. Hawkins, "Board Told to Build Up," B1.

26. Hawkins and Larrabee, "Boshears Strikes at Plans," A1.

27. Ferguson, "Jekyll Critics' Claims Dismissed."

28. Brogdon, "Jekyll Revitalization Kicks Off."

13. LEASES AND LOSSES

1. Hawkins, "Jekyll Authority Questions Leases."

2. Jones, "Senator Calls for Jekyll Rate Hike."

3. Hawkins, "Jekyll Authority Questions Leases."

4. Ferguson, "Jekyll Lease Decision Pending."

5. Hawkins, "Jekyll Authority Questions Leases."

6. Hawkins, "Question on Jekyll Residential Leases." The Bleakly Advisory Group became known as KB Advisory Group in 2021.

7. Ferguson, "Jekyll Lease Decision Pending."

8. Ferguson, "Bill Weighs Jekyll Lease Rates."

9. Ferguson, "Leases to Be Examined."

10. Ibid.

11. Carole Hawkins, "Jekyll Leases Topic of Study," A-1.

12. Ferguson, "Jekyll Lease Study Results Presented."

13. Ibid.

14. Starr, "Advisors: Up Jekyll Leases."

15. Ibid.

16. Ibid.

17. Capek, "Authority Will Vote."

18. JIA minutes, November 9, 2009. While this was the standard option for residential homeowners, there were other proposed options for such things as spousal or family transfers and homestead exemptions.

19. Capek, "Jekyll Adopts New Lease Policies."

20. Capek, "Jekyll Authority Nears Land Lease Terms"; Capek, "Jekyll Leases Given the Go-Ahead."

21. Capek, "Jekyll Leases Given the Go-Ahead."

14. MARSH, LAND, ENVIRONMENTALISM, AND OTHER CONTROVERSIES

1. Hawkins, "Survey Shows Less Land Left," B-2.

2. Wiley, "Jekyll Tries to Define 'Land.'" The Coastal Marshland Protection Act of 1970 was based on Rep. Reid Harris's idea that the marshes belong to the people of Georgia, and any construction that would affect a salt marsh should require a permit. Senator Chapman had sponsored a bill stipulating that two-thirds of the land and salt marshes be left in "their natural state."

3. Wiley, "Jekyll Group Talks Land Categories."

4. Wiley, "Definition of Land Will Chart."

5. Chapman, "Jekyll's Room to Grow at Risk," A-1.

6. Dickson, "Jekyll's Land Mass in Dispute."

7. Dickson, "High Marsh."

8. Wiley, "Jekyll Tries to Define 'Land.'"

9. Bynum, "Jekyll Island Task Force Questions."

10. Dickson, "Jekyll Board May Ask Legislators."

11. Dickson, "Conservationists Bristle."

12. Dickson, "High Marsh," A-1.

13. JIA minutes, August 26, 2013.

14. Dickson, "Deal OKs Limits on Jekyll," A-1.

15. Ibid.

16. Mike Morrison and Dickson, "Jekyll Island Residents Object," A-1.

17. Ibid.

18. Bonnie Newell, interview by Brenden Martin at Newell's home, August 6, 2021.

19. Jamison, "Postal Service Has a Brand-New Bag."

20. Draft summary of Jekyll Island white-tailed deer management recommendations.

21. Dickson, "Board Votes for 4 More Years," A-1.

22. Bynum, "2nd Study Says Too Many Deer."

23. Rehagin, "Alpha Cats," 35–42.

24. Hawkins, "Jekyll Dims the Lights for Turtles."

25. Dickson, "Georgia Sea Turtle Center."

26. Mike Morrison, "Nesting Sea Turtles Avoid Beach," A-1.

27. Stillinger, "Lighting Survey at Jekyll."

28. McDonald, "Pier Road Shop Owners Bring."

29. McDonald, "Jekyll Board Hears Plans."

CONCLUSION

1. Dickson, "68 Years After Its Purchase."

2. Dickson, "Gov. Deal at Jekyll Island," A-1.

3. Memo from Noel Jensen, deputy executive director, Jekyll Island Authority, May 19, 2023.

4. Dickson, "'Go Beyond Beach Access,'" A-1.

5. Rowland, "Jones Hooks Honored by Georgia House."

6. JIA minutes, June 1, 2023.

7. Jones Hooks, interview by Brenden Martin, August 2, 2010, Jekyll Island, Ga.

8. "On Rocky Shore of Jekyll."

9. Constitution State News Service, "Tide at Jekyll Island."

10. Davis, "Erosion Along Georgia Shoreline."

11. Lemos, "Removal of Golden Ray."

12. Hooks interview.

13. Burns, "A Fleeting Stay, an Indelible Legacy," 21.

BIBLIOGRAPHY

INTERVIEWS AND ORAL HISTORIES

Henry Armstrong
Jim Bacote
David Curtis
Bill Donohue
David and Mindy Egan
Larry Evans
Joseph Ferrari
Charles Gowen
Roosevelt Harris
Dr. Ray Hill
Jones Hooks
Vance Hughes
John McTier
Sandra Mungin
Paul Murphey
Warren Murphey
Bonnie Newell
Johnny Paulk
Jean and Len Poleszak
Kevin Runner
Lillian Schaitberger
Tallu Fish Scott
Andre Steiner

BOOKS AND ARTICLES

Allen, Frederick. "Closing of Jekyll Island Threatened." *Atlanta Constitution*, June 12, 1974, 6A.

Allen, Frederick. "EPA Chief Hits Jekyll Inaction." *Atlanta Constitution*, June 18, 1974.

Allitt, Patrick. *A Climate of Crisis: America in the Age of Environmentalism*. New York: Penguin Press, 2014.

"Amendment Seen Requirement for Jekyll Lot Sales." *Brunswick News*, February 4, 1957.

"Anticipated Further Money Drain Prompts Jekyll Recommendations." *Brunswick News*, December 13, 1955.

"Apartments and Negro Project Start on Jekyll." *Brunswick News*, February 5, 1959.

"Applicants Assigned All Jekyll Island Ocean Lots." *Brunswick News*, January 5, 1955.

"Archaeologist Studying Ruins of Major Horton's House." *Brunswick News*, December 12, 1965.

Associated Press. "Faded Island, Still Adored, Weighs Facelift." *New York Times*, March 4, 2007.

"*At Issue*; 51; Quiet Conflict, Brunswick, Ga." 1965-01-00. Library of Congress, American Archive of Public Broadcasting (GBH and the Library of Congress), Boston, Mass., and Washington, D.C. http://americanarchive.org/catalog/cpb-aacip-512-rx93776z41.

"Attractive New Facilities Aim on Jekyll Island." *Brunswick News*, June 30, 1957.

Auchmutey, Jim. "Deals with the Devil: Ransom Plan Is a Footnote to Holocaust." *Atlanta Journal-Constitution*, September 20, 1988.

"Average Person Said 'Latching Onto.'" *Brunswick News*, January 28, 1957.

Bagwell, Tyler. *Jekyll Island: A State Park*. Charleston: Arcadia, 2001.

Barnes, Dianna, ed. *Coastal and Beach Erosion: Processes, Adaptation Strategies and Environmental Impacts*. New York: Nova, 2015.

Bartley, Numan V. *From Thurmond to Wallace: Political Tendencies in Georgia, 1948–1968*. Baltimore: Johns Hopkins University Press, 1970.

"Battle over Development of a Georgia Jewel." *Atlanta Journal-Constitution*, March 25, 2007.

Becker, Elizabeth. *Overbooked. The Exploding Business of Travel and Tourism*. New York: Simon and Schuster, 2016.

"Ben Fortson to Resign as Head of the Jekyll Authority." *Atlanta Constitution*, January 4, 1972.

"Bill Calls for Five-Man Board to Run Jekyll." *Brunswick News*, February 9, 1949.

"Bill Would Give Plot on Jekyll to Each County." *Brunswick News*, February 15, 1950.

Block, Niko. "Maurice Ruddick." In *The Canadian Encyclopedia*. Last modified August 28, 2015. https://

encyclopediecanadienne.com/en/article/maurice-ruddick?themeid=20&id=16.
Bolster, Paul. *Saving the Georgia Coast: A Political History of the Coastal Marshlands Protection Act*. Athens: University of Georgia Press, 2022.
Boring, Bill. "Jekyll Isle, 2d to Heaven, Wrapped in Legend, Fantasy." *Atlanta Constitution*, January 13, 1946.
Brogdon, Louie. "Jekyll Revitalization Kicks Off." *Brunswick News*, September 21, 2010.
Buchanan, Scott E. *Some of the People Who Ate My Barbecue Didn't Vote for Me*. Nashville, Tenn.: Vanderbilt University Press, 2011.
Bullock, Charles S., III, Scott E. Buchanan, and Ronald Keith Gaddie. *The Three Governors Controversy: Skullduggery, Machinations, and the Decline of Georgia's Progressive Politics*. Athens: University of Georgia Press, 2015.
Burns, Rebecca. "A Fleeting Stay, an Indelible Legacy." *31•81, the Magazine of Jekyll Island* 5, no. 2 (Fall/Winter 2022).
"Busbee Vetoes Bill to Bail Out Jekyll Island's Ailing Motels." *Atlanta Constitution*, April 3, 1976.
Bynum, Russ. "Ga.'s Jekyll Island Falling into Disrepair." *StarNews Online*, March 1, 2007.
Bynum, Russ. "Jekyll Island Task Force Questions Just How Big Island Is." *Florida Times-Union* (Jacksonville), May 12, 2013.
Bynum, Russ. "2nd Study Says Too Many Deer on Jekyll Island." *Savannah Morning News* (AP), March 20, 2013.
Capek, Erika. "Authority Will Vote on Jekyll Lease Policy." *Brunswick News*, October 20, 2009.
Capek, Erika. "Jekyll Adopts New Lease Policies." *Brunswick News*, January 28, 2010.
Capek, Erika. "Jekyll Authority Nears Land Lease Terms." *Brunswick News*, February 17, 2010.
Capek, Erika. "Jekyll Leases Given the Go-Ahead." *Brunswick News*, April 20, 2010.
Chapman, Dan. "Developers to Discuss How to Restart Stalled Jekyll Plan." *Atlanta Journal-Constitution*, January 20, 2010.
Chapman, Dan. "Future Is Foggy on Jekyll Island: Battle over Development of a Georgia Jewel." *Atlanta Journal-Constitution*, March 25, 2007.
Chapman, Dan. "Jekyll Developer Incentive Stirs Mud." *Atlanta Journal-Constitution*, July 29, 2007.
Chapman, Dan. "Jekyll Island Figures Just Don't Add Up." *Atlanta Journal-Constitution*, March 13, 2008.
Chapman, Dan. "Jekyll Island: Suit Filed to Stop 'Town Center.'" *Atlanta Journal-Constitution*, November 17, 2007.
Chapman, Dan. "Jekyll's Room to Grow at Risk; Dispute over How Much Area Can Be Developed Reaches State AG Office." *Atlanta Journal-Constitution*, April 27, 2013.
Chapman, Dan. "Legislature 2007: Fight over Jekyll's Future Moves to Senate." *Atlanta Journal-Constitution*, April 11, 2007.
Chapman, Dan. "Legislature 2007: Options Stay Open for Jekyll; Battle for Island's Future Heads to Senate Floor." *Atlanta Journal-Constitution*, April 13, 2007.
Chapman, Dan. "Legislature 2007: State Senators Cast 32–12 Vote to Save Jekyll Island's South End." *Atlanta Journal-Constitution*, April 20, 2007.
Christensen, Mike. "Jekyll's Water Makes Waves." *Atlanta Constitution*, June 16, 1974.
"Coalition Formed in Move to Doom Jekyll Authority." *Brunswick News*, February 15, 1949.
Coastal Marshlands Protection Act (CMPA) of 1970, Ga. L. 1970, p. 939, § 1.
"Cochran's James Dykes Found Dead, Gun Near." *Atlanta Constitution*, December 28, 1966.
"Commission OK's Jekyll Liquor; Oxford Says No." *Brunswick News*, June 15, 1961.
"Committee to Lease Jekyll Is Appointed by Governor." *Brunswick News*, March 2, 1948.
"Compton Leaves Jekyll Authority After Five Years." *Brunswick News*, August 4, 1955.
Constitution State News Bureau. "Jekyll Island Action Filed." *Atlanta Constitution*, June 7, 1947.
Constitution State News Service. "Carter Hit for Vetoing Funds for Jekyll Island." *Atlanta Constitution*, June 4, 1974.
Constitution State News Service. "Tide at Jekyll Island Ties High Mark." *Atlanta Constitution*, January 9, 1974.
"Convict Emerges from Hiding Spot at Jekyll." *Brunswick News*, December 29, 1961.
"Convict Pair Flushed from Jekyll Woods." *Brunswick News*, January 29, 1963.
"Convicts Start Fires on Jekyll Island." *Brunswick News*, March 6, 1953.
Cook, Eugene. "Attorney General Tells of Acquisition of Jekyll Island." *Brunswick News*, May 22, 1948.
Couric, John. "Acquisition of Jekyll Isle Looms as a State-Owned Beach Park." *Atlanta Constitution*, June 3, 1947.
"Court Refuses to Halt Drink Sales on Jekyll." *Atlanta Constitution*, September 1, 1971.
Daniel, Frank. "Jekyll to Show 'Rich' Cottages." *Atlanta Journal*, August 16, 1963.

Daraskevich, Joe. "Reinhard Hardegen, 1913–2018: U-Boat Skipper Sank Oil Tanker off Jacksonville Beach." *Florida Times-Union* (Jacksonville), June 15, 2018.

Davis, Jingle. "Century-Old Millionaires' Club Revived; Jekyll Landmark Being Restored as a First-Class Resort Hotel." *Atlanta Journal and Constitution*, June 29, 1986.

Davis, Jingle. "Develop 'Dull' Jekyll, Planners Urge State." *Atlanta Constitution*, May 27, 1981.

Davis, Jingle. "Erosion Along Georgia Shoreline Threatens Barrier Island." *Atlanta Journal-Constitution*, November 11, 1984.

Davis, Jingle. *Island Passages: An Illustrated History of Jekyll Island, Georgia*. Athens: University of Georgia Press, 2016.

Davis, Jingle. "Jekyll Fighting 'Asphalt Image.'" *Atlanta Journal-Constitution*, August 25, 1985.

Davis, Jingle. "What's Wrong at Jekyll Island?" *Atlanta Constitution*, April 19, 1981.

"Dedication of Jekyll Island Causeway." *Brunswick News*, November 4, 1950.

"Desegregation at Jekyll Asked by Biracial Unit." *Atlanta Journal*, March 13, 1963.

"Development of Jekyll Should Halt." *Wayne County Press*, May 27, 1972.

Dickson, Terry. "Board Votes for 4 More Years of Deer Protection; Jekyll Island Authority to Evaluate Effect on Vegetation." *Florida Times-Union* (Jacksonville), January 20, 2016.

Dickson, Terry. "Conservationists Bristle at New Jekyll Development Plans." *Florida Times-Union* (Jacksonville), August 26, 2013.

Dickson, Terry. "Deal OKs Limits on Jekyll; Compromise Legislation Will Allow Another 20 Acres for Residential Projects on Barrier Island." *Florida Times-Union* (Jacksonville), April 15, 2014.

Dickson, Terry. "Georgia Sea Turtle Center on Jekyll Island Offers Second Chance for Sea Life." *Florida Times-Union* (Jacksonville), May 30, 2009.

Dickson, Terry. "Glynn Lawsuit Attacks Sales Tax; 2 File Challenge to Funds for Jekyll." *Florida Times-Union* (Jacksonville), November 2, 2001.

Dickson, Terry. "'Go Beyond Beach Access'; Jekyll Island Authority to Work with ADA to Make Improvements for Disabled." *Florida Times-Union* (Jacksonville), July 19, 2016.

Dickson, Terry. "Gov. Deal at Jekyll Island: 'Look How Far We've Come'; Island's Self-Sufficiency Celebrated as Officials, Residents Enjoy Rededication." *Florida Times-Union* (Jacksonville), November 17, 2015.

Dickson, Terry. "High Marsh: How High Is It? If Attorney General Says It's Land, Jekyll Could Develop 600 More Acres." *Florida Times-Union* (Jacksonville), June 9, 2013.

Dickson, Terry. "Island Eyes Portion of Glynn's Sales Tax; State-Owned Jekyll Wants Help on Projects." *Florida Times-Union* (Jacksonville), August 21, 2000.

Dickson, Terry. "Jekyll Board May Ask Legislators to Set Firm Acreage Limit on Development." *Florida Times-Union* (Jacksonville), July 16, 2013.

Dickson, Terry. "Jekyll Island Tax Fight Goes to Legislature; Glynn Tax Pinch Seen as Taxpayer Waste." *Florida Times-Union* (Jacksonville), February 6, 2001.

Dickson, Terry. "Jekyll's Land Mass in Dispute Once More." *Florida Times-Union* (Jacksonville), June 28, 2013.

Dickson, Terry. "68 Years After Its Purchase, Jekyll Island Authority Rededicates Island to Georgians After Massive Revitalization." *Florida Times-Union* (Jacksonville), November 17, 2015.

Dickson, Terry, and Frank LoMonte. "Jekyll Authority Chief Quits." *Florida Times-Union* (Jacksonville), February 1, 1995.

Dilsaver, Larry. *Cumberland Island National Seashore: A History of Conservation Conflict*. Charlottesville: University of Virginia Press, 2004.

"Director of JIA Awaits Reply." *Brunswick News*, November 22, 2022.

"Dora: Jekyll Island Light but Widespread." *Brunswick News*, September 10, 1964.

"Downhill for Jekyll Island." *Waycross Journal-Herald*, May 21, 1972.

Draft summary of Jekyll Island white-tailed deer management recommendations, Jekyll Island Authority, July 2014.

Drozeski, Mr. and Mrs. Roland C. Letter to the editor. *Atlanta Journal and Constitution*, July 15, 1956.

Dubay, Robert W. "Marvin Griffin and the Politics of the Stump." In Henderson and Roberts, *Georgia Governors in an Age of Change*.

"Dykes Moves to Spread His Jekyll Island Empire." *Atlanta Constitution*, July 23, 1956.

"Dykes Offers to Give Up Leases at Jekyll Island." *Brunswick News*, August 30, 1956.

Eason, Henry. "Useless Marina Tops Jekyll Agency's Goof List." *Atlanta Constitution*, December 5, 1977.

Egan, David. "Jekyll Island: Revitalize, but Sensitively." *Atlanta Journal-Constitution*, February 11, 2008.

"Escaped Convict Is Object of Hunt on Jekyll Island." *Brunswick News*, October 3, 1960.

"Ex-Jekyll Cleaner Asks Board Hearing for Money." *Brunswick News*, October 30, 1963.
"Ex-Miner Ruddick Sets Return Jekyll Visit as Motel's Guest." *Brunswick News*, July 22, 1959.
Faulkenberry, Leslie. *Project Glynco: A History of NAS Glynco, Brunswick, Georgia*. Brunswick: Glynn County Airport Commission, n.d.
Ferguson, Anna. "Bill Weighs Jekyll Lease Rates." *Brunswick News*, February 19, 2009.
Ferguson, Anna. "Jekyll Critics' Claims Dismissed as Laughable." *Brunswick News*, September 26, 2008.
Ferguson, Anna. "Jekyll Lease Decision Pending." *Brunswick News*, February 10, 2009.
Ferguson, Anna. "Jekyll Lease Study Results Presented." *Brunswick News*, May 12, 2009.
Ferguson, Anna. "Jekyll Plan Well Received." *Brunswick News*, July 15, 2009.
Ferguson, Anna. "Leases to Be Examined." *Brunswick News*, April 24, 2008.
Fiese, Angie. "Jekyll Island." Senate Research Office, *At Issue* (newsletter), September 2013. See Act 630 (1950).
"Fishing Pier Construction Starts at Jekyll." *Brunswick News*, June 27, 1968.
Ford, Elizabeth Austin. *Jekyll Island*. Decatur, Ga.: Wommack Quality Printing, 1960.
"Frequent Visitor Dislikes the Fence." *Jekyll's Golden Islander*, September 19, 1996.
"Fugitives from Jekyll Caught in Camden County." *Brunswick News*, July 28, 1952.
Galloway, Jim, and Bob Kemper. "Political Insider: Chapman Has a Defender on the Jekyll Island Authority." *Atlanta Journal-Constitution*, February 29, 2008.
Galphin, Bruce. "Aldred Says 'Hecklers' Hurt Jekyll." *Atlanta Constitution*, October 19, 1956.
Galphin, Bruce. "Thrasher Raps Jekyll Compromise, Wants Island Taken Out of Politics." *Atlanta Constitution*, February 2, 1957.
Goldstein, Richard. "Reinhard Hardegen, Who Led U-Boats to America's Shore, Dies at 105." *New York Times*, June 17, 2018.
"Golf Course Construction Halted." *Brunswick News*, January 12, 1985.
"Governor Gives Jekyll and Port Plans Backing." *Brunswick News*, January 9, 1957.
"Governor Names Panel to Study Jekyll Island Sale Plan." *Brunswick News*, January 18, 1957.
"Governor Pours Another Quarter Million into Jekyll." *Brunswick News*, June 27, 1957.
"Governor Says He'll Ask Sale of Lots." *Florida Times-Union* (Jacksonville), June 23, 1956.
"Governor Says He Will Assist Jekyll Further." *Brunswick News*, April 5, 1957.
"Governor Seeks to Sell Jekyll." *Brunswick News*, December 10, 1956.
"Governor Shifts Stand on Jekyll." *Brunswick News*, January 12, 1956.
"Governor Signs Bill Creating New Jekyll Board." *Brunswick News*, March 15, 1957.
"Governor Tells Jekyll Board to Hold $180,000." *Brunswick News*, July 25, 1956.
"Governor to Ask Sale of Jekyll Island Lots." *Brunswick News*, November 14, 1955.
"Gowen Pleased with Set-Up for Jekyll Resort." *Brunswick News*, February 14, 1950.
Grant, Donald L. *The Way It Was in the South: The Black Experience in Georgia*. Athens: University of Georgia Press, 1993.
Grass, Doug. "State-Owned Jekyll Island's Money Matters Draw Attention." *Florida Times-Union* (Jacksonville), March 24, 2002.
Greene, Melissa Fay. *Last Man Out: The Story of the Springfield Mine Disaster*. New York: Harcourt, 2003.
"Group Plans Court Action over Jekyll." *Brunswick News*, March 25, 1963.
Hall, Michael. "'New Direction' for Jekyll Historic District Prompts Closing of Decades-Old Businesses." *Brunswick News*, September 23, 2023.
Haq, Gary, and Alistair Paul. *Environmentalism Since 1945*. London: Routledge, 2012.
Harrell, Bob. "Dispossessed of 'My' Jekyll Island." *Atlanta Constitution*, January 18, 1972.
Harris, Kerr, Forster and Company to Ernest Davis, state auditor. September 21, 1972. Mosaic, Jekyll Island Museum.
"Hartley Is Harassing Him, Jekyll Ride Owner Charges." *Brunswick News*, July 17, 1965.
"Hartley Quits State for Jekyll Isle Post." *Atlanta Constitution*, August 5, 1960.
Hawkins, Carole. "Board Told to Build Up Jekyll; $99 Million Would Fix Island, Group Says." *Florida Times-Union* (Jacksonville), September 16, 2008.
Hawkins, Carole. "Expansion Is Linger No Longer; Jekyll Island–Linger Longer End Their Development Partnership." *Florida Times-Union* (Jacksonville), December 9, 2009.
Hawkins, Carole. "Jekyll Authority Defends Its Plans; Members Faced Grilling by the State's Island Oversight Committee." *Florida Times-Union* (Jacksonville), August 31, 2007.
Hawkins, Carole. "Jekyll Authority Questions Leases;

Maybe No Homes Belong on Island, Finance Chairman Suggests." *Florida Times-Union* (Jacksonville), April 16, 2008.

Hawkins, Carole. "Jekyll Defense Now Up to Plan B." *Florida Times-Union* (Jacksonville), March 22, 2008.

Hawkins, Carole. "Jekyll Dims the Lights for Turtles; Ordinance Helps Loggerheads." *Florida Times-Union* (Jacksonville), August 12, 2009.

Hawkins, Carole. "Jekyll Leases Topic of Study; Fewer Homes and Higher Rent Possible." *Florida Times-Union* (Jacksonville), May 18, 2008.

Hawkins, Carole. "Jekyll Residents Question Consultant on Condo Plan." *Florida Times-Union* (Jacksonville), September 30, 2008.

Hawkins, Carole. "Losing Bidder Protests Jekyll's Choice." *Florida Times-Union* (Jacksonville), October 16, 2007.

Hawkins, Carole. "The Question on Jekyll Residential Leases: How High? There Is Concern That the Commercial Properties Will Get a Better Deal." *Florida Times-Union* (Jacksonville), January 1, 2009.

Hawkins, Carole. "Survey Shows Less Land Left on Jekyll Island; Only 35% of the Island's Land Is Allotted for Development." *Florida Times-Union* (Jacksonville), January 15, 2009.

Hawkins, Carole, and Brandon Larrabee. "Boshears Strikes at Plans to Revitalize; Freed from the Jekyll Authority Board, He Is Condemning a Land Deal." *Florida Times-Union* (Jacksonville), September 25, 2008.

"Hearing Sought on Jekyll Firing." *Brunswick News*, May 9, 1963.

"Heavy Jekyll Lift Traffic Requires Span Renovation." *Brunswick News*, January 12, 1961.

Henderson, Harold Paulk. *Ernest Vandiver, Governor of Georgia*. Athens: University of Georgia Press, 2000.

Henderson, Harold Paulk, and Gary L. Roberts, eds. *Georgia Governors in an Age of Change: From Ellis Arnall to George Busbee*. Athens: University of Georgia Press, 1988.

Henderson, Harold Paulk. *The Politics of Change in Georgia: A Political Biography of Ellis Arnall*. Athens: University of Georgia Press, 1991.

Hendrick, Bill. "German U-Boat Commander: *Oklahoma* Was 'a Sitting Duck.'" *Atlanta Journal-Constitution*, February 14, 1999.

"Hendry Nearing Completion of Dredging Work." *Brunswick News*, February 6, 1950.

"Hercules Plant Gets 'E'; Powder Company Officials Attend Ceremony at Brunswick, Ga." *New York Times*, February 3, 1944.

Holcomb, Todd. "Best Player in School History." *Atlanta Journal-Constitution*, October 10, 2017.

Hopkins, Sam. "50-Cent Entrance Fee Proposed for Jekyll Island Visitors." *Atlanta Constitution*, August 28, 1979.

Hopkins, Sam. "Jekyll Board Terminates 2 Motel Mortgage Contracts." *Atlanta Constitution*, December 14, 1976.

"House Committee OKs Jekyll Bill Minus Nightingale." *Brunswick News*, February 12, 1949.

Hurt, Art. "A More Constructive Approach to the Jekyll Island Issue." *Atlanta Journal-Constitution*, February 5, 2008.

"Husband Hunted; Wife Fights for Life." *Atlanta Constitution*, January 5, 1960.

Hussy, Fry, and Bell report, September 28, 1993. Mosaic, Jekyll Island Museum.

"Improving Jekyll." *Atlanta Constitution*, May 27, 1981.

Jamison, Mark. "The Postal Service Has a Brand-New Bag: A Post Office or Mail Delivery, but Not Both." *Florida Times-Union* (Jacksonville), September 11, 2013.

Jarvie, Jenny. "Jekyll Island Personality May Be Split." *Los Angeles Times*, February 18, 2007.

"Jekyll Authority Coming Here for Meeting Today." *Brunswick News*, March 4, 1950.

"Jekyll Authority Holds Meeting at Beach Park." *Brunswick News*, June 25, 1951.

"Jekyll Bill Deserves Support." Editorial. *Atlanta Constitution*, February 3, 1995.

"Jekyll Bill May Die in Assembly Race to Adjourn." *Brunswick News*, February 11, 1949.

"Jekyll Boom Attributed to 'Curiosity.'" *Atlanta Journal*, July 31, 1956.

"Jekyll Bridge Again Blocked." *Brunswick News*, October 19, 1960.

"Jekyll Bridge Failure Brings 10-Hour Delay in Road Travel." *Brunswick News*, June 2, 1965.

"Jekyll Bridge Span Fails." *Brunswick News*, October 13, 1960.

"Jekyll Bridge Still Closed to Tugs, Yachts." *Brunswick News*, December 2, 1960.

"Jekyll Convicts Apprehended by County Officers." *Brunswick News*, December 6, 1951.

"Jekyll Convicts Elude Searching Party on Island." *Brunswick News*, January 8, 1952.

"Jekyll Co-ops Apartment to Get Study." *Brunswick News*, April 1961.

"Jekyll Fugitives Captured at Waynesville." *Brunswick News*, November 18, 1965.

"Jekyll Island Authority Selects Private Partner for Future Revitalization." *PR Newswire*, September 24, 2007.
"Jekyll Island Decline Set for Study." *Atlanta Constitution*, August 8, 1977.
"Jekyll Island Plan Is Wrong!" *Savannah Morning News*, June 6, 1947.
"Jekyll Island Selects New Executive Director." *PR Newswire*, April 30, 2008.
"Jekyll Island's New Fish Pier Plans Drawn." *Brunswick News*, January 5, 1968.
"Jekyll Island State Park Authority Seeks Dismissal of Suit." *PR Newswire*, December 13, 2007.
"Jekyll Island State Park Contracts Thomas Briggs." *Savannah Morning News*, February 1, 1948.
"Jekyll Leaders Urge Residents to Support SPLOST." *Jekyll's Golden Islander*, September 6, 2001.
"Jekyll Motel Embezzler Given 3–5 Year Term." *Brunswick News*, June 21, 1962.
"Jekyll Officials Deny Knowledge of Bars on Island." *Brunswick News*, May 24, 1961.
"Jekyll Owes $2.5 Million for Prisoners." *Brunswick News*, February 6, 1963.
"Jekyll Paint 'Evaporates.'" *Brunswick News*, September 16, 1955.
"Jekyll Prison Camp Returns to Normal After Escapee Try." *Brunswick News*, March 30, 1954.
"Jekyll Says Judge Clears Plan." *Brunswick News*, January 15, 2008.
"Jekyll Sewage System to Serve the Populated Area." *Brunswick News*, September 26, 1961.
"Jekyll Span Fixed; Turtle Repair Near." *Brunswick News*, July 27, 1961.
"Jekyll Sparkles for Lawmakers." *Brunswick News*, February 5, 1960.
"Jekyll Status Preservation Urged." *Atlanta Constitution*, November 1, 1979.
"Jekyll's Water OK, psc Says." *Atlanta Constitution*, June 15, 1974.
"Jekyll to Need Another $500,000; Blalock Reports Jekyll Progress, Answers Critics." *Brunswick News*, September 17, 1955.
"Jekyll Trip as Griffin's Guests Interests Rescued Coal Miners." *Brunswick News*, November 3, 1958.
"Jekyll Unit Is Cautious on Closing." *Atlanta Constitution*, May 5, 1961.
"Jekyll Woman Slain, Husband Takes Life." *Brunswick News*, April 5, 1966.
Jensen, Noel. Memo. Jekyll Island Authority, May 19, 2023.
"JIA: Bradley's Out, Donohue In." *Jekyll's Golden Islander*, August 21, 1997.
Jones, Walter C. "Senator Calls for Jekyll Rate Hike." *Florida Times-Union* (Jacksonville), February 18, 2009.
"Judge Signs Jekyll Isle Racial Edict." *Brunswick News*, June 13, 1964.
Kahri, Andrew W. *The Land Was Ours: African American Beaches from Jim Crow to the Sunbelt South*. Cambridge: Harvard University Press, 2012.
King, P. Nicole. *Sombreros and Motorcycles in a Newer South: The Politics of Aesthetics in South Carolina's Tourism Industry*. Jackson: University Press of Mississippi, 2012.
Krueger, Bob. "Revitalization of Jekyll Island Will Make All Georgians Proud." *Atlanta Journal-Constitution*, December 22, 2009.
Kytle, Calvin, and James A. Mackay. *Who Runs Georgia?* Athens: University of Georgia Press, 1998.
Langford, Jim. "Jekyll Island Development: More Vacationers Could Enjoy Park." *Atlanta Journal-Constitution*, December 10, 2007.
Larrabee, Brandon. "Cry Goes Out to Save South Jekyll Island; Residents and Environmentalists Talk to Senators on Development." *Florida Times-Union* (Jacksonville), April 11, 2007.
Larrabee, Brandon. "Future of Jekyll Starts Today; Senate Panel Will Weigh Lease Extension for Island Authority." *Florida Times-Union* (Jacksonville), April 12, 2007.
Larrabee, Brandon. "Jekyll Developer, Agency Drop Beach Plans." Morris News Service, April 9, 2008.
Larrabee, Brandon. "Jekyll Residents Hope Better Luck in Senate." *Florida Times-Union* (Jacksonville), March 22, 2007.
Larrabee, Brandon. "Jekyll's Residents Relieved by New Law; Perdue Signs a Bill Protecting the South End of the Island from Development." *Florida Times-Union* (Jacksonville), May 31, 2007.
Larrabee, Brandon. "Senator's Claims 'False,' Jekyll Island Authority Chief Says; The Authority Understated Earnings by $11 Million, Jeff Chapman Says." *Florida Times-Union* (Jacksonville), February 28, 2008.
Larrabee, Brandon. "Thumbs-Up Seals Jekyll Deal; Island Authority Lease Extension Passes, Contingent on Master Plan Growth Limits." *Florida Times-Union* (Jacksonville), April 22, 2007.
Layman, David. "Jekyll Chief Resigns." *Brunswick News*, February 1, 1995.
LeCraw, Roy. Letter to the editor. *Atlanta Journal*, August 10, 1956.

Lemos, Gregory. "Removal of Golden Ray Cargo Ship off Georgia Coast Is Largest in U.S. History, Coast Guard Commander Says." CNN, October 26, 2021. https://www.cnn.com/2021/10/26/us/georgia-golden-ray-cargo-ship-wreck-removal-largest-in-us-history/index.html.

Martin, C. Brenden. *Tourism in the Mountain South: A Double-Edged Sword*. Knoxville: University of Tennessee Press, 2007.

Martin, C. Brenden, and June Hall McCash. "From Millionaires to the Masses: Tourism at Jekyll Island, Georgia." In Starnes, *Southern Journeys*.

McCash, June Hall. *The Jekyll Island Cottage Colony*. Athens: University of Georgia Press, 1998.

McCash, June Hall, and Brenden Martin. "The Odyssey of Andre Steiner: Unsung Hero of Jekyll Island." *Georgia Backroads* 8, no. 2 (Summer 2009): 56–61.

McCash, William Barton, and June Hall McCash. *The Jekyll Island Club: Southern Haven for America's Millionaires*. Athens: University of Georgia Press, 1989.

McCoy, Kim, and Willard Bascom. *Waves and Beaches: The Powerful Dynamics of Sea and Coast*. Nashville: Patagonia, 2021.

McDonald, Babs. *Remember Jekyll Island*. Minneapolis: Langdon Street Press, 2012.

McDonald, Lauren. "Jekyll Board Hears Plans for Pier Road Shopping District." *Brunswick News*, January 17, 2024.

McDonald, Lauren. "Pier Road Shop Owners Bring Concerns Before Jekyll Authority Board." *Brunswick News*, October 18, 2023.

McKay, Robert. "Segregation and Public Recreation." *Virginia Law Review* 40, no. 6 (October 1954): 687–731.

"Methodists Ask Halt to Jekyll Liquor Selling." *Brunswick News*, June 7, 1961.

"Miners Enjoy Sun on Jekyll." *Brunswick News*, November 27, 1958.

Montoya, Orlando. "50 Years Later: The 'Quiet Conflict.'" Georgia Public Broadcasting, August 26, 2013. https://www.gpb.org/news/2013/08/26/50-years-later-the-quiet-conflict.

Morrison, Jim. "Bridge Malfunction." *Jekyll's Golden Islander*, April 4, 1985.

Morrison, Jim. "Controversy over Development May Threaten Island Tourism." *Jekyll's Golden Islander*, March 8, 2007.

Morrison, Jim. "Jekyll Bill Lands in Chapman Committee." *Jekyll's Golden Islander*, April 5, 2007.

Morrison, Jim. "Supreme Court Rule for JIA Fire Fee." *Jekyll's Golden Islander*, January 25, 1996.

Morrison, Mike. "Jekyll Revitalization Begins; Great Dunes Opens, and Convention Center Is to Be Built." *Florida Times-Union* (Jacksonville), September 21, 2010.

Morrison, Mike. "Nesting Sea Turtles Avoid Beach at Jekyll Hotel; Westin Has Noncompliant Issues, but It's Not the Only Violator." *Florida Times-Union* (Jacksonville), July 6, 2015.

Morrison, Mike, and Terry Dickson. "Jekyll Island Residents Object to Governing Authority Bargaining Away Their Mail Delivery." *Florida Times-Union* (Jacksonville), September 9, 2013.

Neal, Willard. "Fabulous Jekyll Island Gets Ready for Summer Rush." *Atlanta Journal and Constitution Magazine*, May 19, 1957.

"Negro Farmer Leases Jekyll Beach Motel." *Brunswick News*, December 8, 1960.

Nelson, Jack. "Beer Is Sold at Jekyll After License Is Denied." *Atlanta Constitution*, July 22, 1956.

Nelson, Jack. "Chairman Blalock, Tarbutton Quit Jekyll Board in Wake of Quarrels." *Atlanta Constitution*, April 11, 1956.

Nelson, Jack. "Costly 'Little Executive Mansion' Still Is Not Fit for Occupancy." *Atlanta Constitution*, July 24, 1956.

Nelson, Jack. "Jekyll—A Golden Elephant." *Atlanta Journal and Constitution*, August 31, 1958.

Nelson, Jack. "Jekyll Architect Gains 4 Pct. Fee in Place of $600-a-Month Salary." *Atlanta Constitution*, July 25, 1956.

Nelson, Jack. "Jekyll Authority Employee Bought Supplies from His Own Company." *Atlanta Constitution*, July 26, 1956.

Nelson, Jack. "Jekyll Island Sale Favored, Opposed by State Leaders." *Atlanta Journal*, July 29, 1956.

Nelson, Jack. "Joint Panel Will Study Jekyll Sale." *Atlanta Constitution*, January 18, 1957.

Nelson, Jack. "Liquor and Segregation Fading as Resort Problems." *Atlanta Constitution*, June 29, 1964.

Nelson, Jack. "Longtime Politico Jimmy Dykes Knows How to Deal with State." *Atlanta Constitution*, July 23, 1956.

Nelson, Jack. "Sen. Dykes Moves to Spread His Jekyll Island Empire." *Atlanta Journal and Constitution*, July 22, 1956.

Nelson, Jack. "Solons Demand Jekyll Authority Be Abolished." *Atlanta Constitution*, July 23, 1956.

Nesmith, Jeff. "State Forgets Its Marsh Act." *Atlanta Constitution*, August 1, 1970.

Norton, Terry M. "Sea Turtle Conservation in Georgia

and an Overview of the Georgia Sea Turtle Center on Jekyll Island, Georgia." *Georgia Journal of Science* 63, no. 4 (2005): 208ff.

O'Brien, William E. *Landscapes of Exclusion: State Parks and Jim Crow in the American South*. Amherst: University of Massachusetts Press, 2016.

"Ocean Chews Up Beach, Seawall Erection Rushed." *Brunswick News*, June 20, 1962.

"On Rocky Shore of Jekyll Erosion Bites the Beach." *Brunswick News*, January 28, 1964.

"Ousted Jekyll Board Member Alleges Corruption, Wants Grand Jury Investigation." *Atlanta Journal-Constitution*, September 24, 2007.

Patton, Charlie. "Refurbished Club Reopens at Jekyll for Birthday Year." *Florida Times-Union/Jacksonville Journal*, March 8, 1987.

Pou, Charles. "Dykes Record Bared on Jekyll Hotel Ties." *Atlanta Journal*, July 25, 1956.

Redford, Polly. *Million-Dollar Sandbar*. New York: E. P. Dutton, 1970.

Rehagin, Tony. "Alpha Cats." *31•81, the Magazine of Jekyll Island* 2, no. 1 (Fall/Winter 2017).

Repanshek, Kurt. "How the National Park Service Grappled with Segregation During the 20th Century." *National Parks Traveler*, August 18, 2019.

RGB-27435 001-01-005. Governor-Executive Dept. Governor's Subject Files-1971–1974-Gov. Jimmy Carter County Files, Glynn through Grady. Consignment #1975-0032A.

Rhodes, Thom. "Long-Range Plans for Historic Structures, Interpretation Programs." *Jekyll's Golden Islander*, December 16, 1982.

Riner, Duane. "Jekyll Land Fight Heats." *Atlanta Constitution*, May 14, 1972.

Robinson, Ellen. "Developer—Jekyll Plans on Track." *Brunswick News*, December 11, 2007.

Rowland, Hank. "Donohue May Run Lanier Authority." *Brunswick News*, November 21, 2007.

Rowland, Hank. "Jekyll Developer Says Chapman Wrong." *Brunswick News*, January 10, 2008.

Rowland, Hank. "Jones Hooks Honored by Georgia House of Representatives." *Brunswick News*, March 30, 2023.

"Sale of Lots on Jekyll Held Illegal." *Atlanta Constitution*, February 4, 1957.

Salter, Sallye. "Jekyll Motels Delay Opening." *Atlanta Constitution*, July 26, 1977.

Salter, Sallye. "Jekyll Rejects Condo Switch." *Atlanta Constitution*, October 4, 1977.

Sanders, Crystal R. "Blue Water, Black Beach: The North Carolina Teachers Association and Hammocks Beach in the Age of Jim Crow." *North Carolina Historical Review* 92, no. 2 (April 2015): 145–64.

Seabrook, Charles. *The World of the Salt Marsh: Appreciating and Protecting the Tidal Marshes of the Southeastern Atlantic Coast*. Athens: University of Georgia Press, 2011.

"'Sea Circus' Must Treat Own Waste." *Atlanta Constitution*, May 26, 1972.

"Senate Votes New Jekyll Island Authority." *Savannah Morning News*, February 16, 1957.

Shannon, Margaret. "Jekyll at the Crossroads." *Atlanta Journal and Constitution Magazine*, June 18, 1972.

Shaw, Evelyn. Letter to the editor. *Brunswick News*, February 12, 1995.

Sherr, Evelyn B. *Marsh Mud and Mummichogs: An Intimate Natural History of Coastal Georgia*. Athens: University of Georgia Press, 2015.

Shipp, Bill. "Jekyll Island: Painful Move from Second Rate to First." *Atlanta Constitution*, November 3, 1981.

Shipp, Bill. "The Joke About Jekyll Island." *Statesboro Herald*, April 19, 2007.

Shipp, Bill. "A New Chapter in Jekyll's Sad Story?" *Atlanta Constitution*, June 4, 1981.

"Solons Demand Jekyll Authority Be Abolished." *Brunswick News*, December 10, 1955.

"Solons Demand Probe of Dykes Jekyll 'Empire.'" *Brunswick News*, February 17, 1957.

"Solons Likely to Carry On with Status Quo Jekyll." *Brunswick News*, January 4, 1950.

Sparks, Andrew. "Georgia's Padlocked Island." *Atlanta Journal and Constitution Magazine*, May 25, 1952.

Stantonis, Anthony J. *Faith in Bikinis: Politics and Leisure in the Coastal South Since the Civil War*. Athens: University of Georgia Press, 2014.

Starnes, Richard D., ed. *Southern Journeys: Tourism, History, and Culture in the Modern South*. Tuscaloosa: University of Alabama Press, 2003.

Starr, Mary. "Advisors: Up Jekyll Leases." *Brunswick News*, July 28, 2009.

Starr, Mary. "Former Director Put Jekyll on a New Path." *Brunswick News*, December 27, 2011.

Starr, Mary. "Jekyll Board Hurling Insults." *Brunswick News*, July 30, 2007.

Starr, Mary. "Jekyll's Vision for the Future." *Brunswick News*, September 25, 2007.

"State to Build $75,000 Jekyll Colored Pool." *Brunswick News*, August 22, 1963.

"Steel Strike of 1952." Harry S. Truman Library and

Museum. Accessed November 22, 2022. https://www.trumanlibrary.gov/education/presidential-inquiries/steel-strike-1952.

Stepzinski, Teresa. "Jekyll Bills Land in Chapman Committee; Conservancy Criticizes Bill, Jekyll." *Jekyll's Golden Islander*, March 8, 2007.

Stepzinski, Teresa. "Jekyll Project Aims to Help Sea Turtles; Family Weekend Events to Benefit Planned Georgia Sea Turtle Center." *Florida Times-Union* (Jacksonville), October 5, 2004.

Stillinger, Donna. "Lighting Survey at Jekyll Shows Improvements." *Brunswick News*, August 17, 2015.

St. John, M. L. "Griffin Asks Sale of Jekyll or Swap for Atom Reactor." *Atlanta Constitution*, January 10, 1956.

Stokes, Barbara F. *Myrtle Beach: A History, 1900–1980*. Columbia: University of South Carolina Press, 2007.

Sullivan, Buddy. "Blackbeard Island." In *New Georgia Encyclopedia*. Last modified March 28, 2017. https://www.georgiaencyclopedia.org/articles/geography-environment/blackbeard-island.

Sullivan, Buddy, in association with the Georgia Historical Society. *Georgia: A State History*. Charleston, S.C.: Arcadia, 2010.

Sutter, Paul S., and Paul M. Pressly, eds. *Coastal Nature, Coastal Culture: Environmental Histories of the Georgia Coast*. Athens: University of Georgia Press, 2009.

"Talmadge Appoints Group to Negotiate Jekyll Lease." *Brunswick News*, March 12, 1949.

"Talmadge Approves Plan to Resell Lots on Jekyll." *Brunswick News*, January 29, 1949.

"Talmadge Group Seeking Decision on Jekyll Issue." *Brunswick News*, February 16, 1949.

"Talmadge Seeks Jekyll Study." *Brunswick News*, February 14, 1949.

"They Nabbed This New York Tourist and Sent Him Off to Jekyll Island." *Atlanta Constitution*, June 5, 1962.

Thomas, Gray. "Jekyll Put on Solid Footing." *Florida Times-Union* (Jacksonville), April 26, 1981.

"Thompson Gets into Discussion of Jekyll Island." *Brunswick News*, July 24, 1956.

"Thompson's Folly Revisited." *Florida Times-Union and Journal Sunday Magazine* (Jacksonville), January 4, 1970.

"Thousands Visit Jekyll Opening." *Brunswick News*, December 11, 1954.

"Thrasher, Cook Disagree over Island Lot Sales." *Brunswick News*, February 27, 1957.

"Thrasher Assails Selling of Lots on Jekyll Island." *Atlanta Constitution*, February 4, 1957.

"Thrasher Cracks Down on 'Loose' Jekyll Handling." *Atlanta Journal and Constitution*, March 25, 1957.

"Thrasher Hits Move to Close Jekyll If Mixed." *Brunswick News*, May 21, 1960.

"Tightening of Jekyll Fund Is Ordered." *Atlanta Constitution*, March 30, 1957.

Todd, William Andrew. "Convict Lease System." In *New Georgia Encyclopedia*. Last modified July 17, 2020. https://www.georgiaencyclopedia.org/articles/history-archaeology/convict-lease-system/.

Townsend, Claudia. "Jekyll Authority Seeking Power to Charge Toll." *Atlanta Constitution*, February 3, 1975.

"Trouble Has Struck Lanier Bridge Before." *Atlanta Constitution*, November 9, 1972.

"Two Convicts Shot in Jekyll Escape Attempt." *Brunswick News*, June 9, 1961.

"Two-Week Theft Spree Charged to Island Boys." *Brunswick News*, February 23, 1961.

"Vandiver Asks for $1,218,000 for Jekyll Projects." *Brunswick News*, April 15, 1961.

"Virginia Architect Named to Restore Jekyll Village." *Brunswick News*, July 1, 1966.

"Warehouse Run by Dykes, McMath Sold $2,330 in Supplies to Jekyll." *Atlanta Constitution*, n.d.

"Wayne Prisoner Escapes Detail on Jekyll Friday." *Brunswick News*, July 22, 1967.

Wells, Frank. "Park's Wiggins Clamps Lid on Development at Jekyll." *Atlanta Constitution*, August 9, 1972.

White, Evelyn C. "60 Years Ago, Springhill Mining Disaster Hero Maurice Ruddick Went to Georgia, Where He Couldn't Stay with His Fellow White Miners." *Halifax Examiner*, December 7, 2018.

Wikipedia. "Chitlin' Circuit." Last modified November 29, 2024, 18:18 (UTC). https://en.wikipedia.org/wiki/Chitlin%27_Circuit.

Wiley, Nikki. "Definition of Land Will Chart Jekyll's Future." *Brunswick News*, June 22, 2013.

Wiley, Nikki. "Jekyll Group Talks Land Categories." *Brunswick News*, October 16, 2012.

Wiley, Nikki. "Jekyll Tries to Define 'Land.'" *Brunswick News*, June 16, 2012.

Williams, Sam A. Letter to the editor. *Atlanta Constitution*, June 3, 1981.

"Willing to Sell Jekyll, Talmadge Quoted as Saying." *Atlanta Constitution*, September 11, 1948.

NEWSPAPERS AND PERIODICALS

Atlanta Constitution
Atlanta Journal
Atlanta Journal-Constitution
Augusta Chronicle
Brunswick News
Florida Times-Union (Jacksonville)
Florida Times-Union and Journal (Jacksonville)
Georgia Backroads
Jekyll's Golden Islander
Los Angeles Times
Morris News Service
Munsey's Magazine
New York Times
PR Newswire
Savannah Morning News
Statesboro Herald
31•81, the Magazine of Jekyll Island

ARCHIVAL COLLECTIONS

Atlanta History Center
Coastal Georgia Historical Society
  Richard Everett Collection
Georgia Department of Archives and History
  Vanishing Georgia Collection
Georgia Historical Society
  Sea Island Company Papers
Georgia State University Archives
Mosaic, Jekyll Island Museum
  Jekyll Island Authority (JIA) board minutes
  Jekyll Island Museum (JIM) Archives
  Photograph collection
Roger Beedle diary
Southern Historical Collection, Wilson Special Collections Library, University of North Carolina at Chapel Hill
  Maurice Family Papers
University of Georgia Libraries
  Clifford H. (Baldy) Baldowski Editorial Cartoons
Ed Friend Visual Materials Collection
Hargrett Rare Book and Manuscript Library
Richard B. Russell Library for Political Research and Studies

INDEX

Page numbers in *italics* represent images.